California
State Parks

By the Editors of *Sunset Books* and *Sunset Magazine*

LANE BOOKS · MENLO PARK, CALIFORNIA

HOURS, ADMISSION FEES, AND PRICES
IN THE EDITORIAL CONTENT OF THIS BOOK
ARE AS OF JANUARY 1972.

Research and Text: John Robinson
Supervising Editor: Phyllis Elving

Design: Lawrence A. Laukhuf
Cartography: Roberta A. Perez-Dillow
Topographical Map: Art Technology
Cover: Sunlight filtering through coastal
fog illuminates fragile ferns beneath the
towering redwoods of Jedediah Smith State
Park (see page 10). Photograph by Ray Atkeson.

FIRST PRINTING MAY 1972

Contents

THE STATE PARKS OF CALIFORNIA 4

NORTHERN COAST & REDWOOD COUNTRY   8

SIERRA NEVADA & NORTHERN MOUNTAINS 26

SAN FRANCISCO BAY AREA 40

CENTRAL VALLEY & FOOTHILLS 58

CENTRAL COAST REGION 76

SOUTHERN COAST REGION 94

LOS ANGELES COUNTY 108

SOUTHERN DESERT & MOUNTAINS 116

INDEX 128

SPECIAL FEATURES

Developments to Meet Recreational Needs   7
Lumber Schooners and Dogholes . . . 13
The California Redwoods 17
The Crookedest Railroad in the World . . 19
The First Sierra Skiers 31
The Crowded Road over the Sierra . . . 34
Snowmobiling in California 36
California's Ten Kinds of "Trout" . . . 39
The Bear Flag Incident 44
The Fort Beneath the Bridge 50
Diablo as a Land Survey Base 52
The Central Valley Rivers 65
Pine Grove's Mince Pie Controversy . . 68

The Pacific Flyway 70
The Lakeview Gusher 73
Abalone and Sea Otters 83
The Survival of Point Lobos 86
Four Central Coast Missions . . . 89
The Pismo Clam 93
Solvang—Scandinavia Transplanted . . 98
Collecting Cowhides at Dana Point . . .102
The Dancing Grunion 105
Ocean Fishing in California 107
Restoring Old Buildings 112
Old Pico #4 115
Recreation in the Wilderness 121
A 25-Day Cross-Country Run 122
Color in the Desert 125
The Desert Bighorns 126

The State Parks of California

In California you can enjoy sandy ocean beaches, groves of towering redwood trees, starkly dramatic desert, and lush mountain forests—all in state parks. The California park system reflects the wide variety of terrain and climate of the state itself, offering scenery and recreational opportunities to meet almost any preference.

The state classifies the units in its park system in six categories—state parks, state beaches, state recreation areas, wayside camps, scenic or scientific reserves, and state historic parks. A *state park* generally is sizable and offers good nature experience; usually it has campsites. A *state beach* may be small or extend along several miles; it may be an intensively used area such as is found along the southern coast, or it may be wild and scenic with no development.

State recreation areas are oriented for the most part toward some single form of recreation, usually water; as a rule the emphasis is not on nature experience. The *wayside camp* is in a sense a sort of super-roadside-rest—a place where you can stop overnight in pleasant surroundings enroute to another destination or linger a few days to explore the surrounding country. The *scenic* or *scientific reserve* has the primary purpose of protecting an outstanding scenic resource or delicate ecology.

A *state historic park* has some historic significance. Many are small, with a single point of interest, while others have considerable acreage and include facilities for picnicking and limited hiking. With a few exceptions, state historic parks are open from 10 A.M. to 5 P.M. each day of the year except Thanksgiving, Christmas, and New Year's Day.

The State Historical Landmarks Advisory Committee has identified more than 800 historical landmarks in California; of these only about five percent are included in the state park system and are described in these pages. A booklet listing and briefly describing all of the landmarks is available from The Reservation Office, Department of Parks and Recreation, P.O. Box 2390, Sacramento 95811, for $1 including tax and mailing. (The Department of Parks and Recreation can also furnish general information about the state parks.)

In this book, the state park system has been divided geographically into eight sections. Included in the information given about a park are directions for getting to it; where to write for further information (many parks have useful folders with good maps); and where supplies can be obtained nearby.

Park Rules

Many of the state parks are relatively small areas which receive a great amount of use, so strict rules are neces-

Redwood *groves can be explored at many northern California parks. Short and easy Nickerson Ranch Trail leads through Jedediah Smith Redwoods (see page 10).*

Coastal *parks include both rugged, dramatic sections of shore and warm, sandy beaches. View opposite is at Point Lobos State Reserve (see page 85), looking across Cypress Cove from North Point.*

sary to afford a satisfactory park experience to the public.

You are not allowed to collect your own firewood but must bring your own or buy it from the rangers. You may not collect rocks, flowers, plants, or other specimens, either living or inorganic. Pets must be on a leash not exceeding 6 feet or housed at the campsite. You must have a license and proof of rabies inoculation for a dog.

In virtually all parks you may have fires only in fireplaces furnished, or use a camp stove. In some parks where fire danger is excessive, smoking may be prohibited except in designated areas. No firearms are allowed in state parks, except in those very few where hunting is permitted. You may fish in almost all park waters, subject to Fish and Game Department laws.

Rules pertaining to horses, boats, and trail vehicles vary from park to park.

Fees

By the fee schedule adopted in 1971, $4 per night is charged for campsites with trailer hookups, $3 for developed campsites, and $1.50 for primitive campsites. (In this book the terms "improved," "unimproved," and "primitive" have been used to give you an idea of what to expect; the word "showers" in parentheses with the campground description indicates that there are modern washrooms with hot water, showers, and laundry facilities. "Primitive" means literally that—perhaps there may be only fireplaces and chemical toilets.)

Payment of a campsite fee covers your vehicle and a trailer, if you have one. If you have an additional vehicle such as a jeep or dune buggy, you must pay $1 extra. For dogs there is a charge of 50 cents.

There are no longer reduced rates for off-season camping, but you can pay $10 for a book of 10 tickets for off-season use, good in most parks except a few of the most popular. (In this case, desert park off-season is in summer, but Salton Sea has no off-season.)

Day-use fees are $1 per vehicle, $3 for buses, or 25¢ per person on foot. Normally this includes access to historic museums or other special features which are a part of the day-use area. The usual fee at state historic parks is 25¢ per person 18 or over, under 18 admitted free. Where picnic facilities are to be used (some historic parks have them), the $1-a-day use fee includes access to the other features. A special $10 day-use ticket is available for unlimited use all year.

Boat launching at state ramps is a standard $1, or $2 if picnic facilities are used. An annual ticket for boat launching may be purchased for $10. Concessionaire-operated facilities may charge different rates. Special fees also apply to horse camps, swimming pools, and other unusual features, with special rates for groups.

Reservations

You may reserve campsites in many California state parks, but day-use space cannot be reserved, except for groups. In the park descriptions in this book it has been indicated when reservations are highly recommended because a park is especially popular. If you have sufficient time and you want to go to a park during a popular period, it is wise to make reservations for any park which takes them. Some parks—generally the newer, less popular ones—usually have available space and are operated on a "first come, first served" basis.

Reservations should be requested about 10 days ahead of time, although a little more time is wise in case you have to make another choice. You may get reservation forms by writing to The Reservation Office, Department of Parks and Recreation, P.O. Box 2390, Sacramento 95811. They are also available, along with information on reservations, at most state parks. The park descriptions in this book include the addresses of area managers where you can get information. Requests can also be made by phone.

Major department stores in many cities have "Ticket-ron" facilities which will handle your reservation for a small fee.

Safety

The beaches in the state vary greatly from a safety viewpoint, but it must be kept in mind that the California coast is plagued with riptides which can be serious for the inexperienced swimmer. Shortage of funds is eliminating lifeguards in many parks.

Rattlesnakes are native to California but are not a serious problem. Most park users never see one. In a few parks they may be encountered in outlying areas little frequented by people.

Some of the parks border on great wild stretches. When hiking, be sure you know where children in your group are at all times.

Climate

Certain California weather patterns are consistent from year to year. The state has a wet winter and dry summer, with average annual rainfall diminishing rapidly as you move south. In the northwestern section, precipitation may approach rain-forest proportions, while the southern deserts get only a few inches a year—and sometimes none. The days are warmer in the south, so below San Francisco there may be many fine winter days. Because of the cold offshore current, fog may come in anywhere along the coast in summer. This is less pronounced in the south than in the north.

The Central Valley can get almost as hot as the desert in summer. Temperatures of 105° and higher are not uncommon. The mountains will be cooler, partially because of elevation. Mountain parks will be pleasant on most days in summer, may have an occasional thunderstorm and shower, and will cool off rapidly at night. They may be very cold and have snow in winter, and many are closed then.

NEW DEVELOPMENTS TO MEET RECREATIONAL NEEDS

In 1970, California voters approved Proposition 20—the Recreation and Fish and Wildlife Enhancement Bond Act—authorizing $60 million in bond sales to finance fish and wildlife habitat improvements and provide recreational facilities for an additional 16 million visitor days a year. The projects are all water-oriented and directly connected with the State Water Project, from the headwater dams in the Feather River System, down the 444-mile-long aqueduct, to the final reservoir at Lake Perris southeast of Riverside.

Although only a few of the Proposition 20 developments will be included in the state park system, all will be state-owned and developed with state funds.

From north to south, the 14 projects already approved are as follows:

Upper Feather River Basin: Includes three reservoirs at about 5,000 feet altitude in the eastern Sierra near Portola, in Plumas County. The lakes already are getting fairly heavy use by fishermen; modern campgrounds should be completed by spring of 1974. The lakes will be operated by Plumas National Forest.

Lake Oroville State Recreation Area (see page 61): Funds have been allocated for improved facilities, to be ready in 1976-1977. Oroville will continue to be operated as a state recreation area.

Bethany Reservoir: Located in Alameda County about midway between Livermore and Tracy, 7 miles north of U.S. 50 near Mountain House Road. Facilities, to be available in 1976 or 1977, are to include campsites, picnic areas, boat ramps, and marina. Bethany is to be operated locally.

Lake Del Valle: A 5-mile-long reservoir in Alameda County 7 miles south of Livermore, with about 1,000 acres of lake surface. Del Valle is already in operation by East Bay Regional Park District, with concession stand, family and youth group camping areas, and picnic tables; you can swim, boat, and hike here. Substantial improvements are to be ready by 1975.

Ingram Creek Aquatic Recreation Area: Located in Stanislaus County adjacent to Interstate 5 about 5 miles south of State 33. Ingram will have some small ponds, camping, picnicking, non-power boating, and children's areas. Facilities are to be available in 1974. The area will be operated locally.

San Luis Reservoir State Recreation Area (see page 72): Funds will provide for improvements in access roads and facilities for camping, day use and boating, waterfowl hunting, to be completed in 1977. San Luis will continue to be operated as a state recreation area.

Kettleman City Aquatic Recreation Area: To be located about 5 miles south of Kettleman City. The 70-acre area will have a pool for summer water play and winter fishing. Improvements will include facilities for wayside camping and are to be completed in 1975 or 1976. The site will be locally operated.

Peace Valley Aquatic Recreation Area: A 340-acre land parcel in Los Angeles County with an artificial lake of about 15 acres between the West Branch of the California Aqueduct and State 138, some 4 miles south of Gorman. Facilities for wayside camping and picnicking and horsemen's group are to be ready in 1976.

Pyramid Lake: A reservoir at about 2,500 feet altitude, with 21 miles of shoreline, about 13 miles south of Gorman in Los Angeles County. Development will emphasize day use, with boat ramps in 1973. Facilities at Gorman Creek area for picnicking, swimming, and boating are to be ready by 1974. Administration is to be by the U.S. Forest Service.

Castaic Lake: A fairly large reservoir in Los Angeles County 2 miles north of Castaic off Interstate 5. The lake will have a shoreline of 34 miles. Improvements are to include facilities for camping, picnicking, hiking, riding, and water activities. The lake will be filling by 1973, and facilities will include sandy beaches and boat-in and hike-in camps. Castaic is to be operated by Los Angeles County.

Ritter Canyon Aquatic Recreation Area: In northeastern Los Angeles County about 4 miles west of Palmdale in high desert country. The 15-acre artificial lake will be developed for day use only. Facilities, to be ready in 1975 or 1976, will be locally operated.

Oro Grande Aquatic Recreation Area: In San Bernardino County 30 miles north of San Bernardino, with access from Interstate 15 by the Hesperia Road interchange. Oro Grande comprises 150 acres in a scenic area in the high desert. There is to be a small pool for summer swimming and winter trout fishing, and there will also be access to the aqueduct for fishing. Wayside camping, picnicking, water play facilities will be ready in 1976 or 1977 and will be operated by the county.

Silverwood Lake: A reservoir of about 1,000 acres in San Bernardino County at almost 4,000 feet altitude in partially-forested mountain terrain. From San Bernardino, you drive north 15 miles on State 18 and then 5 miles north on State 138. Limited day-use facilities are to be available in 1972; by mid-1973, campgrounds and other facilities should be nearing completion. San Bernardino National Forest will operate the area with Fish and Game Department assistance.

Lake Perris: A reservoir of about 2,000 acres in rugged hills in Riverside County about 5 miles northeast of Perris, accessible from either U.S. 395 or State 60. Lake Perris has been allocated the largest amount of Proposition 20 funds and is expected to accommodate more than 5 million visitors a year. The lake will start filling in 1973, and some facilities will be ready late in the year, with development continuing until 1976. Provision will be made for camping, hiking, horseback riding, and water sports. A special feature will be trails for bicycling. Perris will be a state recreation area.

Northern Coast & Redwood Country

Two quite different kinds of parks are found in the strip of land along California's northern coast—preserves for groves of giant redwood trees and dramatic sections of coastline.

Aside from the few preserves in the San Francisco Bay area, the only remaining important stands of redwoods are on the north coast. Four redwood parks here have substantial acreages of mature trees—Humboldt, Prairie Creek, Del Norte, and Jedediah Smith. All have big groves with an undisturbed redwood ecology, and eventually the latter three probably will be combined in some way with the Redwood National Park. But there are about a dozen more parks which have redwoods— in some cases sizable second-growth forests, but most with at least a small grove of mature trees.

The trees grow best on river and creek flats, and each redwood park has at least one all-year stream. In summer even the major streams such as the Eel will be shallow, often not deep enough for swimming, but with shoreline beaches and sufficient depth for water play, particularly for children. In the rainy season these same streams can become swollen, dangerous torrents.

Except for Prairie Creek and Del Norte, the redwood parks are found 10 or more miles inland from the coast. Hence you will encounter little fog, and in the late spring, summer, and early fall the weather is close to ideal—ranging from 65 to 85 degrees. In winter these parks will be chilly and damp, although in any season you normally will be able to make daytime stopovers to see the big trees.

The coastal parks have an altogether different character. Here are great headlands and rocky points, with many coves and small beaches breaking the shoreline. On sunny days the parks are a blazing contrast of white surf, dark rocks, and blue ocean. In summer, moisture in the air condenses over the cold offshore currents and is drawn inland by the rising hot air of the interior valleys, so fog is common. Nevertheless, camping space is usually difficult to get.

Annual rainfall increases heavily north of San Francisco. Vegetation is dense but often wind-distorted, while wildflowers mat the open spaces.

Even on this rainy coast, rain is rare in the dry season, but campers should be prepared for cold winds at times and chilly nights. Keep in mind, too, that fall and spring weather are often better than summer, and there are plenty of available campsites at these seasons.

Barelegged paddling is about the extent of water activities on the beaches. Currents are vicious, the water is cold, the surf unpredictable, and footing too often precarious.

Many fishermen work with nets when surf smelt are running, and a few have success surf fishing the beaches for perch; but these fish do not reproduce heavily, and

Beaches *and coves of Sonoma Coast stretch 11 miles (see page 25). View is south from cliffs at Goat Rock.*

Heavy *rainfall and fog from ocean result in lush growth of ferns among redwoods at Prairie Creek park (see page 12), opposite photo.*

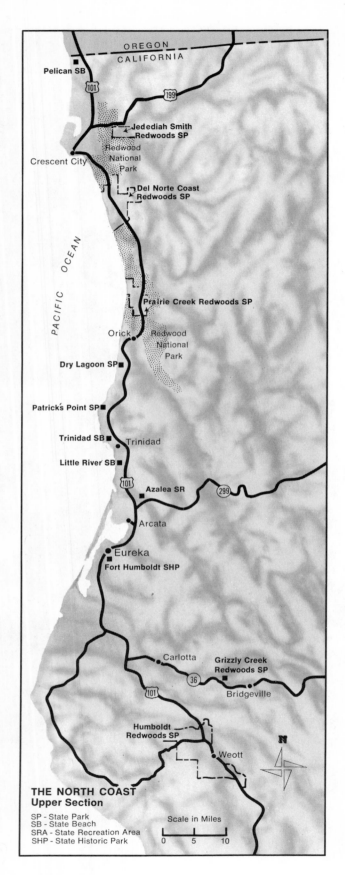

THE NORTH COAST
Upper Section

SP - State Park
SB - State Beach
SRA - State Recreation Area
SHP - State Historic Park

Scale in Miles

0   5   10

their numbers are being reduced rapidly. The most successful line-fishermen are those who know how to work the rock pools for rock cod, cabezon, and such species or else are willing to go to one of the ports for a day of party boat fishing at sea.

Although abalone are still taken from rock pools at extreme low tides, this sport is rapidly becoming the province of the skin-diver.

Pelican State Beach

A small beach right against the Oregon border, Pelican is backed by low dunes and wind-battered Sitka spruce. Driftwood, surf, and great varieties of seabirds contribute to the character of this 5-acre park. This is a good place for beachcombing and sometimes for surf fishing. There are no improvements. Pelican is for those who prefer the wild and undeveloped beach.

Access: Turn west off U.S. 101 just south of the Oregon state line.

Jedediah Smith Redwoods State Park

Big and wild, Jedediah Smith Redwoods has groves encompassing nearly 9,000 acres. Although even a short stopover is rewarding, this is a park in which you should camp to fully appreciate its redwoods.

Facilities are near the park entrance, but the groves extend south about 4 miles. The Six Rivers National Forest spreads outward many more miles from the park boundaries, making this area one of the best in the state for exploration by amateur woodsmen.

Jedediah Smith is popular in summer, and since the Smith River—one of the state's best steelhead and salmon streams—flows across two sides of the park, summer family campers are replaced almost immediately in the fall by fishermen.

The park is warm and dry in summer and has heavy rainfall in winter.

Activities: Camping, picnicking, hiking, nature study, swimming and stream play, fishing. The campground is near park headquarters in the redwoods, with 107 improved campsites (showers) available for picnicking when unoccupied. Camping limit is 10 days in summer.

Several foot trails traverse the redwood groves, and there are one or two old roads which can be negotiated by passenger cars with care.

Because of the extensive wilderness which surrounds the park, wildlife is abundant, ranging all the way from bears and deer down to chipmunks and raccoons. Mention of the latter should be a warning to any camper, as they are notorious food thieves.

There is steelhead and salmon fishing from October to February, and fly fishing for trout is usually good from late August until the first heavy rains.

For further information: Area Manager, Hiouchi Area State Parks, P.O. Drawer J, Crescent City 95531.

Access: Take U.S. 199 just north of Crescent City where it branches from U.S. 101; the park entrance is about 11 miles northeast of town.

Supplies: Nearby Hiouchi store, or Crescent City.

Del Norte Coast Redwoods State Park

A spectacular combination of redwoods, beaches, cliffs, and rain forest is presented by Del Norte Coast Redwoods State Park. Only a few other parks share with Del Norte the combination of sequoia forest and scenic seacoast, and this park also offers protected camping areas away from the coast.

Aside from Kruse Rhododendron Reserve, this is the best park to visit to see outstanding displays of native rhododendrons from April to July. Western azaleas are also found here, but not in such great profusion as the rhododendrons.

Rain forest growth in the redwoods is also distinctive, and excellent specimens of all this ecological complex are everywhere. Wildlife includes a broad range of animals, even an occasional bear or Roosevelt elk.

More than 6,000 acres are included in the park, which is adjacent to many square miles of Del Norte National Forest. Altitudes range from sea level to 2,500 feet.

The park is closed November through March because of rainfall.

Giant redwoods *are seen at every turn on old Howland Hill road in Jedediah Smith Redwoods State Park.*

Wilson Beach *at south end of Del Norte Coast Redwoods State Park offers picnicking and sunbathing. Driftwood here may be used for fires if you can find pieces small enough. Much of park is on bluffs high above ocean.*

Activities: Camping, picnicking, hiking, stream play, stream fishing for trout (no salmon fishing during spawning season), rock and surf fishing, beachcombing and tide pool study. There is a day-use area at the south end of the state park on the beach at the mouth of Wilson Creek.

Camps are in Mill Creek Valley some distance below the east side of the highway, with 145 improved sites (showers). Mill Creek runs through the campground. Two-thirds of the sites accommodate trailers with no hookups but a sanitation station. Picnicking is permitted at empty campsites. Space is almost always available.

The interesting trail system includes Damnation Creek trail, which descends 1,000 feet to the ocean in a distance of a mile. Except for Wilson, the ocean beaches are small and rocky; all ocean swimming is dangerous because of currents and cold water.

For further information: Area Manager, Hiouchi Area State Parks, P.O. Drawer J, Crescent City 95531.

Access: The park entrance is on the east side of U.S. 101 about 5 miles south of Crescent City near the top of the grade.

Supplies: Crescent City.

Prairie Creek Redwoods State Park

If you are looking for a park where you can get away from it all, Prairie Creek Redwoods comes close to being ideal. Its 12,000-plus acres encompass dense redwoods, rain forest, several streams, and one of the West's best wild beaches—8 miles long and looking much as it must have a thousand years ago.

Altitudes range from sea level to more than 1,200 feet. There are many hiking trails for exploration, and camp and picnic sites are commodious and well located for a variety of tastes. In late spring, summer, and particularly early fall, the weather is excellent, with cool nights and daytime temperatures which occasionally range upward to 85 degrees. The park is open all year, but wet in winter.

Wild and exceptionally scenic Gold Beach, backed by dramatic bluffs, does have some gold in its sand. At one time this was the scene of a gold rush, but it was expensive and difficult to separate gold from sand.

Several Roosevelt elk herds inhabit the park, which is a reserve for these animals, once almost extinct. They are larger than the Tule elk which roamed the Central Valley; their natural range was north into Canada along

Roosevelt elk *graze in the "prairie" above Redwood Highway at Prairie Creek State Park. The elk have become accustomed to people and don't mind photographers if they do not come too close.*

the coast and east to the Rockies. Although the animals are accustomed to sightseers, they may be hostile if approached too closely, particularly the bulls and cows with calves.

Prairie Creek has exceptional wild rhododendron and azalea displays in spring and early summer and many wildflowers throughout the season on the prairie.

The park's redwood groves gradually have been augmented since the first acquisition of about 200 acres in the 1920's and, mainly through the efforts of the Save-the-Redwoods League, there are now more than 75 memorial groves. The redwood ecology is especially good, because the redwoods range down close to the sea, and the 75-inch annual rainfall creates a virtual rain forest.

Activities: Camping, picnicking, hiking and riding, stream water play for paddlers, a wide range of nature programs, stream and surf fishing. Ocean swimming is dangerous because of surf, currents, and cold water. Fishermen work the creeks for rainbow and cutthroat trout in summer, salmon and steelhead in winter.

There are two campgrounds—a 25-unit area on the beach with unimproved campsites and a 65-unit area (showers) off the prairie on the edge of small timber, with a few sites in the open. This section has improved sites with all facilities. The picnic area is just to the north, near the park entrance, on the edge of the redwood groves. There is a visitor's center, and campfire programs are conducted in summer.

More than 40 miles of trails meander through the park. The Revelation guided nature trail for the blind is an unusual feature; a trail guide in Braille is available at park headquarters. An excellent self-guided nature trail for the casual visitor starts near headquarters. The James Irvine trail, 4½ miles long, loops through Fern Canyon, where five-fingered ferns carpet perpendicular canyon walls 50 feet high.

For further information: Area Manager, Prairie Creek Redwoods State Park, Orick 95555.

Access: The prairie and headquarters are visible on the west side of U.S. 101 about 6 miles north of Orick. Directions are well marked with signs, and the large entrance sign is lighted at night.

Supplies: Orick, 6 miles south.

Dry Lagoon State Park

A wild and dramatic thousand acres of coastal headlands, beach, and dunes, Dry Lagoon State Park encompasses 8 miles of coast. The park includes Big Lagoon and Stone Lagoon, inland bodies of water separated from the ocean by sand bars.

Weather at Dry Lagoon is typical of the north coast, with much fog in summer. Climate may be excellent in spring and fall, stormy in winter.

Activities: Picnicking, beachcombing, surf and lagoon fishing (trout). Facilities consist of parking and chemi-

LUMBER SCHOONERS AND DOGHOLES

The redwood forests once stretched almost unbroken from Monterey to beyond the Oregon border. As the easily accessible forests of the San Francisco Bay Area and parts of Marin County were decimated, cutting moved up the north coast. The wealth in timber was irresistible, but because there were no adequate seaports and no roads between San Francisco and Eureka, an entire new set of skills had to be developed to get the lumber to market.

Early attempts to use the little coves and inlets as seaports were often disastrous, and hundreds of ships were wrecked on the sharp reefs in attempts to get out the lumber. Eventually the most usable of the "dogholes" along the coast were identified, and mills grew up near them. A special kind of vessel—the lumber schooner—became a familiar part of the San Francisco and north coast scene, and only in the past few decades has the last of them disappeared. (See San Francisco Maritime State Historic Park, page 49).

These little vessels usually were flush decked forward, with all their superstructure in the stern, and powerful engines for maneuvering in the strong currents. Shallow drafted and easily maneuverable, they could poke close to shore through rocks and reefs.

Loading was by cable slings, flimsy wharves which often had to be rebuilt each year after winter storms, and often long greased chutes supported by suspensions engineered by local handymen. These chutes had gates near the seaward end which controlled the flow of timber onto the ship's deck.

cal toilets only, except at Stone Lagoon, where there is a paved access road with parking and picnic tables.

Access: To reach Stone Lagoon, drive a half mile south of Freshwater Lagoon on U.S. 101; there is no sign. To reach Dry Lagoon go 2 miles south of Stone Lagoon; a sign marks the area.

Patrick's Point State Park

A small, wild, but well-developed promontory jutting into the Pacific, Patrick's Point is a fine place for those who thrive on sea air and the sound of booming surf. Careful placement of facilities and roads makes the park's 245 acres seem much larger. Some open meadows and headlands covered with rich coastal vegetation offer a profusion of wildflowers in spring and summer, including many native azaleas. There are dense copses of Sitka spruce and alders in places.

The long sweep of Agate Beach, backed by steep, golden cliffs, is good for hiking and sunbathing. Contrary to usual park rules, you may take agates here. The coast here is dangerous, so stay out of water over

Unspoiled *beach at Trinidad usually is even less crowded than this. Trinidad Head is at upper left in photo.*

Old logging equipment *at Fort Humboldt gets a close examination by young girl. City of Eureka provides the exhibit.*

knee-deep. Sea lions frequent the offshore rocks at the south end of the park.

A self-guided nature trail loops through the Octopus Tree Grove. These gnarled and deformed ancient Sitka spruces show the effects of storm and growth problems encountered in their long lifetimes.

Best weather here is spring, early summer, and fall, but summer fog sometimes breaks for several days. The park is wet and windy in winter. Patrick's Point is a popular park in season.

Activities: Camping, picnicking, beachcombing, rock and surf fishing. Abalone, Penn Creek, and Agate Beach campgrounds offer 123 improved sites (showers), with picnic grounds at Lookout Rock. Red Alder and Mussel Rock picnic areas are for groups on reservation. Cliff trails lead to the beach and fishing spots.

Twelve trails wind through the park, some of them through vegetation extremely dense. Climbing on the cliffs is hazardous; despite your exploring urge, stick to the marked ways.

Some of the trails lead down to ledges above the surf where you can fish for ling cod, greenlings, sea trout, and cabezon. Occasional ocean perch are caught from Agate Beach.

For further information: Area Manager, c/o Prairie Creek Redwoods State Park, Orick 95555.

Access: The park is west of U.S. 101, with the turnoff 30 miles north of Eureka at the interchange marked Patrick's Point Drive. Watch for signs a short distance in.

Supplies: Trinidad, or other nearby points.

Trinidad State Beach

Although right on the edge of a town, Trinidad State Beach has a wild, haunting beauty that should satisfy even the most demanding nature lover. The beach is curving, with many rock formations jutting out from the bluffs behind. Dramatic Pewetole Island is situated just offshore.

Weather here is typically north coastal—wet in winter, foggy in summer.

Activities: Picnicking, beachcombing, surf fishing, no swimming. The adjacent town of Trinidad has party boats for deep sea fishing.

A small picnic area is located on the bluffs near the park entrance in a sunny, protected spot. A trail from here leads down to the beach.

This park currently gets little use. Plans call for the addition of a small campground, a nature center, more trails, and an arboretum by 1973.

Access: You take U.S. 101 to the Trinidad exit, then continue to the park via the Trinity and Stagecoach roads.

Little River State Beach

If you are a clamming enthusiast, Little River is the popular beach at which to pursue your sport. Though this is a relatively small beach of about 100 acres, it stretches a mile along the ocean at the mouth of Little River and is backed by big dunes.

Typical north coast weather prevails, with much fog in summer. The park has no facilities, there is no camping, and swimming is very dangerous.

In 1849 the starving Josiah Gregg party broke through here after struggling for a month to get to the coast from Weaverville.

Activities: Picnicking, surf fishing, and clamming. The dunes and lagoon at the mouth of the river are enjoyed by children. Do not go off established roads with vehicles, as it is very easy to get stuck in the sand.

Access: The beach is visible from the freeway, and offramps lead to it about 4 miles south of Trinidad on U.S. 101.

Azalea State Reserve

If you visit Azalea State Reserve around Memorial Day, you will probably find the western azaleas, *Rhododendron occidentale*, at their peak. Period of best bloom varies by two to three weeks, depending upon weather.

From the parking lot on Azalea Avenue, two trails take you among masses of creamy blossoms hanging overhead everywhere. Together, the trails total more than 1½ miles through the azaleas. East Trail has a scenic overlook of the area. A self-guided nature trail leaflet is available.

The reserve has three picnic sites with ramadas and restrooms. Group hikes led by a naturalist can be arranged through the park's area manager, Fort Humboldt State Historic Park, 3431 Fort Avenue, Eureka 95501.

Access: The reserve is reached via North Bank Road either from U.S. 101 or U.S. 299 a few miles north of the town of Arcata.

Fort Humboldt State Historic Park

At Fort Humboldt State Historic Park you can see old logging equipment which handled big redwood logs and imagine yourself operating a highline in the loggers' heyday. The city of Eureka has financed the exhibit, pending availability of state funds to reconstruct the old fort.

Signs mark the locations of the old buildings which the federal government built in 1853 to protect the settlers from Indian uprisings triggered by the encroachment of gold miners. A young army captain named Ulysses S. Grant served a tour of duty here. There is a small historical museum in back of the park district headquarters. Ask for the mimeographed material on the fort's history.

Access: The park is located on a bluff overlooking Humboldt Bay in the southern part of the city of Eureka. Turn east off Broadway (U.S. 101) onto Highland Avenue and drive about a tenth of a mile.

Grizzly Creek Redwoods State Park

An off-the-beaten-track redwood park, Grizzly Creek is situated in what was once a very wild area and is still only lightly populated. But don't expect to meet any of the grizzlies which once swarmed here—they have long since disappeared.

Two live streams run through the park, one of them the Van Duzen River. Grizzly Creek's 234 acres include a virgin redwood grove and more than a mile of river front, at an altitude of 400 feet. This is the farthest inland of the state's redwood parks.

The park is wet in the rainy season, but otherwise the visitor enjoys temperatures of 60 to 70 degrees in the spring and up to 75 degrees in summer and early autumn.

The peripatetic Josiah Gregg came through here in 1850, and the spot where the park's picnic ground is now located was for many years a stop for stagecoaches and teamsters.

Activities: Camping, picnicking, hiking, fishing, stream water play for children, nature study. A campground is strung along the river bank, with 30 improved campsites (showers) in somewhat open settings. The tree-shaded picnic area, farther downstream near the beach, is available for overflow camping.

There is a 1½-mile hiking trail up the redwood slopes and a 1-mile self-guided nature trail. In summer the rangers conduct nature walks and campfire programs, and there are displays of rocks, birds, and flora at headquarters.

Trout fishing is spotty during the summer months, but when the river is right, steelhead fishing is good from mid-February to mid-April.

For further information: Area Manager, c/o Humboldt Redwoods State Park, P.O. Box 100, Weott 95571.

Access: Turn off U.S. 101 at Alton onto State 36 and go 18 miles east on a well-paved but winding road. Do not plan to continue east on State 36 beyond the park if you have a trailer, as the road is narrow, rugged, and winding through the Bully Choop Mountains.

Supplies: Bridgeville or Carlotta, each about 10 miles distant, or Fortuna, a sizable town about 20 miles away on U.S. 101.

Van Duzen River *in summer is attractive for wading at Grizzly Creek Redwoods, farthest inland of the redwood parks.*

Humboldt Redwoods State Park

When you visit Humboldt Redwoods State Park, you see the world's finest reserve of the coast redwood, *Sequoia sempervirens*. This park's popularity is well deserved, for the overpowering majesty of the groves must be experienced to be appreciated.

Piece by piece, conservationists and state funds have put together here more than 43,000 acres of park, much of it pure stands of virgin redwoods. Stretching intermittently for more than 31 miles along the South Fork of the Eel River, it offers dozens of places to view the big trees.

The finest coastal redwood forests were those on river flats in canyons where there was deep soil, protection from sea winds, and adequate water. Because these were also easiest to log off, few survived. Some, in fact, were logged off for farms in the early days before it was learned the lumber was valuable. But, because of the difficulties of transport, these groves along the South Fork of the Eel survived into the first decades of the twentieth century, when alarmed conservationists began to act to protect them. Today the park complex ties together more than 70 memorial groves.

The Avenue of the Giants has become world famous. When the Redwood Highway down the Eel Canyon was converted to freeway, the old road—often across the river from the new road—was retained as a parkway. Here you can drive for miles over the curving, two-lane route with its gigantic trees crowding close to the roadside. You can even see where slices were taken off the trunks years ago to widen the way for trucks and buses. There are many places you can pull out and walk among the trees—but watch for fast moving cars and trucks.

The Rockefeller Forest, given to the state many years ago by the Rockefeller family, is the most valuable tract of timber in the world. Bull Creek, which runs through this forest, boasts many trees over 350 feet high and includes a number of natural oddities.

The Eel is a temperamental river. In summer a shallow, slow-moving stream, it can become a raging, dangerous torrent in winter when flooded with rain.

Situated some miles in from the coast, the park has little fog in summer and is usually warm, sometimes hot. Since it is in a heavy rainfall area, you can expect it to be damp and sometimes foggy and chilly in winter and early spring, but even in these months it is usually suitable for casual visiting.

Activities: Climax redwood forest nature study, hiking, riding, camping, picnicking, water play, fishing in season.

There are three major campgrounds, all of them in dense forest and two of them easily accessible from U.S. 101. Burlington, near park headquarters and the center of the park, has 58 improved campsites; Hidden Springs, about 3 miles south, has 155 (showers). Another campground, Albee Creek, is a few miles to the west up Bull Creek in the Rockefeller Forest, with 32 unimproved sites. Still farther west a few miles is a group horsemen's camp with its own riding trail.

The park has four family picnic areas and the large group picnic area at Williams Grove, which must be reserved; group camping is also permitted here.

More than 100 miles of trails thread the area (where they cross the river, bridges are not in place during the high-water season).

The river beaches can be reached from a number of points, particularly from the established camp and picnic areas. Depending on the activities of the winter floods, there may be deep holes, but generally the river is only a few feet deep in summer, making it ideal for children.

Each of the two larger campgrounds has regular nature

programs, talks, and walks. Additional information is available at park headquarters.

The entire area is popular in winter for steelhead and salmon fishing.

For further information: Area Manager, Humboldt Redwoods State Park, P.O. Box 100, Weott 95571.

Access: The park is easily reached either from north or south on U.S. 101. Park headquarters at Weott is 47 miles south of Eureka, 26 miles north of Garberville.

Supplies: Garberville, Eureka, or a number of smaller towns scattered through the park area.

Benbow Lake State Recreation Area

A pleasant and popular stopover for a day along the Eel River, Benbow Lake State Recreation Area has been completely remodeled and modernized in recent years. The dam which makes a lake in summer is the park's main feature; normally it is installed the last week in May (weather and river permitting) and removed after Labor Day.

The park includes open river shore, with wooded slopes across the river where a new campground has been built.

Activities: Camping, picnicking and sunbathing on well-kept lawns, swimming, boating (non-powered boats), no water-skiing. There are no lifeguards.

Picnic areas are excellent, with new tree plantings. The campground has 22 unimproved sites. The park is open all year, but there is no winter camping.

For further information: Area Manager, c/o Richardson Grove State Park, Garberville 95440.

Access: Three miles south of Garberville, take the Benbow offramp from U.S. 101.

Supplies: Small concession for launching light boats, rental of water play equipment.

Richardson Grove State Park

Richardson Grove is a relatively small redwood park (about 800 acres), but you can't fail to find it—the Redwood Highway goes right through it. Eventually the highway will be rerouted across the river.

Richardson offers camping, picnicking, a beach on the Eel River, one of the best redwood nature displays in the park system, and some excellent interpretive programs. A small area along the highway is given over to a restaurant, a gift shop, a market, and even a post office.

Climate here is consistently mild in summer and likely to be wet and chilly in winter, but the park is open all year and is worth a visit any time when weather permits.

This park was named in memory of 1920's conservationist California governor Friend W. Richardson.

THE CALIFORNIA REDWOODS

Redwood trees apparently were much more numerous throughout the northern hemisphere in past geologic ages, but today they are unique to California. Groves of *Sequoia sempervirens*, or coast redwood, are preserved in a number of state parks in the north coastal part of California. A close relative, but not a true redwood, is the massive *Sequoiadendron giganteum*, or Big Tree; it grows in the Sierra Nevada range, and groves can be seen at Calaveras Big Trees State Park (see page 36).

Changes in rainfall and climate over a 50-million-year period gradually restricted the redwoods to the areas in which they now grow. Presumably there are other regions that receive about 50 inches of rainfall annually, are cooled by ocean air, and have deep enough soil to meet the growth requirements of these trees; but so far no country has established its own redwood forest—which would take 2,000 years to grow to the full maturity of the California groves.

The great columnar trunks and high, dense crowns of the trees create a cathedral-like atmosphere in the coast redwood forests. Because of the foliage density of redwoods in pure stands, the ground below is al-

most always in shade, discouraging bushy undergrowth. But shade-adapted plants—particularly ferns, which also need moisture—create a rich green carpet. Wildlife is unobtrusive, consisting primarily of insects, snails, and rodents.

Fossil remains of redwoods have been found in many places in the West, in Alaska, in northern Japan, and in Europe. The northern trees were first thought to be typical redwoods, but as more evidence was gathered they were identified as belonging to a separate genus—*Metasequoia*. These trees were thought to have become extinct 20 million years ago; then in 1945, unusual trees in remote areas of central China were identified as living examples—*Metasequoia glyptostroboides*—of these fossil trees. Today the Chinese government has set aside these groves as a national preserve.

Metasequoia glyptostroboides is not a true redwood, though it is called the Dawn Redwood. Its branching pattern is different from that of the California redwoods, it does not grow as large, it drops its leaves in winter, and it can survive in much colder climates.

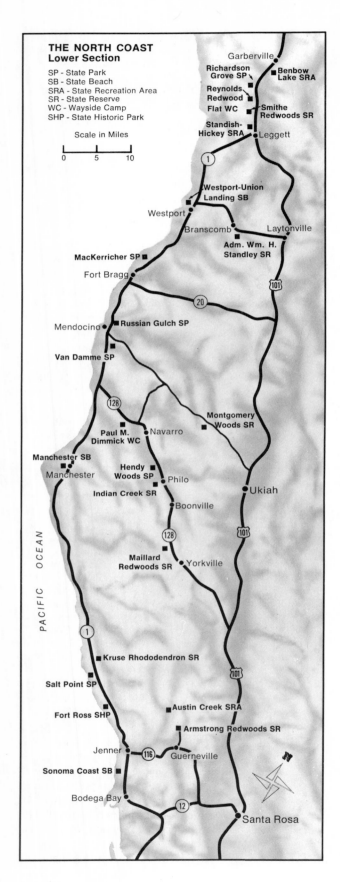

THE NORTH COAST
Lower Section

SP - State Park
SB - State Beach
SRA - State Recreation Area
SR - State Reserve
WC - Wayside Camp
SHP - State Historic Park

Scale in Miles

0   5   10

Activities: Camping, hiking, picnicking, sunbathing and water play along the river (no lifeguards), nature study. There are several hiking trails. The picnic area is among trees near the river.

Three campgrounds offer a total of 185 improved sites (showers). Huckleberry and Madrone are on higher ground above the grove and west of the highway; Oak Flat is on flat ground across the river. (The park folder has an excellent map.)

For further information: Area Manager, Richardson Grove State Park, Garberville 95440.

Access: On U.S. 101, 8 miles south of Garberville.

Supplies: In the park.

Reynolds Wayside Camp

If you are looking for a spot to camp overnight along the Redwood Highway, you will find at Reynolds Wayside Camp a sizable campground with 50 unimproved sites offering good facilities. The campsites are also used for picnicking.

Reynolds Wayside Camp comprises almost 400 acres of redwood, Douglas fir, and oak forest, with access to the Eel River and salmon and steelhead fishing in winter.

Access: The park is 8 miles north of Leggett on the west side of U.S. 101.

Smithe Redwoods State Reserve

An easy stopover on U.S. 101 almost 3 miles north of Leggett, Smithe Redwoods State Reserve features a small grove of mature redwoods and a 60-foot waterfall. A quarter-mile hike leads to the waterfall, and there is a footpath leading down to the Eel River. The park is a memorial to Frank and Bess Smithe, who contributed the land. It has a few picnic sites.

Standish-Hickey State Recreation Area

Nearly a thousand acres adjoining U.S. 101, Standish-Hickey is in character similar to redwood parks along the Eel River but boasts only one mature redwood—the dense forest is all second growth Douglas fir, redwood, and various deciduous species, with some outstanding madrones.

A great variation in terrain is encompassed by the park, with steep slopes dropping far down into Eel Canyon. Weather is pleasant in summer, wet in winter.

This land originally was owned and logged by Standish-Hickey interests. One mature redwood escaped logging and was named in honor of Captain Miles Standish of the *Mayflower*.

Activities: Camping, hiking, picnicking, swimming, sunbathing, water play, fishing in winter season for steelhead and salmon.

THE CROOKEDEST RAILROAD IN THE WORLD

Its engine puffing satisfyingly, Super Skunk crosses Noyo River on its trip from Willits.

Up in the northern coast ranges, the California Western Railroad still operates "the crookedest railroad in the world." The Skunk and Super Skunk travel from Willits to Fort Bragg over a twisting 40-mile route.

The train got its "skunk" name in 1925. That year the company began providing passenger service with a self-powered, gasoline-engined car, which, to the natives accustomed to coal fumes, smelled like a skunk. Since then the early models have been replaced by diesel-driven units, but the company has kept the name "skunk."

Today the Skunk is the single-car unit which makes the trip once each way daily, winter and summer, although schedules vary seasonally. It makes all stops when flagged. The Super Skunk was added in 1965, because the line had become popular with outsiders who just wanted to take the ride. An old-time Mikado 2-8-2 steam locomotive almost a hundred years old, completely rebuilt and refurbished and pulling colorful passenger cars, it makes the trip across and back daily from late May to mid-September, during Easter week, and on Saturdays several weekends in spring and fall. It makes just one stop on the way across and is the only regularly scheduled, standard-gauge steam train passenger service in the West.

Reservations must be made well ahead of time to ensure yourself of a ride on the Super Skunk. For information on current schedules, fares, and reservations, write to the California Western Railroad, Box 907-B, Fort Bragg 95437.

Three campgrounds have a total of 162 improved sites (showers). Rock Creek and Hickey are near the highway; Rock Creek is in dense second growth, Hickey in a more open area. Redwood campground is on the slopes across the river on terraces. A campfire and picnic area is located near Hickey camp, with a small amphitheatre and several short hiking trails. One trail leads to a lookout point near the southern park boundary. The 5-mile Mill Creek loop is steep and rugged.

For further information: Area Manager, c/o Richardson Grove State Park, Garberville 95440.

Access: Standish-Hickey is on the west side of U.S. 101 just north of Leggett.

Westport-Union Landing State Beach

A small, scenic beach of 32 acres, Westport-Union Landing is located on the wild coast just north of the sleepy, historically colorful town of Westport. It has coastal cliffs, with a small cove and beach.

The park is completely undeveloped except for unpaved roads and parking and is for day use only.

Activities: Picnicking, rock and surf fishing, diving for abalone.

Access: The park is on the west side of State 1 about 2 miles north of Westport. There is no sign, and the park is difficult to identify, as many camping vehicles use pullouts all along this stretch of highway.

MacKerricher State Park

The northernmost of a trio of magnificent coastal parks clustered along a short section of the Mendocino coast, MacKerricher has headlands, beaches, surf, heavily forested uplands, and even a small lake, all on approximately 300 acres. The beach extends south to Pudding Creek behind an elevated lumber company right-of-way.

MacKerricher, like Van Damme and Russian Gulch to the south, is popular and rarely has campsite vacancies in summer, despite its three campgrounds—so apply for reservations. The weather is typically north coastal, with considerable fog in summer and very wet winters, but temperatures are usually pleasant.

Lake Cleone, once a tidal lagoon and now landlocked,

is an unusual feature for this type of coastal park. It is planted with trout each year, and catfish planted a few years back are thriving.

Activities: Camping, picnicking, hiking, beachcombing, fishing and boating (non-power only) on Lake Cleone, surf fishing, nature interpretation with a campfire center. There is no swimming—the park includes no safe beaches, and the lake is shallow and weedy.

The campgrounds are Pinewood, Cleone, and Surfwood, with the latter two near the lake in open timber, Pinewood in denser forest. They have a total of 143 campsites, all improved (showers). A sanitation station for trailers and campers is provided. There is a picnic area on the shores of the lake, and a 6-mile loop trail goes almost to Pudding Creek.

MacKerricher is a popular park for skin-divers, who go out after abalone, but these shellfish are pretty well fished out near the shore.

Ocean fishing includes both surf and rock fish; the lake has trout and catfish. Several of the streams in the vicinity of the park offer steelhead and salmon fishing in season, and party boats for deep sea fishing operate out of nearby fishing harbors.

For further information: Area Manager, Mendocino Area State Parks, P.O. Box 127, Mendocino 95460.

Access: The park entrance is 3 miles north of Fort Bragg off State 1.

Supplies: A grocery store near north edge of park and Fort Bragg. A snack bar and boat launch concession at the lake rents bicycles and various small craft for use on the lake.

Russian Gulch State Park

Coastal beauty that rivals Point Lobos, redwoods, a scenic beach, a waterfall, a pygmy forest, and even a self-guided nature trail for automobiles make Russian Gulch one of the outstanding state parks.

Pygmy Forest is one of several along this section of coast where peculiar soils inhibit plant growth. Fully formed and mature pines and cypresses, normally 50 to 60 feet high, here grow only 3 or 4 feet high.

The Devil's Punch Bowl is an interesting example of the result of wave action, although not as dramatic as visitors sometimes expect. The sea has cut a tunnel here several hundred feet under the land, the inland part of which has collapsed, making a large pit into which sea water ebbs and flows through the tunnel. Wildflowers along the rim are spectacular, apparently stimulated by the ocean spray.

Once a tidal lagoon, *Lake Cleone at MacKerricher State Park is now landlocked by dune movement, is fresh water. You can boat here with small craft and fish for planted trout and catfish.*

As at all north coast parks, weather at Russian Gulch can be foggy in summer, but it is usually warm, and there is much good weather in spring and fall. Temperatures in summer range from 30 to 40 degrees cooler than in the interior valleys. The park is open for campers from March 15 to November 1, for day use all year. During the closed camping period, nearby Van Damme and MacKerricher are available.

Russian Gulch is sizable, with more than 1,100 acres extending inland from the scenic headlands. The park is bordered by Jackson State Forest on the east.

Activities: Camping, picnicking, sunning and other beach activities in the cove at the mouth of Russian Gulch Creek, hiking and nature study, stream and rock fishing, skin-diving.

The main campground, with 30 improved sites (showers), is up the creek canyon, protected from sea winds; some sites are on the edge of a meadow, some in dense alder groves. A group camp with 40 sites is nearby, available on reservation. A small picnic area is provided at the beach, and there is a somewhat larger one on the headland above the cove beneath Bishop pines.

A narrow but easily negotiable road follows the creek for several miles, with various areas numbered for identification with the trail pamphlet. At the head of this road Falls Loop Trail circles 3½ miles for a view of the 52-foot high falls. Another trail leads to the Pygmy Forest, and there are several trails around the headland and to the Devil's Punch Bowl. The trails and nature study for both coastal and inland ecology are excellent, with a great variety of wildlife.

Rock fishing is possible at a number of points, and trout are taken in the creek. Because it is a spawning stream, steelhead fishing is not allowed. Some visitors bring small boats and fish for salmon in nearby waters, but venturing to sea in such a craft may be dangerous for the inexperienced because of fog and surf. Party boat fishing is available at a number of nearby towns.

For further information: Area Manager, Mendocino Area State Parks, P.O. Box 127, Mendocino 95460.

Access: The park entrance is 1 mile north of Mendocino on State 1.

Supplies: Mendocino or Fort Bragg.

Van Damme State Park

Van Damme State Park encompasses much of Little River and its scenic canyon, a beach, a pygmy forest, and land heavily forested with second-growth trees.

Little River is a small stream in summer (not to be confused with the one north of Arcata), flowing down a canyon with steep sloping walls covered with sword ferns and other rain forest species. The park includes the cove at the creek mouth and extends eastward several miles in a long parcel of 1,800 acres.

Climate is mild, and most of the park is protected from sea winds. Considerable fog may be expected in summer, and rainfall is heavy in winter. Many valley people come here to get away from summer heat.

As early as 1864 a lumber mill was operated on the site of the present park, producing 20,000 feet of lumber daily from redwood logs hauled down the canyon on skid roads. Somewhat later the owners, dissatisfied with the availability of ships to take their lumber to market, induced a ship-builder to set up a shipyard on the north side of the cove, and eventually 13 ships were built there. With their profits, the partners built palatial homes nearby—one of them survives as the Little River Inn.

Charles Van Damme, born at Little River in 1881, went to San Francisco, made a fortune in the ferryboat business, and returned to buy the property after it was logged out. He allowed his land to be used for public camping, and in 1934, after his death, the family gave the first parcel of land to create the park. Since then, it has been considerably expanded with other acquisitions.

Activities: Camping, picnicking, hiking, fishing. The main campground, with 74 improved campsites, is near the mouth of the canyon, protected from winds, with most sites among trees. The group camp area is closer to the road. Campfire programs are held from July to Labor Day.

Although this is one of the very few north coast beaches which is reasonably safe for swimming, the water is a cold 52 degrees. Even the most hardy usually find a quick dip sufficient.

Fishing is not exceptional, although sometimes there is a run of salmon or steelhead near the coast in fall and winter. Rock fishing at the park and nearby is better, and skin-divers base at the park for abalone fishing.

A paved road, narrow (virtually one-way in places) but easily negotiable, follows the old skid road for about a mile. The park furnishes an excellent nature trail guide which you can follow as you drive from stop to stop. Several interesting trails branch out from the road, including one to the pygmy forest.

For further information: Area Manager, Mendocino Area State Parks, P.O. Box 127, Mendocino 95460.

Access: The entrance is off State 1 about 2 miles south of Mendocino.

Supplies: Mendocino or Fort Bragg.

Admiral William Standley, Montgomery Woods, and Mailliard State Reserves

Small pockets of virgin redwoods in Mendocino County about 15 to 25 miles in from the coast, Admiral William H. Standley, Montgomery Woods, and Mailliard are reserves for trees which were overlooked in logging operations for one reason or another. These three parks preserve the original redwood ecology and its associated plant life untouched by man.

None is developed for public use, nor is it likely they will be for some time, if ever. Terrain is generally rugged. Present policy is to keep them as their names indicate—redwood reserves.

Here and there along the roadsides are widened spaces for parking, and sometimes a picnic table or two. Hiking, exploring, and picnicking without fires are permitted. All three areas have small streams, and there may be native trout in them, but they are wary.

Admiral William H. Standley: A small redwood area (45 acres) with about a half mile of frontage on the South Fork of the Eel, this reserve was named for a naval officer born in the county. There is a small picnic area along the river. The reserve is just east of the town of Branscomb and is accessible by a county road which connects Laytonville on U.S. 101 and Westport on State 1. The only sign is at the park.

Montgomery Woods: More than 800 acres of fine large redwoods make up this park. There are several small streams. Woodwardia ferns are outstanding here. From U.S. 101 just north of Ukiah, you go 14 miles over a county road. The only sign is at the park.

Mailliard: Named for conservationist John Ward Mailliard, Jr., whose family still retains large ranch holdings in the adjacent valley, this reserve includes a total of 242 acres. The headwaters of the Garcia River run through it. (The river is a spawning stream for salmon and steelhead, and fishing is prohibited.) The access road off State 128 is 8 miles east of Boonville or 5 miles west of Yorkville. Turn south at the old wooden bridge onto Mendocino County Route 122 (Signal Ridge Road to Anchor Bay) and drive about 4 miles to the park over good road. There are no signs except at the park.

Paul M. Dimmick Wayside Camp

Paul M. Dimmick Wayside Camp makes a handy place for the trailer camper to use as a base for exploring the surrounding redwood country and the superb Mendocino coast. You will also see tent campers who come to Dimmick for a quiet place to relax.

A small area of 12 acres between the highway and the Navarro River, Dimmick is in dense redwood second growth which was cut over so long ago that the trees look big except in comparison to the old stumps.

Climate is excellent here in late spring, summer, and early fall—warm and sunny, just in from the coastal fog belt. Like all redwood parks, this one is damp and chilly in winter, and it also is often flooded by the river. The park is open from May to October.

Activities: Camping, picnicking, stream play for children, steelhead and salmon fishing in season. Sometimes there are a few swimming holes in the Navarro River.

There are 28 improved campsites along the river and a separate picnic area with 12 sites. The Masonite Com-

pany has large holdings along the highway adjacent to Dimmick and has provided access at many points for casual campers (mostly vehicle campers), with no facilities except parking.

The Navarro is a popular steelhead fishing stream, and occasionally it has silver salmon runs.

Access: The park is off State 128, about 7 miles north of Navarro.

Supplies: General store in village of Navarro.

Hendy Woods State Park

For the camper or picnicker who wants a quiet place to stop, Hendy Woods is a good choice. Not so well known as some of the state parks, it usually has available campsites. A live stream runs through the park, and there are two virgin redwood groves.

Although a major highway runs through it, the valley is sparsely populated. Coast range ridges rise high on both sides, with Hendy Woods' 700 acres situated on a flat a short distance off the road.

Climate is warm to hot in summer, mild in spring and fall; there is heavy rainfall in winter. Any time of year in good weather the park is enjoyable for picnicking, with the added bonus of fall and winter fishing nearby.

Activities: Camping, picnicking, hiking, fishing, water play for children in summer in Navarro River, nature walks in summer every Saturday morning.

Hendy has two campgrounds, Azalea and Wildcat, both in mixed redwood and Douglas fir forests which provide good privacy (showers). About 25 picnic sites are furnished a short distance away along the river.

Summer trout fishing is usually poor, but there is steelhead and salmon fishing from the park boundary northeast to the ocean during the fall-winter season.

For further information: Area Manager, Mendocino Area State Parks, P.O. Box 127, Mendocino 95460.

Access: Turn south from State 128 about 3 miles north of Philo and go half a mile to the park entrance.

Supplies: Philo.

Indian Creek State Reserve

A small redwood grove comprising 15 acres, Indian Creek State Reserve is just west of Philo on State 128. The rather obscure entrance is just south of Indian Creek Bridge. There is a live creek, but there are no facilities. A parking area is provided.

Manchester State Beach

A relatively wild, sloping beach just north of Point Arena, Manchester provides a chance for the surf caster to practice his skill and for the beachcomber to roam. A 2-mile beach strip is backed by a section of open

Redwoods *grow best near fresh water, and streams are a common feature of the redwood parks. Children here are playing in stream at Indian Creek Reserve, small park off State 128, a good place to stop for a basket lunch.*

coastal ledge with facilities. Point Arena and its lighthouse are visible to the south.

Manchester is apt to be windy, often foggy in summer, and usually cold and often stormy in winter.

Activities: Camping, picnicking, beachcombing, fishing. Campsites are primitive, located behind the dunes and in the lee of a line of cypress. Facilities are relatively new; there are dirt roads, and the 46 campsites are available for picnickers when not occupied. Camping limit is 15 days. Space is usually available.

The sharply shelving beach is dangerous for surfing or swimming. There is good surf fishing when fish are running, and sometimes surf smelt are caught.

For further information: Area Manager, Mendocino Area State Parks, P.O. Box 127, Mendocino 95460.

Access: The park entrance is on the west side of State 1, about a mile north of Manchester.

Supplies: Manchester.

Kruse Rhododendron State Reserve

From about April to June, you can see a profusion of rhododendron blossoms at Kruse Rhododendron State Reserve. More than 300 acres are set aside to preserve the *Rhododendron macrophyllum*, or California

rosebay, as it grew before Europeans first arrived in California. When the plants are in bloom, you may wander along paths beneath big trusses of rosy blooms hanging from shrubs up to 20 feet high.

Although its name identifies it as a California shrub, this is the western rhododendron common to Pacific Coast forests north to British Columbia. The name should not be confused with *Rhododendron occidentale*, which is the western azalea and often is found in the same vicinity. The latter is creamy white with a different type bloom, although it is actually a member of the rhododendron family. (See Azalea State Reserve, page 15.)

The reserve has good trails, parking, and restrooms, but there are no picnic facilities.

Access: The reserve is on State 1 north of Salt Point 3 miles. There is a sign at the entrance but none in advance, and the entrance on the east side of the highway is at a sharp turn uphill; continue about a mile to the reserve on a steep but good gravel road.

Salt Point State Park

A new and relatively undeveloped state park along the wild coast, Salt Point has scenic coastal headlands, small beaches, rolling open coastal shelf, and dense Bishop pine forests.

Climate is mild in late spring, summer, and early fall, but it may be windy; summer fog is common, as are heavy storms in winter.

Activities: Camping, picnicking, hiking and beachcombing, fishing. A campground with 31 primitive units and dirt roads is on the slopes back of the point at the edge of pines; 25 picnic sites are scattered near the coast.

Because of the small beaches, surf fishing is not good, but there are many places for rock fishing. Skin-divers take abalone. Gualala River about 12 miles north is a famous steelhead stream.

For further information: Area Manager, Fort Ross State Historic Park, 19005 Coast Highway 1, Jenner 95450.

Access: The park is off State 1, with the entrance on the west side of the highway 8 miles north of Fort Ross.

Supplies: Jenner or Gualala.

Fort Ross State Historic Park

Fires in 1970 and 1971 destroyed much of Fort Ross State Historic Park, also a national historic monument. The old stockade and blockhouses are now all that is left to memorialize this Russian foothold in California, known to the Russians as Colony Ross and to the Mexicans as Fuerte de los Rusos.

The fascinating replica of the original church burned to the ground in 1970, and another fire in 1971 destroyed the roof of the commanding officer's quarters, closing its museum. Restoration is planned when funds are available.

From 1812 on, Fort Ross was for a number of years the headquarters and supply base for Russian traffic in sea otter and seal along the north Pacific Coast. Captain John A. Sutter bought the property from its Russian owners in 1841, and it gradually fell into disrepair with the downfall of his personal fortune. The site and dilapidated structures became state property in 1906, and portions of the old fort were restored in the 1950's after careful research.

The state property takes in 355 acres around the site, including a coastal strip with a cove which has a small beach and a few picnic tables. A special group of picnic tables on the beach is provided for skin-divers and abalone fishermen.

Access: Although the State Division of Highways has plans for routing State 1 around the fort, the road presently passes directly through it. Parking is provided.

Fort Ross is 11 miles north of Jenner via a scenic drive through wild coastal scenery equal to the Big Sur country of the central coast.

Armstrong Redwoods State Reserve

Although classified as a state reserve, Armstrong offers a great deal in addition to the redwoods. It is the only state park in the Russian River country with camping and a big day-use area as well as the giant redwoods. Swimming in the river near the park supplements these activities, and Austin Creek State Recreation area is on the other side of the river (see below).

Weather here is generally mild year-round, and the park is just back from the coastal fog belt, although it may be damp and chilly in the rainy season.

Activities: Camping, picnicking, hiking, nature study. The 1,200-seat Redwood Forest Theatre has stage and musical productions during the summer, and with the popularity of outdoor weddings it has become so much in demand that a reservation list must be kept. (You have the use of the area for two hours, there is an electrical outlet for an organ, and you may have receptions in the picnic area. An entrance fee of $1 per car is charged the same as for day use, but the responsible person can arrange to be billed for the entire party.)

The campground of 20 improved sites (showers) is around a meadow at the edge of the forest. No trailers are permitted. Nearby in deep groves is a 100-unit picnic area. Both facilities are very popular and get heavy use in the summer.

A self-guided nature trail loops through the big tree area, which includes the Colonel Armstrong and Parson Jones redwoods. In addition, summer nature walks are conducted three times a week.

Two branches of Fife Creek wind through the park but offer no fishing.

For further information: Area Manager, Russian River Area State Parks, P.O. Box 385, Guerneville 95446.

Access: The park is 2 miles north from the center of Guerneville on Armstrong Woods Road.

Supplies: Guerneville.

Austin Creek State Recreation Area

Austin Creek is really an extension of Armstrong Redwoods, but whereas Armstrong has only about 700 acres, Austin has more than 4,000, with a complete change of terrain. Whereas Armstrong is dark and almost gloomy with the dense growth stimulated by the deep rich soil and abundant water, Austin is brilliantly sunlit, rolling coastal mountain country. Much of it is oak grass, with many open fields, and there is dense growth of madrone, Douglas fir, and alder in the canyons. Three live creeks run through the recreation area, and there are about 100 springs. The air is clear, and you can find quiet and privacy here.

Austin is warm in summer and, unlike Armstrong, not damp and chilly in winter, making it usable year-round although winter use may be somewhat curtailed when the creeks are high.

Activities: Camping, picnicking, fishing, hiking, and riding, with emphasis on the latter two.

Redwood Lake is a small artificial lake near the center of the park, with 25 unimproved campsites and a few picnic sites. Here you will find ancient madrones which probably will dwarf any you have seen elsewhere. There are several other primitive hike-in camping areas, with Horse Haven set aside for equestrian campers.

The streams contain native trout, but they are elusive. During the season, when conditions are good, you may catch steelhead and salmon.

For further information: See Armstrong Redwoods State Reserve (above).

Access: After entering Armstrong (see above), stay to the right until you see a sign near the picnic ground which says Redwood Lake Campground. From here you negotiate a narrow, steep, winding but surfaced road for 2½ miles until you come out on top of the first ridge, about 2,000 feet above. The road is not passable with trailers, heavy campers, or heavy vans.

Supplies: Guerneville.

Sonoma Coast State Beach

A constantly changing panorama of small, shining beaches, rocky headlands, and massive rock stacks off-shore is presented by Sonoma Coast State Beach. This park consists of a string of beaches and coves extending along State 1 from the north end of the fishing village of Bodega Bay to the mouth of the Russian River, with more than 11 miles of ocean frontage.

Goat Rock and the surrounding rocky coast near the mouth of the Russian River are dramatic. The dune area just south of Salmon Creek has experimental plantings of European beach grass to stabilize sand movement.

Although often rainy and chilly in winter, these beaches have many pleasant off-season days, and the park is used all year. Coastal fog can be expected often in summer, but the days are warm. Spring and fall are usually superb.

Duncan's Landing is a dangerous portion of this coast; it is fenced and marked with a sign. The configuration of the sea bottom sometimes creates huge swells which wash over the rocks here. There is a lesser danger at some other points, but tide changes can trap adventurous rock climbers if they are not aware. The cold water, suddenly shelving beaches, surf, and currents make going beyond shallow surf foolhardy, particularly for small children.

Activities: Fishing, beachcombing, picnicking, camping. There are 30 improved campsites at Wright's Beach, with a 10-day limit in summer—not advisable in winter because of storms. These facilities are available for picnicking when not occupied.

Picnic facilities are also provided at Rocky Point and near Goat Rock behind the dunes, but most visitors picnic without facilities wherever they like, as there are dozens of small beaches and sheltered coves.

Fishing includes surf, rock, and surf-net. The latter is a popular pastime, and you can see the colorful net work-ers at many places when the smelt are running. Salmon Creek at the south end of the park is open during the steelhead season from the ocean to the highway bridge.

For further information: Area Manager, Russian River Area State Parks, P.O. Box 385, Guerneville 95446.

Access: The beaches all lie on the seaward side of State 1; many are marked by signs. Twenty-four parking areas are provided.

Dramatic *scenery and profusion of wildflowers are features of the Sonoma Coast beaches most of the year.*

Sierra Nevada & Northern Mountains

Forming a north-south barrier for more than 400 miles in the eastern part of the state, the rugged Sierra Nevada range rises to a height of 14,495 feet at Mt. Whitney in the southern section of the range. Much of this country is virtually inaccessible wilderness, but at a group of state parks here you can camp and hike in forests of conifers and fish in mountain streams and lakes.

The state parks are concentrated in the central part of the range along the western slopes. Several are near beautiful Lake Tahoe, high in the mountains at the California-Nevada border. North of the Sierra, the state parks extend into the Cascade and Klamath ranges.

Hiking and fishing are two major pastimes at the parks in this part of the state. Usually there is at least planted-trout fishing in the vicinity of the state parks here. Nearly all of the parks border on great expanses of national forest or other primitive areas.

At altitudes of 3,000 feet and much higher, all of these parks will have warm days in summer but usually cool nights. (For most of them, sleeping bags constructed for temperatures down to 30 degrees are a good idea. If you use a cot, provide yourself with a pad or other insulation to go between your bag and cot.) Heavy snow-falls in winter mean that most of the parks are open for camping only five to six months of the year, but in response to public demand some are now being kept open for winter camping (see individual park descriptions). Snow melting in spring keeps the streams running all year and fills hundreds of lakes.

Several historic parks in this part of the state offer insight into the state's mining past. Bodie, in the southern Sierra, is a mining ghost town from the 1870's and 1880's. Shasta, west of Redding, was a mining supply center, and Malakoff Diggins in the central Sierra was the world's biggest hydraulic mining operation.

Castle Crags State Park

Located on both sides of Interstate 5, with vehicle and pedestrian undercrossings, Castle Crags State Park ranges from about 2,000 feet altitude along the Sacramento River up to more than 6,000 feet at the summit of the great granite crags from which it takes its name.

The campground is popular in summer for one-night stopovers, but the park offers a wide variety of activities and terrain. Climate is warm in summer, sometimes hot, with cool nights; but winters are cold and wet, often with heavy snow and sub-freezing temperatures. Rainfall is 70 to 90 inches annually.

Activities: Camping, picnicking, hiking, rock and cliff climbing, swimming, fishing. The park is open from April to October, with 15-day camping limits. The campground has 64 improved sites (showers), which may be

Rubicon and Phipps peaks dominate skyline above Emerald Bay on Lake Tahoe. Two state parks—Emerald Bay and D. L. Bliss—enclose the bay (see page 35).

Eroded cliffs at Malakoff Diggins, opposite photo, still hold tons of gold. Hydraulic mining dug pit more than 200 feet deep (see page 31).

used for picnicking when unoccupied. The sites are situated on the slopes above headquarters, mostly in conifer forest. A picnic ground near the river provides 21 picnic sites. Bears may be a nuisance, so food should be stored in the car trunk.

Rangers conduct guided nature hikes on Thursdays and Vista Point talks on Sundays. The rare Brewer's spruce grows here, and there is a natural mineral spring near the river. Several points in the park afford dramatic views of Mount Shasta to the north.

Many streams in and near the park offer good trout fishing, and the Sacramento River at the park's lower levels is popular with fishermen, who take trout, steelhead, and salmon in season. The river has a few swimming holes.

Trails lead to several areas, giving access to adjacent national forest land in some cases, but long-range hikers should be experienced. The back country is virtually unsettled and wild all the way to the seacoast. Slightly southeast about 20 miles are the Trinity Alps and the Trinity Alps Wilderness Area, with its many lakes.

One trail climbs into the Crags, giving fine vantage points of the surrounding country. Rock climbers sometimes practice in the Crags, but this sport, too, is for the experienced.

For further information: Area Manager, Castle Crags State Park, Castella 96017.

Access: The park entrance is west of Interstate 5, about 6 miles south of the town of Dunsmuir and 25 miles north of Shasta Lake.

Supplies: Small shopping center near park entrance, including gas station.

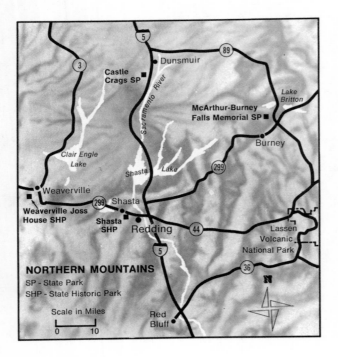

McArthur-Burney Falls Memorial State Park

One of the more popular mountain parks is McArthur-Burney Falls Memorial in northern lava-plateau country, heavily forested with conifers. Burney Falls, dropping thunderously down a sheer 129-foot cliff into a pool of emerald green water, is a spectacular feature of this state park. Fed by great springs which commence within the park, the flow is more than 200 million gallons of water each day.

The park has excellent summer weather at its 3,000 foot altitude, and it usually is full in summer. In addition to the falls, the park's recreation value is greatly expanded by Lake Britton on Pacific Gas and Electric Company land at the state park's northern boundaries. Lassen Volcanic National Park is about 30 miles to the south, and Lava Beds National Monument is a day's round trip to the north.

Days are pleasantly warm in summer, with cool nights; there are occasional summer thunderstorms. Fall and spring may be crisp, with nights quite cool. Some snow can be expected in winter.

Activities: Camping, picnicking, hiking, swimming, stream and lake fishing, boating, water-skiing, nature study.

The park is well developed and maintained. Pioneer and Rim campgrounds provide 118 improved campsites (showers) with fairly good privacy. Summer camping limit is 15 days, but the park is open all year. There is no piped water in winter. A picnic area near the park entrance and another near the beach offer 51 units.

Burney has a number of trails, some leading into adjacent P.G. & E. and national forest land. A footbridge off the Headwaters Trail takes the hiker across Burney Creek above the falls to a self-guided nature trail and the best view of the falls; it is about a half-mile walk. From the parking lot near headquarters, there is another trail which drops down into the canyon below the falls—about an hour's easy trip for even the casual walker. On a hot day, following this trail is like entering an air-conditioned room, for the water coming over the falls is a constant 48 degrees.

The park has a campfire circle near headquarters for interpretive talks and programs, and there are nature walks several days a week in summer.

Wildlife ranges from bears and cougars down to many small rodents, as much of the country roundabout is still relatively unsettled. Large mammals are rarely seen in summer, however, as they are wary of people. Occasionally a bald eagle is sighted.

The lake offers bass and perch fishing; trout are planted in the creek. Swimming at the beach is only for the experienced; the bottom slopes downward rapidly from the shore, and there are no lifeguards.

A marina concessionaire offers mooring, rents boats and tackle, and sells bait.

Burney Falls *tumbles over porous basalt ledge, with many secondary falls coming directly out of the rock. Pyramidal section in center gradually is being cut away. Rare black swifts nest in cliffs around the falls.*

For further information: Area Manager, McArthur-Burney Falls Memorial State Park, Route 1, Box 1260, Burney 96013.

Access: From Interstate 5 at Redding, drive 64 miles northeast via State 299 and State 89.

Supplies: Concession near park entrance with snack bar, gift shop, and some groceries in season; otherwise at Burney, 13 miles away.

Weaverville Joss House State Historic Park

In Weaverville you can visit perhaps the western hemisphere's finest remaining example of a Taoist temple. The Joss House still serves a small congregation of elderly Chinese.

The Weaverville Joss House dates back to 1873, when it was constructed as a replacement for a previous temple which burned. The interiors of the Joss House are authentic and splendid.

The historic park is open every day of the year (except Christmas, New Year's, and Thanksgiving), and tours are conducted every half hour from 10 A.M. to 5 P.M. in summer. A small fee is charged adults.

Joss House *exterior is explained by park ranger to tour group at historic park. Building still serves as Taoist temple.*

Next door is the County Historic Museum, also worth visiting.

Access: The Joss House is on the south side of Main Street in Weaverville (State 299W) at Oregon Street, just west of the town center.

Shasta State Historic Park

An important supply and transportation center during the days of the northern gold rush, Old Shasta became a ghost town when the mines petered out and the great hydraulic operations to the west were stopped in 1884. Now part of the town has been designated as Shasta State Historic Park.

More than 100 freight wagons came into town each day during Shasta's peak in the 1850's, carrying supplies to be transferred to 2,000 pack mules and taken into the rugged back country. Mule skinners called Shasta "the head of 'whoa' navigation." The buildings were set well back from the main street to accommodate the press of animals and vehicles.

The town was the county seat for many years, but with its commercial decline and the construction of the railroad farther east, it lost its importance. Restoration of the old courthouse was begun in 1922 by private groups and continued by the state, and the building was opened to the public in 1950. Interiors have been restored and many mementoes of the boom years added. The jail downstairs and the double gallows in the rear recreate vividly another facet of the Old West. The Masonic Hall down the street may be the oldest in the state. Built in 1853, it is still in use.

Currently the park includes only about 11 acres, but attempts are being made to acquire more land.

A parking apron is provided in front of the old courthouse, and ranger interpretive specialists are on duty. A few picnic tables are available. The courthouse is open from 10 A.M. to 5 P.M. daily (except Thanksgiving, Christmas, and New Year's); a small fee is charged.

Access: The park is located on both sides of State 299W some 6 miles west of Redding.

Plumas-Eureka State Park

Nearly 5,000 acres of park in the middle of a scenic recreation area which extends for many miles in all directions, Plumas-Eureka is situated in the northern part of the Sierra Nevada. The park surrounds the ghost town of Johnsville, part of which is state owned, and is the only California park which memorializes hard-rock mining days. Park boundaries include Eureka Peak,

Johnsville's *main street is lined by buildings of past century when this was a mining town. Now it is a ghost town, and it is included in Plumas-Eureka State Park. Center building was the engine house for Johnsville Fire Department.*

where the Plumas-Eureka mine operated for years, following veins with 65 miles of tunnels.

Altitude of the park is about 4,000 feet at headquarters, but much of its acreage is higher. Summer weather is pleasant, with cool nights; the climate can be wintry by October and on into mid-spring. Snowfall often is heavy, and although the park is open all year, in the off-season it gets mainly day use. There is a ski area of sorts. Snow may be lacking, although Johnsville is said to be the cradle of skiing in the United States (see next column).

Activities: Camping, picnicking, hiking, lake and stream fishing, nature and historic interpretation, some snow activity in winter, but off the beaten track.

Upper Jamison has 67 improved campsites (showers) on Jamison Creek in a grove of yellow pines. Reservations are available in summer. Picnic facilities are being developed, but vacant campsites may be used for picnicking. The campground is not open in winter.

Trails, old roads, and fire roads make a great network for hikers all through this portion of the Sierra and connect it with the Tahoe National Forest Lakes Basin Recreation Area to the south. There are several peaks that can be climbed.

Fishing is good in many creeks and lakes in and near the park. Eureka Lake on Eureka Peak offers good lake fishing and is accessible by paved road much of the way —the last mile and a quarter is rough fire road.

The Plumas-Eureka Mine stamp mill near park headquarters has been shored up and preserved from collapse, and further restoration is going on. This kind of hard-rock mining structure has almost disappeared from the scene today.

The museum and hard-rock mining exhibit at park headquarters is a "must" to see for students of California history and the westward movement. (Guided tours are offered to classes—teachers should contact the park and make arrangements.) The park day-use fee covers admission; hours are from 9 A.M. to 5 P.M.

For further information: Area Manager, Plumas-Eureka State Park, Johnsville Star Route, Blairsden 96103.

Access: Park headquarters are at Johnsville, 6 miles west from the intersection of routes 70 and 89 near Blairsden.

Supplies: Blairsden, or any of several other resort centers in the area.

Malakoff Diggins State Historic Park

A 1,600-acre pit was carved into the earth by huge hydraulic "monitors" during gold mining about a century ago northeast of Nevada City. Today the great manmade cliffs of the Malakoff Diggins—now a state historic park —are eroded and colorful. The park also includes the entire ghost town of North Bloomfield, once center of the hydraulic operation.

THE FIRST SIERRA SKIERS

During the hard winters of the 1850's and 1860's, miners trapped by deep snow in the northern Sierra around Johnsville and nearby camps found a diversion in the sport of skiing. Scandinavians in the group introduced skiing to the miners, and Johnsville claims to be the birthplace of skiing in the United States.

The miners raced down the slopes on skis that were 12 feet long and weighed 25 pounds. Slopes chosen were as nearly perpendicular as practicable. Contestants lined up at a selected point at the top and all took off—literally into the air with one great shove of their poles—when a starter struck a drum or fired a pistol.

The course was straight downhill—usually about a half mile long. Since the races were held only when the snow was hard, speeds of 70 and 80 miles per hour were common. At nearby La Porte, Tommy Todd set a record of 87 miles per hour in 1873, and that record still stands.

La Porte claims to be the home of the first organized ski club in America—the Alturas Snowshoe Club, founded in 1866—but other towns quickly organized their own. The old Eureka Mine in Plumas-Eureka State Park has the distinction of having provided the first ski lift—miners rode the chain buckets uphill.

Malakoff, worked from 1866 to 1884, was the largest hydraulic mining operation in the world. Water fed through giant nozzles at tremendous pressures washed away whole hillsides here, digging a pit more than 200 feet deep. One of the hydraulic monitors is on display at the park historic center. Hydraulic mining was brought to a halt in California by a court decision in 1884, after floods and debris caused by such operations threatened to destroy croplands. The Sacramento River bottom at Marysville was raised 16 feet—3 feet above the town level; this effect at many river towns meant not only that the levees had to be built much higher but that riverboat transport was greatly curtailed.

Wind and rain and time have softened Malakoff's features, smoothed the hard edges, tinted the minerals and soil, and reestablished some vegetation. Now the land has a ghostlike beauty, haunting in its starkness. The museum here has an excellent interpretive display on the hydraulic-mining days. The pit is a short hike away. Mining engineers have estimated that another half billion in gold still lies in the ancient riverbed gravels. Only $3.4 million was taken out—about 10 cents to the yard.

Once some 1,800 people lived in the town of North Bloomfield, but today only a small cluster of nineteenth-century buildings remain. Several buildings have been restored and given period furnishings. At McKillican and Mobley general store "everything from ribbons to

T-rails" was sold. The museum is in a building which was once more lively as the miners' dance hall.

But Malakoff is more than just an historic park, since it includes about 2,600 acres of middle-Sierra country at altitudes of 3,300 feet. Much of the surrounding land is national forest; there are streams and a small lake and camping and picnicking facilities.

Climate is dry and warm in summer and mild in spring and fall, but usually nights are cool in all three seasons. The park may be cold and have snow in winter.

Activities: Camping, picnicking, hiking, fishing, nature study, historical study. A campground is situated above the park headquarters in a wooded area, with 30 unimproved sites. The park is open all year, with a 30-day camping limit. Sites are usually available except during holiday weekends in summer.

Malakoff has two picnic areas—one in town and another near Blair Lake, with a group area for 80 persons available by reservation. An additional "Clampicnic" area on the edge of North Bloomfield is available courtesy of the E Clampus Vitus chapter of Grass Valley-Nevada City.

Blair Lake is artificial, with planted black bass and catfish. During summer rangers give evening history interpretive talks, and once a year in June local communities cooperate in staging the big homecoming celebration at the park.

For further information: Area Manager, Malakoff Diggins State Historic Park, North Bloomfield, Graniteville Star Route, Nevada City 95959.

Access: There are two accesses to the park, both curving mountain roads with considerable gravel mileage. Off State 49 just above Nevada City, turn north on Bloomfield Road and go about a mile to a T-intersection where a sign indicates the park direction to the left; from here it is about 12 miles upgrade. Camping vehicles and trailers should use Tyler Road off State 49 about 12 miles north of Nevada City; you go southeast about 14 miles.

Supplies: Nevada City, Grass Valley, North San Juan.

Donner Memorial State Park

A superb backdrop of high Sierra ridges surrounds Donner Memorial State Park, a 6,000-foot-high area that includes about 2 miles of Donner Lake shoreline around the mouth of Donner Creek. The 350-acre park is forested with lodgepole and Jeffrey pines, with some white and red fir.

Included in the park are important historic sites pertaining to the tragic Donner Party trapped here in heavy snows during the winter of 1846-47.

Summer weather here usually is mild in the daytime, cool at nights; the climate is progressively cooler as the season advances, and there is heavy snow in winter. The park is open from May to October only.

Activities: Camping, picnicking, hiking, fishing, nature and history study, swimming. Three campgrounds, all a short hike from the lake, have a total of 154 improved campsites (showers). Camping limit is 10 days, and reservations are needed. Parking is available at several points for the 50 picnic units scattered along the lake.

The park has a few trails, and a museum housed in a handsome, modern building is the center for various interpretive programs, including movies. Exhibits here give many details on the Donner Party and also depict Sierra geology, local Indian culture, and construction of the first transcontinental railroad through the inhospitable Donner Pass to the west. A self-guided interpretive trail loops from the museum.

The lake is popular with fishermen for kokanee salmon, mainly trolling from boats, and also contains cat-

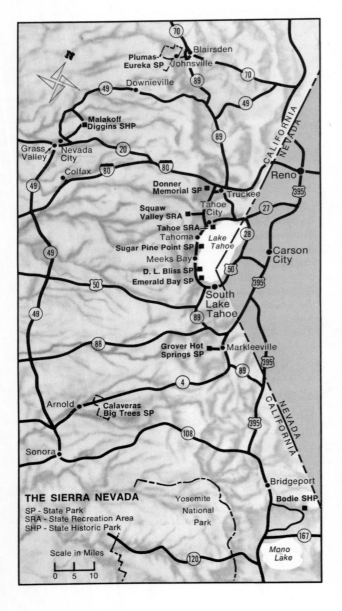

THE SIERRA NEVADA
SP - State Park
SRA - State Recreation Area
SHP - State Historic Park

Scale in Miles
0 5 10

Majestic *setting for picnicking is on shore of Donner Lake at Donner Memorial State Park. Sierra ridges surround park.*

Squaw Valley *takes on a different look after the winter snows melt and skiers depart. Squaw Peak is in distance.*

fish. Trout fishermen like Donner Creek. Several small beaches provide sunbathing and swimming and small boat grounding.

For further information: Area Manager, Sierra Area State Parks, P.O. Box 2127, Olympic Valley 95730.

Access: A sign marks the offramp to the park from Interstate 80 at the east end of Donner Lake.

Supplies: Commercial recreation center nearby and Truckee a few miles away.

Squaw Valley State Recreation Area

An elongated bowl surrounded by Sierra peaks rising to about 9,000 feet, Squaw Valley was the scene of the 1960 Winter Olympic Games. It is a popular winter sports area, and part of it is designated as a state recreation area.

The valley floor is at an elevation of 6,200 feet. Squaw Peak dominates the head of the valley. In winter the area is heavily covered with snow, the white mantle broken only by dark conifers and a few bare rock outcroppings. At this season all other activities are subordinated to skiing, and dozens of lifts fan out from the valley floor. Other lifts at higher altitudes take skiers even higher. Development now is proceeding toward access to adjacent valleys, so it will be possible for skiers to go far beyond Squaw, then return to the

high ridges on supplementary lifts and ski down the slopes into Squaw again.

The state park portion of this vast winter sports area is only about 1,300 acres, but much of it is on the valley floor. You should not overlook its summer attractions. There are planted trout in Squaw Creek, a 10-unit primitive campground high on the slopes for hikers and horsemen, and about 50 picnic tables scattered around the valley floor.

Almost all of the park facilities are operated by concessionaires, which makes them difficult to distinguish from privately-owned establishments. In addition to the winter sports facilities, visitors will find lodging, groceries, movie theater, restaurants, all-year ice arena, tennis court, and horse rentals.

For further information: Area Manager, Sierra Area State Parks, P.O. Box 2127, Olympic Valley 95730.

Access: From Interstate 80 west of Truckee, take the State 89 offramp south and drive about 9 miles, then turn west on the Squaw Valley access road and continue about a mile.

Tahoe State Recreation Area

A little lakeshore park of 14 acres right in the middle of Tahoe City, Tahoe State Recreation Area is almost

THE CROWDED ROAD OVER THE SIERRA

In 1857 the feasibility of the State Wagon Road over the Sierra was still being argued in Sacramento. To force the issue of road improvements, Colonel Jared B. Crandall, operator of the Pioneer Stage Line from Folsom to Hangtown, took a six-horse Concord over the mountains from Hangtown (now Placerville) and announced a weekly run up to Genoa, Nevada.

This was "Johnson's Cutoff"—the Echo Pass route which today is generally followed by U.S. 50. Even before 1857 this had been one of the immigrant routes. But it was an unexpected factor that made the road of vital importance—miners struck silver in 1859 at Virginia City, Nevada.

With the discovery of the rich silver veins, Johnson's Cutoff became a crowded thoroughfare. Wagons struggled through mudholes and over the rocky canyon terrain, up the high pass, and down the steep slopes to Lake Tahoe. Here they swung around the east side of the lake, just as the highway still does, over Spooner Summit, and north into Virginia City.

Virginia City had thousands of men working in the mines. The closest supply point was San Francisco, and there were no railroads. During these years the freight wagons, often pulled by 16 horses or mules, passed in a solid stream through Tahoe Valley, with faster-moving pack trains traveling along the road edge. Among all the other commodities, the machinery for the first Lake Tahoe steamer was hauled over this route.

No driver dared to drop out of line. If he had a breakdown, he would have to wait until after dark to get back on the road. Passenger stages, mail, and Pony Express moved at night. Because of the difficulties of breasting the traffic when returning empty, many came back over Carson Pass, now State 88.

---

always crowded. The park has 39 improved campsites with 10-day limits (showers), but extra vehicle campers somehow seem to crowd in and around the park boundary. The park is open from May to October only.

A small pier is available for fishing if boat activity is not too heavy; there are boat launching, mooring, and rentals. Included in the park are a small beach and picnic area with 8 sites. All supplies are available within walking distance.

Access: The park entrance is a half mile north of the junction of routes 89 and 28.

Sugar Pine Point State Park

Dense forests, about a mile and a half of Lake Tahoe shore, and fine groves of the trees for which it is named are among the attractions of Sugar Pine Point State Park. Relatively new and not yet completely developed, Sugar Pine has much the same character as D. L. Bliss-Emerald Bay (see next page), with slightly more acreage, although it is not quite so scenic.

The park's sugar pines are representative of a species not nearly so profuse as the more common yellow pine but more dramatic and shapely. The long cones are much in demand for Christmas decorations, and this somewhat rare species has been decimated. It provides a soft but tight-grained, easily worked lumber which is highly prized for certain specialized purposes such as making molds.

Sugar Pine Point is very similar in climate to the other mountain parks in the vicinity—warm and pleasant in summer with cool nights, cold with heavy snow in winter, but somewhat better protected than the other parks in the area.

Activities: Camping, picnicking, hiking, fishing, nature study, swimming, tennis. The campgrounds above the highway provide 175 improved campsites (some with showers) in heavy forest. One portion is designated for both summer and winter camping. The park is open all year, with camping limits 10 days in summer, 30 in winter. A trailer sanitation station is available.

Because of Sugar Pine Point's more protected location, it is the only state park in the Tahoe area offering winter camping; 75 campsites are set aside for this purpose. Parking spaces and roadways are kept open except during extreme storm conditions; restrooms are heated, with hot water available. Shower rooms are not open during the winter.

The day-use area below the highway has a 75-unit picnic ground with parking. This part of the park is a preserve for the sugar pines and cinnamon-bark juniper. Here also are an interpretive center, a beach, and a small pier.

Several hiking trails have been laid out—two of them follow either shore of General Creek, which runs through the park to empty into the lake near the interpretive center. One trail continues into the Desolation Valley Wilderness Area high above.

General Creek has rainbow, eastern brook, and German brown trout, as do several other streams in the vicinity and in the wilderness area. The lake has Mackinaw lake trout and kokanee salmon. Some fishermen deepline for the former, but surface trolling and bank fishing are popular.

The interpretive center-museum is located in the Ehrman mansion, which the state acquired with the property. Wildlife and ecology of the area is explained at the interpretive center, and some rooms in the mansion retain the appearance they had in the 1900's, when this was the finest summer house on the lake. Several tennis courts on the grounds are available on reservation.

For further information: Area Manager, Sierra Area State Parks, P.O. Box 2127, Olympic Valley 95730.

Access: The park is north of D. L. Bliss-Emerald Bay on both sides of State Route 89 between Tahoma and Meeks Bay.

Supplies: Tahoma or Meeks Bay.

Emerald Bay State Park
D. L. Bliss State Park

Six miles of frontage on Lake Tahoe and Emerald Bay, massive virgin pine groves, and granite outcroppings make Emerald Bay and D. L. Bliss a superb mountain park area. The two units operate as a single park, with headquarters for both parks at Bliss, but there are separate ranger stations at Emerald Bay also.

Altitude at the park is nearly 7,000 feet. Days usually are warm in late spring, summer, and early fall, but there may be occasional summer thunderstorms. Winter climate is cold, with much snow, and the park is open only from about mid-May until mid-September.

Activities: Camping, picnicking, hiking, fishing, nature study, swimming, and controlled boating and water-skiing on the lake.

In the Bliss portion there are three campgrounds with a total of 168 improved campsites (showers); in the Emerald Bay unit at Eagle Point there are two more campgrounds with another 100 sites. Campsite reservations are always necessary. A group camp with a 40-person capacity is available on reservation, and on the north shore of Emerald Bay a primitive camp with 20 sites is provided for boaters (who should familiarize themselves with regulations for the bay). Commercial boat launching facilities are available about 6 miles to the north.

The day-use area at Eagle Falls at the head of Emerald Bay has parking with a short hike to the Emerald Bay viewpoint and trails leading down to the lake and to views of Eagle Falls. The forest service furnishes picnicking facilities nearby.

A feature of the day-use area is the Vikingsholm "castle," built in 1929 and designed by a Swedish architect who had instructions to construct an eighth-century Norse fortress. The ground floor is open to the public from July 1 to Labor Day. From the parking lot it is a 1-mile hike down to Vikingsholm, near the lake level; the trail continues as part of the Rubicon Trail around Emerald Point.

Lester Beach, just north of scenic Rubicon Point, is the best and most popular swimming beach, but there are several other small cove beaches along the lake shore.

Best lake fishing is in Emerald Bay below Maiden Rock and at Rubicon Point. Several streams in the vicinity have native and planted trout.

Excellent nature interpretation programs are offered during the summer, and there is a short self-guided trail near Balancing Rock. Among the park's trails, the Rubicon Trail offers outstanding views along the edge of Emerald Bay and around the Point.

For further information: Area Manager, Sierra Area State Parks, P.O. Box 2127, Olympic Valley 95730.

Fortresslike *castle of Vikingsholm is close to shore of Emerald Bay on Lake Tahoe; it is open during summer months.*

Access: State Route 89 on the west side of Lake Tahoe winds through both parks, and the main park entrance is on the east side of the highway about a mile north of Emerald Bay. The parks are well marked.

Supplies: Many small communities along the lake shore to north and south, within a few miles.

Grover Hot Springs State Park

A true alpine park in the central Sierra higher than 6,000 feet, Grover Hot Springs is set in a mountain meadow beneath granite ridges that rise another 4,000 feet. Its own hot springs pool gives the park its name. Vegetation here includes scattered groves of yellow pines, alder, and quaking aspen.

The climate is on the chilly side; days are usually warm in summer, but nighttime temperatures average 50 degrees, and frost is not uncommon in early June and late September. Snowfall is heavy in winter.

Activities: Camping, picnicking, hiking, and stream fishing. Toiyabe and Quaking Aspen campgrounds contain 76 improved sites between them (showers). Near the park entrance is a day-use area with 30 picnic units.

Camping is popular in summer, and reservations are advisable. The campgrounds are closed from October until May, but the park remains open all year. Some hardy souls come in winter to take a dip in the warm pool and then cool off in the snow.

The entire area is sportsmen's country, and many streams provide good trout fishing. Several trails offer stiff climbs to the tops of the surrounding ridges.

For further information: Area Manager, Sierra Area State Parks, P.O. Box 2127, Olympic Valley 95730.

Access: From Markleeville on State Route 89, drive west about 3 miles on county route E-1.

Supplies: Markleeville.

SNOWMOBILING IN CALIFORNIA

Snowmobiles in California must be registered and carry a valid identification plate before they may be used on any public or private property. Information and registration forms are available at State Department of Motor Vehicle offices throughout the state.

Five dollars of the original $18 registration fee and a biennial $10 fee go into a trust fund for use by the State Department of Parks and Recreation. The state legislature has directed that the park department's share of the money be used to plan and develop safe and environmentally acceptable snowmobile trails in the mountains and to maintain and administer an effective program of conservation.

Glaciers *and the Stanislaus River have carved granite ledge at Calaveras Big Trees State Park.*

Calaveras Big Trees State Park

Groves of imposing Big Trees are found at only one state park—Calaveras Big Trees. A beautiful mountain park of 5,500 acres in the central Sierra Nevada at elevations close to 5,000 feet, Calaveras was originally set aside as a preserve for one of the few remaining stands of the *Sequoiadendron giganteum*. Never profuse, these trees were threatened by loggers who were cutting them for grapestakes and fence rails.

The North Fork of the Stanislaus River runs through the park, which is densely forested with fine stands of mature conifers. Terrain here is extremely varied, with high ridges and deep, forested canyons. Recently the road which previously went only to the river has been extended and paved another 5 miles to give access to the South Grove of redwoods, untouched and finer than the North Grove near the park entrance.

Although related to the coast redwood (*Sequoia sempervirens*), the Big Tree is a separate genus, only found in about a 250-mile stretch of the western Sierra slopes. (There are stands in Yosemite and Sequoia national parks.) It does not grow in forests as dense as the coast tree but is bulkier and lives longer. There is evidence that the North Grove was the first grove of these trees

Huge stump *at Calaveras Big Trees is 24 feet across, has stairway you climb to top. Stump is on nature trail in North Grove of park. Big Trees are found only on western slopes of the Sierra Nevada.*

seen by Europeans; later some of them were logged. On the guided nature trail in this grove is a huge stump with a stairway to its top, which allows you to perceive the size of the trees better than just by looking at a growing tree. As a publicity stunt, a dance was once held on this stump's 24-foot-wide surface.

On summer days the park sometimes is quite warm, up to 85 or 90 degrees, but temperatures are usually somewhat lower, with cool nights. Because the park is farther south in the Sierra Nevada than most of the state's mountain parks, and somewhat lower in altitude, it is usable most of the year. During its occasional winter snowfalls over a three-month period, it gets a great amount of "snow bunny" activity.

Activities: Camping, picnicking, hiking, swimming, fishing, nature study, snow play in winter. Two campgrounds provide 129 improved campsites (showers). Squaw Hollow gives more quiet and privacy than North Grove but is less convenient to park activities. Camping limit is 15 days in summer, and reservations are important; winter camping is allowed at North Grove, particularly suitable for vehicle campers, when conditions permit.

Near the park entrance, adjacent to North Grove,

there is a large picnic area. Nine miles away near the trailhead at Beaver Creek is another large picnic area with sites scattered along the road in small clearings served by parking strips. A third picnic area and parking are located in the center of the park near the big bridge over the river.

Calaveras has several hiking trails around the slopes and along the river canyon. The self-guided nature trail at the North Grove near the highway gets a great deal of casual use. Another self-guided nature trail loops through the South Grove, which is a mile-long hike from parking at Beaver Creek. Interpretive pamphlets are available at the trailhead.

There is a recreation hall near the North Grove for various park activities and nature interpretation. A large outdoor campfire amphitheatre is located here, and church services are held at the amphitheatre on Sundays in summer.

The river provides water play for youngsters, and there are deep swimming holes just above the bridge. Here an ancient glacier-scraped granite ledge has been eroded by the river over the years, creating deep potholes for swimming and smooth granite faces for sunbathing.

Both the river and Beaver Creek offer trout fishing.

For further information: Area Manager, Calaveras Big Trees State Park, P.O. Box 686, Arnold 95223.

Access: The park entrance is 4 miles east of Arnold, on the south side of State Route 4.

Supplies: Arnold, a recreation center, which also has a public golf course.

Bodie State Historic Park

"Goodbye, God, I'm going to Bodie" was the saying in the 1870's and 1880's when this town had a population of 10,000 womanless miners and was known over the West for its wickedness. It had more than its share of badmen, and "the worst climate out-of-doors." Prosperity ended when the hard-rock mines ran into borrasca in the early 1880's, and the town went rapidly into decline.

Literally a ghost town for many years, much of it destroyed by fire, Bodie had about a hundred buildings remaining when it became an historic park in 1962. Although badly weathered by the dry winds and the 20-foot snows in winter at 8,400 feet elevation, many of the old buildings are still in surprisingly good repair. The park department's policy, for the time being, is to maintain them in a state of "arrested decay." Bodie is only open from May 30 until Labor Day. Day-use hours are from 9 A.M. to 6 P.M.

The park folder is a guided historic walk through the old town, with 36 points of interest. Rangers have set up displays and are available for interpretive assistance.

Smoking on the history walk is allowed only in designated places, and you should stay out of the buildings for your own safety. If you explore around the town, beware of old mine shafts.

There are 8 primitive campsites, but considerable overflow is allotted for camping vehicles.

Access: From U.S. 395, about 6 miles south of Bridgeport, turn east on Bodie Road. The 13-mile gravel road is rough and dusty in summer, but summer generally is the only time you can get in. An alternate route is to turn east onto State 167 from U.S. 395 just north of Mono Lake; after 7 miles, turn north onto an unimproved road and continue for 10 miles. Check locally on the road conditions. Washouts are common; the snow falls deep and early and remains late into spring.

Venerable facade *at Bodie State Historic Park is the front of the town's Odd Fellows Lodge Hall. Self-guided interpretive walk through town leads to 36 historic sites. Bodie is near Nevada border in the southern Sierra.*

CALIFORNIA'S TEN KINDS OF "TROUT"

Cold-water lake and stream fish caught on a line and called "trout" all belong to the *salmonidae* family—but beyond this basic classification there are many variations that can make identification difficult. The true trout belongs to the genus *salmo,* while several "trout" you may catch in the West are really chars (*salvelinus*). The Atlantic salmon is a *salmo,* closely akin to the western steelhead, while the western salmon belongs to the genus *oncorhynchus.*

Members of the *salmonidae* family are best identified by their "adipose fin"—the stumpy little fin about half-way between the dorsal and the tail. Another characteristic is the big mouth, which starts right at the tip of the head.

California has 10 species of fish (besides migratory "salmon") which may be caught within a very general category of "trout fishing" techniques. Two of these California "trout" are introduced members of the char family, and the mountain whitefish (*prosopium*) is neither char nor trout. In recent years the kokanee has become an important sporting fish in some lakes, yet it is a true western salmon.

The 10 kinds of fish are as follows:

Rainbow (salmo): Generally silvery and brightly marked, without red markings except for a side stripe, rainbows are distributed in streams and are the most common species for planting. Usually they are small in streams, but they can grow to 15 pounds or more in big lakes.

Steelhead rainbow (salmo): The steelhead can be classified as a rainbow that migrates into the ocean and grows larger and stronger. When returning from the ocean to spawn, these fish are gray and silver, with subdued markings, but after several weeks in fresh water they regain the rainbow markings. They are found is most live streams along the coast from San Luis Obispo north and are much sought after by fishermen for their size and fighting ability. Runs are seasonal.

Cutthroat (salmo): Usually these are distinguished by a pair of red streaks—the "cut throat"—on the membrane between the jawbones. Cutthroats have larger spots than other trout. Usually they have teeth on the base of the tongue. There are two varieties: the coast cutthroat, found in California only from the Eel River northward (and on into the Pacific Northwest); and the ancient-impounded kind in eastside Sierra streams and lakes.

Brown (salmo): Dark brown or olive brown on the back, shading to golden on the sides, these fish were brought to California many years ago and widely planted. The brown is a tough fighter when hooked, but very wary. Because of its wariness it survives longer and grows big enough to dominate the waters it lives in, eating great quantities of small fish.

Golden (salmo): Highly colored with shades of yellow and red sides and belly, the golden trout is California's state fish. Spotting is sparse against a clear background on the back, more pronounced on dorsal and tail than it is on other trout. Originally found only at high altitudes in the upper Kern River system, this fish has been planted widely in lakes and streams in the Sierra at elevations of 8,000 feet and up. Because it survives well at such high altitudes and thus requires hard climbing to catch, the golden trout is for the angler comparable to the bighorn sheep for the hunter.

Dolly Varden (salvelinus): Olive green or muddy gray, shading to a white belly, the Dolly Varden is not as brilliantly marked as the rainbow. It has pale yellow or pinkish spots. This fish is widespread in northeastern states, but so far as known in California it lives only in the McCloud River system. Supposedly, the fish was given its name by women in the party that first identified it—they named it after a dressmaking material that was popular in the early 1900's.

Eastern brook (salvelinus) An introduced char, the Eastern brook is normally dark olive on back and sides and is spotted like a rainbow, but many spots are light. The belly is golden. There are lines on the back and particularly on the dorsal fin—an important identifying mark. This fish does best at higher altitudes. It is called "eastern" because originally rainbows were "brook" trout in the West.

Lake or Mackinaw (salvelinus): Dark gray, sometimes varying from pale to very dark with large pale spots, this is a long, narrow fish in comparison with other trout. It lives in lakes in deep water. A char imported to California, it was planted in Tahoe and Donner lakes in 1895. It is predatory.

Mountain whitefish (prosopium): Not a trout, this fish resembles one superficially, with silvery sides and light brown back and fins; it has no spots. Though it has a very small mouth, the adipose fin identifies it as being in the *salmonidae* family. Many trout anglers throw these fish back, thinking they are suckers. A good sport fish, found only in the eastside Sierra Nevada streams, the mountain whitefish makes very good eating.

Kokanee salmon (oncorhynchus): The sockeye salmon of the north coast, this fish has dark blue back and silvery sides. It has no spots. Its mouth is somewhat smaller than *salmo,* and soft. It turns deep red as spawning season approaches. The species which has been planted in California is a land-locked variety which is relatively small—up to 16 inches. Of more than two dozen experimental plantings in California lakes, only about 10 at higher altitudes have been successful. The name comes from the Kokanee River in British Columbia.

San Francisco Bay Area

Within a 50-mile radius of the city of San Francisco are some of California's finest state parks. Here you have your choice of fine redwood groves, a string of beaches, and mountain parks. There are several excellent historical parks.

It is unusual for such a densely settled area to have been able to reserve so much land for recreation purposes. The broken topography and the many water barriers in this part of the state have been partially responsible. The less accessible places remained relatively undeveloped and were available when the need for public parks was realized. As a result, you can swim, hike, walk the beach, picnic, and camp close to major metropolitan areas. You can enjoy superb views from the top of Mount Diablo and Mount Tamalpais. You can spend a day on an island in San Francisco Bay, and you can watch the animals at the Oakland Zoo.

The historic parks here include Sonoma's mission and some structures from the period of transition between Mexican and United States jurisdiction in California; one of the state's early capitols, at Benicia; and a memorial to writer Jack London. In the city of San Francisco, one park offers a look at maritime history (you can tour four old ships) and another a chance to operate scientific exhibits (at the Palace of Fine Arts).

Like the parks themselves, the climate in the Bay Area is varied. San Francisco and the coastal side of both peninsulas are usually fog-ridden in summer, but winter rainfall will be heavier in the coastal mountains on both sides of the Golden Gate than in the city itself. The east side of the bay will be from 10 to 15 degrees warmer in summer than the west side and may be considerably cooler in winter.

The northern California beaches are generally poor for swimming, but they are more scenic than the swimming beaches of the southern part of the state and offer many sequestered coves.

Sugarloaf Ridge State Park

A pleasant coast-range park of 1,500 acres, Sugarloaf Ridge consists of an elevated valley surrounded by ridges and volcanic upthrusts of the Mayacamas Mountains. Sonoma Creek passes through the park. Vegetation is partially oak-grass, but there are Douglas fir groves on the slopes. Park facilities are located in the flat valley.

Climate may be warm in summer, very pleasant in spring and fall, and often wet in winter. Altitudes are 600 to 2,400 feet.

Activities: Camping, picnicking, hiking, stream fishing for trout in early spring. The campground has 50 unimproved sites, mostly under trees surrounding a large meadow. The access road has been surfaced but is steep,

Dense *forest of redwoods and Douglas fir at Butano State Park (see page 56) is mostly second growth, but cutting was long ago and forest cover is again lush.*

View *of San Francisco and Alcatraz Island is from steep shore of Angel Island (see page 49), opposite photo.*

winding, and narrow; it is not recommended for trailers. Slope slippage during the rainy season sometimes closes the road in winter.

Picnickers may use unoccupied campsites. The park is open all year (unless the road is impassable), with limits of 10 days in summer, 30 days in other seasons. About 15 miles of trails into the mountains are available for hiking.

For further information: Area Manager, Sonoma Area State Parks, P.O. Box 167, Sonoma 95476.

Access: From State 12 about 6 miles south of Santa Rosa, turn northeast onto Adobe Canyon Road and proceed 4 miles to the park entrance.

Supplies: Kenwood on State 12, Santa Rosa, or Sonoma.

Jack London State Historic Park

A memorial to the California writer who was also roustabout, oyster pirate, and seaman, Jack London State Historic Park is located in the hills above the community of Glen Ellen. The House of Happy Walls, the house built by London's wife after his death, is now

Upper meadow *at Sugarloaf Ridge was once site of small ranch. Trails lead through wooded slopes in background.*

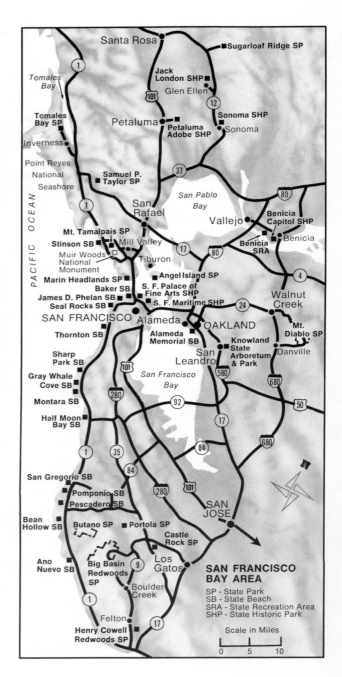

preserved as a museum on his life. A pleasant mile-long hike away are the ruins of Wolf House, the house London planned but never lived in. Wolf House was burned the night after it was finished, presumably by vandals who resented London's outspokenness. The great rock walls and chimneys still stand on a knoll overlooking the valley, and there are several interpretive displays. Nearby is a grove of redwoods.

London died in 1916 at the age of 40. His grave, marked by a lava boulder simply engraved "Jack London," is a short climb off the trail to Wolf House.

The 48-acre park preserves the beauty of the Valley of the Moon country London loved, and which he used as a subject of his novel *Valley of the Moon*. The wooded slopes and open meadows make this a pleasant place for walking. No picnic facilities are provided, but basket picnickers are welcomed. A large parking apron is provided at the park entrance. The park is open from 10 A.M. to 5 P.M. daily except on Thanksgiving, Christmas, and New Year's. A single admission charge admits you to Sonoma (below) and Petaluma Adobe (page 44) historic parks as well.

Access: Turn off State 12 a few miles west of Sonoma to Glen Ellen and continue uphill about a mile to the park entrance, following the park signs.

Sonoma State Historic Park

The Sonoma region was important during a period when three countries—Russia, Mexico, and the United States—were making their influence felt in northern California. A state historic park in Sonoma preserves several structures from that time.

The last in the chain of Franciscan missions in California was established here in 1823—the state park includes the restored mission building. Ten years later Sonoma became the headquarters of General Mariano Vallejo, sent by the Mexican governor to investigate Russian activities at Fort Ross. Vallejo was the Mexican administrator for northern California at the time of the Bear Flag Revolt in 1846—a statue in the town plaza commemorates the hoisting of the Bear Flag by an army of 33 Americans to declare California a republic. The Vallejo home and the barracks that housed soldiers of the Mexican and then the United States army are both part of the state park.

General Vallejo was jailed by the Bear Flag revolters but quickly released, and shortly thereafter he was elected the area's first senator in the new state government. His impress is everywhere. He was in charge of secularizing the short-lived Sonoma Mission in 1834, and in 1835 he founded the city of Sonoma. He himself laid out the plaza as a place to drill his soldiers.

The Sonoma Mission, across from the northeast corner of the plaza, no longer functions as a church but is furnished as a museum. The present church dates from 1840, but the padres' quarters were built in about 1825.

Wolf House *ruins stand as monument to writer Jack London. His mansion burned down the night it was completed.*

Across the street to the west is the two-story Sonoma Barracks building, built in about 1837. West on Spain Street is the site of Vallejo's first home, *Casa Grande*, which burned in 1867. The servants' wing remains, and there is a museum.

Also bordering the plaza, though not part of the state park, are the Jacob Leese House (1847); *El Prado*, the Salvador Vallejo House (1840's); the restored Toscario Hotel; and the Blue Wing Inn, first hotel in northern California.

The General Vallejo Home, which he called *Lachrymae Montis* ("Tears of the Mountain"), is about a mile away—go west 2 blocks from the Plaza to Third Street, then proceed north to the monument entrance. Vallejo built this house after the American takeover, and its architecture is a direct reversal of the California style—an eastern seaboard-style home. His storehouse was built of brick and timber. Now it is a museum on the general and his family.

A single admission charge of 25 cents covers entrance to the mission, the museum on the Casa Grande site, and

The capture of the Sonoma Barracks and the imprisonment of Mexican General Mariano G. Vallejo and his staff in 1846 by three dozen adventurers has been greatly glamorized in later accounts. The Bear Flag revolt is important principally as the first overt action by Americans against the Mexican government. The Bear Flag Revolutionary Party raised their flag to declare California a republic free of Mexican rule, but less than a month later the United States intervened, and the Bear Flag was replaced by the U.S. flag.

The flag itself was quickly made from a yard-wide strip of rough cloth, with a strip of red flannel material sewn along one edge. Mrs. Abraham Lincoln's nephew, William L. Todd, painted a star in one corner in memory of the Texas Lone Star Republic and drew a rough representation of a grizzly bear in the center above the words "California Republic."

The banner was raised in the Sonoma Plaza on June 14, 1846, and remained flying there until July 9. During the time the Bear Flag was in public view, townspeople of Sonoma made much fun of it, saying it resembled a pig more than a bear.

The United States already was in a state of war with Mexico at the time—a fact of which the Bear Flag revolutionaries were unaware because of the slow communications of the period. Without United States intervention, a rival republic in the West might have been established; there are historians who believe this really was a dream of John C. Fremont, with himself as president. There is no evidence to show that Fremont sponsored the Bear Flag Rebellion, although his presence at nearby Marysville no doubt encouraged the group of insurrectionists. A few days later he did give them active support.

The idea of an independent western republic—including what are now the western states, Texas, Mexico, and Central America—died hard. Its proponents were still active in California as late as the Civil War.

California. Construction of the huge redwood and adobe administrative center for Vallejo's 100-square-mile ranch took a decade, from 1836 to 1846. The building originally consisted of two wings, with a large courtyard and massive gates in front.

The interior is furnished with period-style pieces. An interpretive specialist is on duty to answer questions, and a park folder gives information about the adobe. Plan on spending two or three hours to tour the site adequately.

Recent improvements include landscaping and paths, a large parking apron, and modern restrooms.

In 1971 the adobe was designated a National Historic Landmark by the National Park Service. The park is administered as part of Sonoma State Historic Park, and a 25 cent ticket admits you to both.

Access: Take the Sonoma-Napa turnoff from U.S. 101 at Petaluma to State 116; there is an historical landmarks sign. Follow State 116 east for .6 mile, turn north onto Casa Grande and continue 2 miles to the intersection with Adobe Road—you will see the monument directly ahead. The parking area is located 200 yards to the right.

Tomales Bay State Park

A strikingly beautiful park of about 1,000 acres, Tomales Bay consists largely of a reserve for one of the finest remaining virgin stands of the picturesque Bishop pine, *Pinus muricata*. Most of the visitor-use areas are along the edge of Tomales Bay, where dark, 50-foot cliffs edge close to the blue water and wind-distorted pines are silhouetted against the sky. Just to the south is the developing Point Reyes National Seashore.

The area is somewhat protected by its location on the bay instead of the ocean. Fog is not so prevalent in summer and is apt to disappear earlier in the day, but the best weather is in spring and fall. There are sometimes cold winds on the plateau and in the picnic grounds. The park is open the year around, from 8 A.M. to 5 P.M. in winter, from 8 A.M. to 9 P.M. in summer.

Activities: Picnicking, sunbathing, swimming, fishing. Heart's Desire Cove has a small beach, a buoyed swimming area, and parking. Additional parking is available at the 20-unit picnic grounds on the bluffs above. A 1-mile trail leads from the picnic area through the pines to a grove named for California botanist Willis L. Jepson.

Fishing is a combination of surf and casting, as the bay waters are usually calm.

Access: The park is 4 miles west of Inverness on Sir Francis Drake Boulevard.

Samuel P. Taylor State Park

Samuel P. Taylor State Park has redwoods, a creek, and an interesting history. A paper mill, a hotel, and what

the Vallejo Home. The same ticket can also be used for Jack London Park (see page 42) and the Petaluma Adobe (see below).

About 2 miles east of town is the winery where the Hungarian Count Agoston Haraszthy and Vallejo experimented with European grape cuttings to start California's wine industry in 1853. The winery still produces the Buena Vista bottlings, and visitors are welcome.

Petaluma Adobe State Historic Park

Even though only the western half of General Vallejo's Petaluma adobe still remains, this massive two-story building is one of the largest adobes still standing in may have been one of the first public campgrounds in the United States have been located here.

Because of the park's proximity to the heavily populated suburban areas of San Francisco, camping space is at a premium much of the time. Climate here is pleasant most of the year. The park is somewhat back from the coastal fog belt, but often it does have fog in summer; it is damp during the rainy season.

Samuel Taylor was a pioneer logger and industrialist who built a paper mill on the creek in 1856. He is said to have gotten his start in business in 1853 when he found a hogshead of eggs floating in San Francisco Bay, quickly bought some bacon, and started selling bacon and eggs. Nothing remains of his mill today except the foundations, but it gave its name to the creek.

Taylor was so fond of the area that when a narrow-gauge railroad gave easy access in 1874, he built a hotel about where the present park headquarters building is located, and space nearby was set aside for camping. This became known as Camp Taylor long before it became a state park.

Activities: Camping, picnicking, hiking, swimming, riding, nature study, fishing. Two campgrounds have a combined total of 73 improved sites (showers), with limits of 10 days. There is a horsemen's camp at Devil's Gulch (corral, hitching racks, water troughs) with a capacity of 35 people.

The park has a self-guided nature trail and a museum, and summer nature walks are held every day except Sunday. Four days a week programs are held at the Campfire Circle near the upper campground.

Taylor has three family picnic areas with a combined total of 128 sites, each with its own table and stove. In addition there is a 100-person group site available on reservation. Most of the picnic sites are located in groves of large second-growth redwoods.

Several hiking trails are available, for both the easy-going and the rugged hiker. One goes to the lookout station on Barnabe Peak, which is just inside the park boundary. Others connect with trails through adjacent Marin Municipal Water District property and also lead to several small lakes. The California Riding and Hiking Trail passes through Taylor and connects the park with Mount Tamalpais and points beyond.

Trout are planted in Paper Mill Creek in early spring but usually do not survive through the warmer days that follow. The creek has a swimming hole near the lower end of the park, and children play in its shallows in many places.

For further information: Area Manager, Marin Area State Parks, P.O. Box 227, Point Reyes Station 94956.

Access: Take the Sir Francis Drake Boulevard offramp west from U.S. 101 at San Rafael and follow the boulevard about 12 miles to the park.

Supplies: Small local establishments along the road close to the park, or nearby towns, including San Rafael.

Stinson State Beach

A long strip on the ocean side of the Marin Peninsula, Stinson is a wide beach backed by low dunes. The beach is 3 miles long, with rocky sections at its south end. An older park, Stinson is well developed and has capacious facilities behind the dunes.

The climate is capricious, often foggy in summer, and

Viewpoint *on trail at Tomales Bay State Park overlooks bay. Just below is Heart's Desire Beach day-use area.*

winds may be cold. Spring and fall days are usually clear, and you may even find good weather in winter.

A day-use park, Stinson is open all year. Its hours of use are 9 A.M. to 6 P.M. on standard time, 9 A.M. to 10 P.M. Daylight Saving Time.

Activities: Picnicking, beach activities, beach hiking, swimming, surfing, and fishing. The picnic areas are somewhat protected behind the dunes and are attractively set in groves of trees; 100 tables and 40 barbecue pits are provided. There is a snack concession in the park, and there are several large parking aprons.

Lifeguards are present in summer, but surf may be dangerous and there may be riptides, particularly in winter and spring.

The variations in the beach provide both surf and rock fishing for a wide range of north coast fish.

Access: The park is 24 miles north of San Francisco via State 1; the park entrance is on the west side of the highway in the southern part of the city of Stinson Beach.

Mount Tamalpais State Park

At 2,571 feet, Mount Tamalpais is not an especially high mountain. But it rises virtually from sea level, and on clear days it affords superb views of the entire San Francisco Bay area.

The large expanse of state park land here is mostly on the western slopes of Mount Tamalpais. The park completely surrounds Muir Woods National Monument and includes right-of-way and a small area near the East Peak summit, the higher of the mountain's two peaks. (West Peak is a military reservation.)

The park's potential for public use is greatly expanded by the national monument and the surrounding Marin Municipal Water District watershed land. One portion of the state park extends to the sea. The coast here is precipitous and not suitable for any recreation except hiking, but small Muir Beach, previously beyond the park's southern limits, has just been added to the state park land.

The park has a very wide range of wildlife, including cougar and deer, and raccoons may be a nuisance to campers. Vegetation ranges from oak-grass on the slopes to redwood groves in the canyons. Muir Woods is an outstanding mature redwood forest.

With Muir Woods and the surrounding watershed land, a great natural preserve has been created, stretching from the extremely rocky seacoast almost to San Francisco Bay. There are literally hundreds of miles of riding and hiking trails through the area.

The area is often foggy in summer, but it can be hot at midday; it may be chilly and windy sometimes on the higher slopes. Occasionally there is light snowfall in winter near the peaks.

The Mountain Theatre off the summit road is a local institution, having first been established for outdoor plays

High spirits *and Stinson Beach surf combine for an exuberant outing at the coast. Beach is wide, 3 miles long.*

in 1913. In the early 1930's, Civilian Conservation Corps workers improved and expanded the theatre so it now seats 5,000 people. On the third Sunday in May, the Mountain Play Association presents its annual play here, and amateur productions are staged at several times during the summer as well.

Activities: Camping, picnicking, hiking, riding, some beach activity at Muir Beach. Swimming is dangerous, and there are no lifeguards. There is a small concession stand, and there are a few picnic tables. The beach may be used for fishing.

The campground is in the Pantoll Area near park headquarters at about 2,000 feet altitude. Sites are un-improved, located a short walk in from the parking area in dense tree growth. Two group campgrounds at Alice Eastwood Camp are available on reservation.

In addition to the small picnic area at Muir Beach, picnic sites are available at the Bootjack Area on Panoramic Highway leading up from Mill Valley, at the Pantoll Area, and near East Peak, where there is a large parking apron. Trails encircle the peak and go to the summit.

Pebbly beach *of Rodeo Cove at Fort Cronkite is between two sections of Marin Headlands State Park; Army allows public use, and beach is popular. Bird Rock in distance is most seaward extension of north side of Golden Gate.*

For further information: Area Manager, Marin Area State Parks, P.O. Box 227, Point Reyes Station 94956.

Access: The best approach is by taking State 1 from U.S. 101 at Mill Valley and continuing to Panoramic Highway above Mill Valley. It is about 7 miles from U.S. 101 to park headquarters and 4 miles farther to summit parking. The road is good but winding. At park headquarters, Panoramic Highway splits into Ridgecrest, which goes to the summit, and Stinson Beach Highway, which continues to the coast.

Supplies: Mill Valley or Stinson Beach.

Marin Headlands State Park

Two sections of rocky, precipitous coastline along the north shores of the Golden Gate make up Marin Headlands State Park. Kirby Cove, just west of the Golden Gate Bridge, has a group campground available by reservation only. A 1-mile hike leads to a public day-use area here. There is no access to Tennessee Cove. The state acquired these lands, totaling about 600 acres, by transfer from U.S. Army holdings; as yet there has been little development for use.

The Army allows public use of Fort Cronkite Beach at Rodeo Cove between the two parcels of state park land. This is a beautiful black sand beach, usable for sunbathing and beach activities. Swimming is dangerous, however, and there are no lifeguards. Gravel parking areas are provided, and there are restrooms.

Access: Take the southern Sausalito exit from U.S. 101. The most used route leaves the road to Sausalito a quarter mile from the freeway and heads back under U.S. 101 and through a one-way tunnel controlled by traffic lights. Another road which connects with this road on Army land near the coast loops back along the rim of the Golden Gate and joins U.S. 101 at the same interchange. This is a slower route, but the two routes may be combined as a short scenic drive.

Four San Francisco Parks

Several state parks in San Francisco are operated locally. The Palace of Fine Arts is an historic park that now

Last *of the lumber schooners, the* C. A. Thayer *at the Hyde Street Pier is part of San Francisco Maritime Park.*

houses a science museum, Baker and James D. Phelan are state beaches popular for picnicking and other beach activities, and Seal Rocks State Beach offers a view of sea lions.

Palace of Fine Arts: A San Francisco landmark since it was constructed in 1915 as a temporary structure for the Panama-Pacific International Exposition, the Palace of Fine Arts was completely restored in 1967. Now it houses a science exploratorium, a museum in which you touch and hear exhibits as well as see them; demonstrations in science, technology, and human perception are presented. The museum is open Wednesday through Sunday from 1 to 5 P.M. The Palace is located near San Francisco Marina on Baker Street between Jefferson and Bay. Its attractive grounds include a small lake.

Baker Beach: A sandy strip of beach on the west side of the Presidio, Baker is reached from Lincoln Boulevard. Facilities are limited, but the beach is heavily used. Surf fishermen sometimes catch striped bass.

James D. Phelan Beach: Southwest of Baker Beach at the end of Sea Cliff Avenue, James D. Phelan Beach is operated in conjunction with a city-owned beach. The beach is open to swimmers from 10 A.M. to 6 P.M., to

Peaceful park *with lake surrounds restored Palace of Fine Arts, last surviving building of the Panama-Pacific International Exposition of 1915. Inside the majestic building is a science exploratorium.*

fishermen at other times. There are concessions, limited picnic facilities, lifeguards in summer and during other heavy use periods, and a dressing-room building with a sun deck on top.

Seal Rocks Beach: A longtime San Francisco tourist attraction, Seal Rocks State Beach serves as a wildlife preserve. The "seals" actually are Steller sea lions, and they have dwindled in number. You can see them from fall through spring. This area is just offshore from the Cliff House at Point Lobos Avenue and Great Highway.

San Francisco Maritime State Historic Park

You can combine a ride on a cable car with a look into San Francisco's maritime past when you visit a floating park at the foot of Hyde Street.

The Powell-Hyde cable car line terminates in Victorian Park. From this part of the state park it is an easy walk to the long Hyde Street Pier, where four old ships are moored. They are preserved as the San Francisco Maritime State Historic Park, and you can go aboard all four. The park is also a stopover on San Francisco's

scenic 49-mile drive, and close at hand are a Maritime Museum, Fisherman's Wharf, and the shopping complexes of Ghirardelli Square and The Cannery.

The ships have been reconstructed and made seaworthy by master ship-builders who have given attention to even the smallest details in order to restore them to the way they looked when they were working units of the fleet. There is a nominal admission charge to the wharf, which is open from 10 A.M. to 10 P.M. daily.

Wapama is a steam schooner, 205 feet long, built in 1915. It was engaged in the coastal trade, carrying both lumber and passengers.

C. A. Thayer is a three-masted schooner built in Eureka in 1895; for many years the schooner worked in and out of the "dogholes" along the coast in the lumber trade (see page 13).

Relic of the Bay ferries is the old side-wheeler *Eureka*, at one time the largest and fastest double-ended ferry in the world. She carried her last load of commuters from San Francisco to Sausalito in 1941.

The scow schooner *Alma*, built in 1891, is typical of the craft which served as the trucks of that day. Hundreds of these sail-driven, shallow draft vessels once plied the bay, in and out of landings impossible for other ships.

Angel Island State Park

You travel by boat to reach Angel Island State Park in the San Francisco Bay. This is the state's only island park open to the public, and to get to it you can ride a ferry from Tiburon or a tour boat from San Francisco —or take a private boat.

Angel Island is relatively small—only 740 acres—but the terrain is varied and scenic. Its highest point is 776-foot Mt. Caroline Livermore, rising exactly in the center of the island. Climate is similar to that of San Francisco, although somewhat warmer and less foggy in summer.

The island was a military reservation from 1850 to 1946; before that it was a horse and cattle ranch. Superstitious sailors and pirates in early days claimed they often saw ghosts or angels along the shores of the island —hence the name. Ayala Cove, the entrance to the island, is named for Don Juan de Ayala, first Spanish explorer to enter the bay. He anchored here in 1775.

Activities: Picnicking, hiking, beach activities, fishing, sightseeing. Ayala Cove has a beach and picnic facilities —take your own food, as there are no food concessions. You cannot go into the water because of pollution. Private boats may use the public docking facilities.

A concessionaire operates sightseeing elephant trains on weekends, and there are a number of trails around the island, including a summit trail.

Fishermen who work the Cove catch perch, rock cod, sand sharks, and an occasional bass, but Raccoon Strait adjacent to the Cove is a migratory channel for stripers.

Access: For departure from Tiburon via ferry, take the Belvedere-Tiburon turnoff from U.S. 101 and proceed

Ferry prepares to take on passengers at Tiburon for scheduled trip to Angel Island State Park, in background.

southeast on State 131 about 5 miles to downtown Tiburon. Turn right onto Main Street and continue a half block; parking is provided off Tiburon Boulevard.

Departure from San Francisco via tour boat is from Pier 43 at Fisherman's Wharf; after stopping at Angel Island the boat continues to Tiburon and then makes a return trip.

Benicia State Recreation Area

Much of Benicia State Recreation Area is marshland, but higher land along the upper San Francisco Bay and

at the west end of the park provides areas for day-use activities. The facilities are to be expanded when funds are available.

Activities: Picnicking, beachcombing, sunbathing, fishing. The park is open during daylight hours. An automatic turnstile collects your fee and admits you to the 85-unit picnic area and the beach. From a small pier in the park you can fish for striped bass, flounder, and sturgeon.

Access: Follow signs south from the Columbus Parkway turnoff from Interstate 680 west of Benicia.

THE FORT BENEATH THE BRIDGE

Beneath the southern tip of the Golden Gate Bridge span is Fort Point, which served for many years as a U.S. Army fort and was built on the site of an old Spanish fort. Today the fort is open to the public, and more than 100,000 visitors tour it each year. In 1968 it officially became the Fort Point National Historic Site. Considerable restoration is planned by the U.S. Park Service in the near future.

The fort is now being operated by the Fort Point Museum Association, which acts in cooperation with

Once *Fort Point dominated entrance to San Francisco Bay; now it is almost hidden under bridge.*

the park service. It is open to the public from 1 to 4 P.M. every day of the week. No admission is charged at present, although when the federal service takes over a nominal fee will be charged.

Juan Bautista de Anza landed here in 1776, and in the 1790's the Spanish built an impressive adobe structure—El Castillo de San Joaquin. A battery of 11 brass 9-pounder cannons was shipped in, but somehow they never got mounted. They still lay on the beach when the American-Mexican War started in 1846. In his usual flamboyant fashion, Captain John C. Fremont slipped over from Sausalito one night and spiked them, reporting to his superiors that he had eliminated the fort's future effectiveness. The American flag was raised over El Castillo 8 days later.

No time was lost in replacing El Castillo with an even more massive brick complex—the buildings which you see today. However, no defensive shot was ever fired from the fort, and in the first decade of the twentieth century it was declared obsolete. When the Golden Gate Bridge was under design in the 1930's, removal of the fort was considered; but chief design engineer Joseph E. Strauss added the small arch at the south end of the bridge to save the fort.

The fort museum is full of articles from various periods in military history, including two cases of medical equipment from the Civil War, many old flags, and examples of the 128 and 65-pound cannon balls fired by the fort's guns. There is also an 1835 Army Escort Wagon which the United States was still using in World War I and later; a 12-pound Napoleon from the Civil War; an 18-pound mountain howitzer; and one of the original Spanish cannons from El Castillo —a 1684 model.

Prize of the collection is a 1754 French cannon from the time of Louis XIV, beautifully embossed with many fleurs-de-lis, the name of King Louis and all his titles, and the motto which appeared on all French cannons of the time—"The Ultimate Argument of Kings."

Benicia Capitol State Historic Park

From late 1852 until 1854 the town of Benicia served as California's capital. Now the old capitol building is preserved as a state historic park.

The Benicia capitol, rushed to completion in late 1852, housed only two partial sessions of the state legislature before Sacramento became the capital. During the more than 100 years of its existence it has served many purposes—as church, school, jail, public auditorium, and city hall. Today it has been restored to its appearance when it was constructed. Inside, the original winding stairs, the oil lamps, and the furnishings of the legislature chambers convey the atmosphere of an important public building of the day. There are many artifacts related to California history in the 1850's.

The building is open from 10 A.M. to 5 P.M. daily except on Thanksgiving, Christmas, and New Year's. There is a small admission fee.

California's first and second legislative sessions met in San Jose in 1849 and 1851, and then the third legislature moved to Sacramento just in time to have their enthusiasm for that city dampened by a great flood. They began the fourth session in Vallejo. Benicia had been vying with the other cities for the capital from the beginning, basing its appeal on its location for easy land and water communication. As the northern base for the U.S. Army at that time, it did have somewhat advanced facilities. The remainder of the fourth session and part of the fifth met in Benicia, but in 1854 the capital was moved to its permanent location in Sacramento.

Soon to become part of the historic park is the nearby Fischer House, part of a large prefabricated hotel brought from the East Coast by ship in 1849. Much of it burned in 1856, but the undamaged wing continued in use as a residence until this century. It will be furnished in the style of the period.

Access: The historic park is in downtown Benicia at First and G Streets.

Mount Diablo State Park

On a clear day, you can see for hundreds of miles in several directions from the vantage point of Mount Diablo. Despite the mountain's barren appearance from a distance, an attractive state park here offers hiking, picnicking, group camping—and the view.

The park comprises 7,000 acres, mostly on the south side of the summit but extending north as well. Many of the slopes are chaparral, broken by oak-grass combinations, but big trees grow in many places in the canyons and on the eastern slopes. A grove of Coulter pines in one canyon marks this tree's extreme northern range. Digger pine, live oak, blue oak, big leaf maple, sycamore, laurel, alder, and cottonwood are found in the park.

Although it is less than 4,000 feet high, Diablo rises from plains virtually at sea level. It is the Coast and Geodetic Survey base for surveys of virtually all the land in northern and central California and much of Nevada. There is a marker at the summit and a small interpretive display.

The climate is variable. Sometimes coastal overcast extends this far inland, but the mountain is usually free of fog. Summer days are usually pleasant but can be warm through temperature inversion. Snow on the high slopes is not uncommon in winter, and very clear days usually indicate cold north winds at the higher levels.

Activities: Camping, picnicking, hiking, nature study, snow play sometimes in winter. The California Hiking

Mt. Diablo's *main peak, at right, affords superb views, is land survey base. To the left is Black Point.*

DIABLO AS A LAND SURVEY BASE

Mount Diablo was one of only three points selected by United States survey parties in the 1850's as bases from which to establish land measurements and deeds for the entire state. The others are Mount San Bernardino above Redlands and a high point in Humboldt County.

Once a surveying reference point is set, a north and south line called a meridian is established. Then an east and west line called a base line is determined. The land is then laid out in "townships" 6 miles on a side—36 square miles. Townships extending outward from the base lines are called tiers—tiers north and tiers south. Townships extending outward from the meridian line are called ranges, east and west.

You will sometimes see markers in national forests with land measurement symbols—for example, T.21S., R.18E., Sec. 26, Mt. Diablo. This would locate the site in the 21st tier south of the Mt. Diablo baseline and the 18th range east of the meridian. The "Sec. 26" is one of the 36 square miles in the township, comprising 640 acres.

The United States system was unique when it was inaugurated by Congress soon after separation from the British empire. It was devised to satisfy the need to survey great areas with no recorded markers such as existed in Europe. Much of the East is laid out in "metes and bounds"—the old English system—but the township system takes over in the Midwest and the West.

and Riding Trail passes through the park.

Juniper, Junction, and Live Oak campgrounds provide 80 family campsites (some with showers), with group camp areas available on reservation at Laurel Nook and Wildcat. Barbecue Terrace is a horsemen's group camp, and Upland is a permanent Boy Scout camp. Water is available at the park's campgrounds but should be used sparingly.

Approximately 250 family picnic units are scattered over the mountain slopes, generally in small clusters. Many of the campsites and picnic sites are on viewpoints. Reservations may be made for group picnics.

The park's trail system totals 20 miles, but some trails extend on through adjacent unused land. An interesting but rugged trail goes to North Peak, a short distance beyond the park limits. The Rock City self-guided nature trail introduces the visitor to samples of the park's flora and geology, and in spring wildflowers usually present a colorful display.

The park is open all year, with a 15-day camping limit; day-use hours are from 8 A.M. until dark.

For further information: Area Manager, Mount Diablo State Park, P.O. Box 258, Diablo 94528.

Access: The North Gate Road and the South Gate Road join about halfway up the mountain. The former starts near Walnut Creek, but the easier access is via the South Gate Road from Danville on Interstate 680. Take the Diablo Road-Danville offramp east to Diablo Road and follow signs about 10 miles to the south checking station. The road up the mountain is paved but somewhat narrow and very winding.

Supplies: Danville or Walnut Creek.

Knowland State Arboretum and Park (Scientific Reserve)

The small but imaginatively designed Oakland Zoo is one of the attractions of Knowland State Arboretum and Park, operated by the city of Oakland. You can watch monkeys playing in a 50-foot-high cage here and spend a pleasant hour or two seeing bears, lions, elephants, and other animals. Uncaged parrots peer at you from natural surroundings. One concessionaire operates a zoo of baby animals which is very popular, and others offer food, a "skyride," a miniature-train ride, and a small amusement park.

On the slopes above the zoo is the "Oaks of the World" project, where 30 different species of oaks are growing. More are being planted as specimens are obtained. You also can stroll through several other specialized botanical preserves.

About 40 picnic units are located under the trees near the park entrance, and three group picnic areas are available on reservation.

The park is open from 8 A.M. until dusk every day, the zoo from 10 A.M. to 4:30 P.M. weekdays and 10 A.M. to 5 P.M. on weekends. An entrance fee of 50 cents per car is charged except when schools are in session, when entrance is free. Admission is always free on Mondays.

The park was named after Oakland publisher Joseph Knowland, an ardent conservationist who served for many years on the State Park Commission.

Access: The park is near San Leandro via Interstate 580. Take the 98th Avenue offramp and follow signs.

Alameda Memorial State Beach

Alameda Memorial State Beach is a relatively small state property operated by the East Bay Regional Park District as a part of a beach complex of 383 acres with about a mile and a half of beach. It has bathhouses, a concession stand, a day camp area, and picnic and barbecue facilities. An innovative "Old Wharf" classroom has excellent dioramas of Bay Area aquatic life and is particularly suited for children. Guided tours can be arranged.

Access: The beach is at the bay end of Webster Street in Alameda.

Imaginatively designed *monkey cage is part of zoo at Knowland State Arboretum and Park in Oakland, state owned but under city management. The park's wide variety of attractions includes botanical preserves, picnic grounds.*

San Mateo County Coast State Beaches

Ten state beaches scattered along about 50 miles of San Mateo County coast are popular destinations for picnicking and beach activities. They are administered as a single park unit—the San Mateo County Coast State Beaches—from headquarters at Half Moon Bay. Most of the beaches are fairly narrow, some below low coastal bluffs but a few under steep cliffs. All except Thornton and Ano Nuevo are directly accessible from State 1. All but Sharp Park have parking areas and restrooms. Only Dunes, Francis, and Thornton have drinking water. Persistent summer fog and cold water do not keep these beaches from receiving heavy use. Swimming is not safe at many; there are riptides, strong currents, and unpredictable surf. Even at those beaches which are reasonably safe for swimmers, there will probably be no lifeguards because of the lack of funds.

Fishermen who know the coast enjoy good sport at many points. Some of them take surf and rock fish at the state beaches, but luck will vary.

From north to south, the San Mateo Coast Beaches are as follows:

Thornton Beach: Recent improvements make Thornton Beach one of the best of the San Mateo County state beaches. It has a well-kept day-use area, trails to the beach, and a large paved parking apron. Permanent restrooms and a few picnic sites are located on cliffs above the beach, and there is a small developed picnic area up a draw north of the parking area. Drive south on Skyline Boulevard from San Francisco (49-Mile Scenic Drive) and turn right at Alemany Boulevard.

Sharp Park: Though it has no facilities, Sharp Park is said to have good striped bass runs in season. In the town of Sharp Park, take Paloma Avenue to Beach Road.

Gray Whale Cove: Previously inaccessible, Gray Whale Cove has been turned over to a concessionaire who has provided a stairway to the beach. A concessionaire-operated parking lot is on the cliffs above the beach. Gray Whale Cove is south of Devil's Slide on State 1; it is marked by a "Beach Parking" sign.

Pescadero Beach, *shown here at high tide, is one of 10 state beaches in 50 miles of San Mateo County coast.*

Montara: Narrow Montara beach is situated beneath steep cliffs, but there is good access to it at one point. The beach is at the town of Montara on State 1.

Half Moon Bay Beaches: Included in the Half Moon Bay Beaches are *Roosevelt, Francis, Venice,* and *Dunes* beaches. Francis is the best developed, with a sizable picnic area and rough one-night camper or trailer facilities (standard fee). Riding on trails behind the beaches is popular—local stables rent horses—but horses are not permitted on the beaches.

San Gregorio: Situated at a small break cut through the coastal cliffs by San Gregorio Creek is San Gregorio beach. The creek's little delta provides an area where children can paddle in shallow water and play with inflated toys. San Gregorio has a large parking area, easy beach access, and a snack concession in summer. The area is off State 1 just south of the turnoff into the town of San Gregorio.

Bean Hollow—*Arroyo de Los Frijoles*—*is typical of the San Mateo County Coast Beaches. It has rocky promontories, dunes, and narrow sand strips with many secluded nooks and coves for exploring.*

Pomponio: A small lagoon is a feature of Pomponio, about a mile of beach with a sizable picnic area. Trails lead from the east side of the highway to the beach through an underpass. Pomponio is south of Half Moon Bay off State 1.

Pescadero: A narrow beach and narrow upland between ocean and highway, Pescadero has picturesque rocky promontories and small, secluded pocket beaches. There are large dunes at the north end. Gravel-surfaced pull-outs are provided for parking. A few picnic tables have been placed on the bluffs, but the protected beach areas are more popular with picnickers.

The park department has plans to establish the marsh area east of the highway as a shore-bird reserve. This is an important nesting area, and you should remain on the outer edge only.

Pescadero offers surf, rock, and stream fishing when fish are running, as Pescadero Creek empties here. Some razorback clams are dug in season.

The beach is opposite the turnoff from State 1 to the town of Pescadero.

Bean Hollow (Arroyo de los Frijoles): A picturesque small beach with low rocky promontories jutting into the water, Bean Hollow includes the old Pebble Beach. A few picnic tables are located on the bluff. This popular beach is off State 1 about 23 miles south of Half Moon Bay.

Ano Nuevo: Most of the state ownership is the island offshore, which is visible from one or two spots on State 1. Ano Nuevo Island is primarily a scientific reserve, and there are no facilities for boat landing. Any intrusion can result in the death of young sea lions and invalidate scientific studies.

Portola State Park

In a natural bowl on the west side of the San Francisco Peninsula's coastal mountains, Portola State Park covers about 1,800 acres and is forested with Douglas fir and second-growth redwoods. Pescadero Creek runs through the park, but shortage of funds has eliminated the dammed swimming hole which once attracted many visitors to the park.

Climate here may be foggy during mornings and evenings in summer, and the park will be cold and damp in the winter rainy season.

Activities: Camping, picnicking, hiking, stream play, planted trout fishing in spring, nature study. The campground is in groves of big trees and has 55 improved campsites (showers). There are also 106 family picnic sites and two group picnicking areas available on reservation. The park is open all year, with a camping limit of 15 days.

Rangers conduct nature walks and talks on Fridays and Saturday nights. The park has about 15 miles of hiking trails.

For further information: Area Manager, Santa Cruz Mountain Area State Parks, P.O. Box 761, Felton 95018.

Access: From Skyline Boulevard (State 35) about 7 miles south of State 84, turn west on Alpine Road.

Supplies: Grocery store outside park entrance.

Castle Rock State Park

Slightly more than 500 acres of rather wild and rugged terrain in the coastal mountains west of Saratoga, Castle Rock State Park is relatively undeveloped. It has a trail system and a hike-in group camp (reservations only), but no rangers are on duty.

For further information: Area Manager, Santa Cruz Mountain Area State Parks, P.O. Box 761, Felton 95018.

Access: The park is off State 35 about 1 mile south of its junction with State 9.

Hikers pass among ghostly trees of Castle Rock State Park. Dramatic rock formation gives this park its name.

Butano State Park

More than 2,000 acres of heavily wooded slopes on the western side of the Coast Range are included in Butano State Park. The park is back of Pescadero at an average elevation of 500 feet. Here you will find dense forests of Douglas fir and redwood, mostly second-growth although there are many mature trees. Little Butano Creek runs through the park, and there is a small fern canyon.

Butano was added to the park system in the 1960's and is not yet well developed. It is on the edge of the coastal fog belt, so fog can be expected nights and mornings in summer. The park's best seasons are spring and fall. It is wet and cold in winter.

Activities: Camping, picnicking, hiking. A campground with 40 unimproved sites is in a forested area on slopes back from the park entrance; dirt roads go through the campground. No trailers beyond 35 feet can be accommodated, and 19 sites are 50 to 300-foot "walk-in" types for tent campers only. There is no separate picnic ground, but unoccupied campsites may be used for picnicking. The park is open all year, with a 15-day camping limit. It gets considerable use as an "overflow" camping area supplementing nearby parks. Including fire roads, 40 miles of trails are available for hiking in the park.

Access: Take the Pescadero turnoff from State 1. Turn right on Cloverdale Road east of town and proceed for about 5 miles; the last 1½ miles of road are gravel (good condition).

Big Basin Redwoods State Park

Big Basin is the oldest park owned by the state. Included in its expanse are several creeks, many waterfalls, windswept uplands, and dense groves of mature redwoods. The state acquired the original 3,800 acres in 1902 and named it "California Redwood Park." (Yosemite was a state park even earlier, but it later became a national park.) The name was changed to "Big Basin Redwoods" in 1927, and it has been gradually expanded over the years to nearly 12,000 acres. Now it serves hundreds of thousands of visitors annually. Camping space may be at a premium in summer and on good-weather weekends any time of the year.

Its mild climate makes Big Basin State Park usable much of the year, except during the heavy rainfall season in the winter.

Activities: Camping, picnicking, hiking, riding, nature study. Ten campgrounds provide 243 improved campsites for families and space for 450 people in group areas (these must be reserved). Camping limit is 15 days, and the park is open year-round. One campground is walk-in, several accommodate camping vehicles, and a vehicle sanitation station is provided. Scattered through the park are 175 family picnic sites.

About 35 miles of trails follow the stream valleys or

Feeding deer *delights young visitor to Big Basin State Park. This is California's oldest state park.*

lead up to high points. Riders may use 15 miles of the trail network, and horses are available for rental outside the park boundaries. One hiking and riding trail goes to Castle Rock State Park, 14 miles away. Near park headquarters there is a short self-guided nature trail through a grove of large trees.

Interpretive specialists conduct nature walks and talks in season. Near headquarters is a small museum with displays on local wildlife.

For further information: Area Manager, Santa Cruz Mountain Area State Parks, P.O. Box 761, Felton 95018.

Access: The best route is from Boulder Creek—leave State 9 here and follow signs for about 9 miles to park headquarters. This road loops through the park and rejoins State 9 about 8 miles farther north, but the northern route is not recommended for trailers and camping vehicles.

Supplies: Boulder Creek. In summer a concessionaire operates a restaurant, snack bar, gift shop, and gas station at the park.

Trail leads *into redwood forest of Henry Cowell park. Situated to the north of the town of Santa Cruz, the park has facilities for both picnicking and camping; you can fish in the San Lorenzo River here.*

Henry Cowell Redwoods State Park

At Henry Cowell Redwoods State Park you can walk through a large grove of redwoods and stands of mature Ponderosa pines—very unusual for this region. The park is situated on a valley bottom in the Santa Cruz Mountains at about 500 feet altitude; it includes about 1,800 acres and has two streams—Eagle Creek and the San Lorenzo River.

Although Cowell has a campground, its major use is during the day by visitors who come to walk the excellent self-guided nature trail through the grove near park headquarters. Another trail leads up to the Cathedral Redwoods grove.

Climate is mild here much of the year but can be damp and chilly in winter because of heavy rainfall in the mountains.

About a hundred acres of the park was the old Santa Cruz County Big Trees Park, a popular Victorian-era outing spot reached by narrow-gauge excursion trains. Samuel Henry Cowell gave the state most of the park land in 1953.

Activities: Camping, picnicking, hiking, nature study, riding, fishing in season. The campground is on the east side of the park and is reached by the Graham Hill Road from Felton. It has 50 improved campsites, accommodating trailers up to 36 feet in length.

A huge picnic area with 220 family sites and group areas available on reservation for 500 people are situated near park headquarters. Many sites overlook the river.

Trails offer 15 miles of hiking, and horses may be ridden in the park; they are available for rent from a stable in Felton.

The river offers steelhead fishing from Boulder Creek to the river mouth from November to February, but it is closed to trout fishing in the summer.

For further information: Area Manager, Santa Cruz Mountain Area State Parks, P.O. Box 761, Felton 95018.

Access: The main park entrance is on the east side of State 9 just south of Felton.

Supplies: Cafeteria and gift shop in park, otherwise Felton.

Central Valley & Foothills

The broad Central Valley extends up and down the state for more than 400 miles, enclosed on all four sides by mountains. Here and in the surrounding foothills, you can pursue water sports at reservoir parks, enjoy the wooded setting of river parks, and look into the past at historic parks.

Two major rivers flow through this region—the Sacramento and the San Joaquin rise hundreds of miles apart and finally join, forming the Delta region, before eventually going into San Francisco Bay. The Central Valley actually consists of both the Sacramento and San Joaquin valleys. Bordering the valley are the Sierra Nevada to the east, the Coast Range to the west, the Tehachapis to the south, and the southern Cascade and Trinity ranges to the north.

Four reservoir parks (classified as "state recreation areas") are located on the east side of the valley above dams which control flooding and preserve the Sierra run-off for irrigation. Another reservoir park, San Luis, is on the west side of the valley. All of these reservoirs are great sheets of water only a few hundred feet above sea level. These parks are hot in summer—often very hot—but attract fishermen and boating enthusiasts.

The river parks are relatively small, but here you will find almost the only remnants of the bank forests that once lined the valley rivers. (Most of the trees were cut down to supply steamboat fuel or to leave clearings for farmland.) These parks are hot in summer, but they are cooler than the surrounding regions. Except for the Sacramento, the rivers are shallow in summer, but usually they are still deep enough for water recreation, and there are sandy beaches.

The historic parks in this part of the state include remnants and reminders of gold rush days. Here, in the foothills of the Sierra, Marshall Gold Discovery State Park marks the site where gold was found in 1848. The mining town of Columbia is also preserved as a state park, with many restored buildings that help recreate the atmosphere of the hectic boom days.

William B. Ide Adobe State Historic Park

A pleasant area of 3 acres on the banks of the Sacramento River, the William B. Ide Adobe Park commemorates the home of the first (and only) president of the Bear Flag Republic. Shaded by an immense valley oak, the restored home and outbuildings built by Ide look today as nearly like the originals as the state's restoration experts could make them. The interiors as well as the exteriors have been restored.

The exact date of the adobe's construction is not known, but it was shortly after the first gold rush days of 1848 when Ide and his sons garnered enough dust and

White oak, *one of the largest in the state, dwarfs the William B. Ide Adobe, built in gold rush days.*

Any *warm day you are likely to see water-skiers on Soda Bay at Clear Lake (see page 62). View opposite is from park's Bayview Campground.*

Pioneer John Bidwell *chose homesite in valley near Chico Creek for his mansion, and city of Chico has grown up around. Old home, once center of social life for northern Sacramento Valley, is now an historic park.*

nuggets in the placer mines to become prosperous. Their home was built at the head of the river navigation in those days, where the California-Oregon Trail crossed the river to link Sacramento and the Mother Lode with Shasta and the Northern Mines.

The park has a small picnic area. There is limited access to the river, with mooring facilities near the site of the Old Adobe Ferry.

Access: In the northern outskirts of Red Bluff, the park is on Adobe Road off State 36. The turnoff is well marked from Interstate 5.

Woodson Bridge State Recreation Area

Woodson Bridge is essentially a camping park, but the activities possible here are expanded by the adjacent Tehama County Park's excellent day-use area. The county park has a beach on the Sacramento River and a boat launching ramp. The state park consists of about 400 acres of land on both sides of the Sacramento River; the west side is undeveloped but includes Kopta Slough, an old river channel where you can fish.

One of the parcels of land along the Sacramento which retains its natural wooded character, Woodson Bridge has mature groves of oaks and cottonwoods.

In summer it is often hot here, although the park is cooler than the surrounding farm country and gets use by a few campers who enjoy its peaceful atmosphere. Greatest use is from October through May, when the climate is cooler and various salmon and steelhead runs occur. Occasional heavy rains can be expected in winter, but frosty nights are rare.

Activities: Camping, picnicking, limited hiking and swimming, sunbathing, boating, fishing. The campgrounds are east of the river, in groves of big trees, and have 48 improved sites offering semi-privacy (showers). Picnic facilities are available in the county park adjoining Woodson Bridge.

Woodson Bridge's big attraction is the fishing along this stretch of river for big steelhead and salmon, an occasional run of stripers, and catfish, largemouth bass, and bluegills in the slough. Most fishing is from boats, but the rangers will suggest places to fish from the banks.

For further information: Area Manager, North Valley Area State Parks, 525 Esplanade, Chico 95926.

Access: The park entrance is on the north side of county route A-9 (South Avenue), a few hundred yards east of the river. It is 3 miles west of Vina on U.S. 99E and 6 miles east of Corning on Interstate 5.

Supplies: County park at the east end of the bridge has a cafe and store, a trailer park with hookups, boating mooring and rentals. Ice and general supplies can be obtained in Vina or Corning.

Bidwell Mansion State Historic Park

The Chico home of prominent California pioneer John Bidwell is now preserved as an historic park. Bidwell was a leader in agriculture in the state, and his mansion is a relic of opulent ranch life of another era.

Bidwell came to California in 1841 at the age of 22 with the Bartleson party—the first organized group of settlers to cross the Sierra. He worked for Captain John Sutter for five years, and later he became prosperous after he laid out some gold claims on the Feather River in 1848. Bidwell became a member of the State Senate, and he bought the 25,000-acre Rancho del Arroyo Chico.

Bidwell made many innovations in California agriculture and is said to be the father of the California raisin industry. He was elected a U.S. Congressman in 1865 but ran for governor five times on the Union Party ticket without success, and in 1892 he also failed in his attempt to gain the presidency on the Prohibition ticket.

While in Congress, Bidwell met and married Annie Ellicott Kennedy, and their home became a sort of cultural center for northern California. Many prominent guests were entertained here. The home today is furnished as a museum of the Bidwells' life style, and it also contains Annie Bidwell's collection of Indian baskets.

The mansion is open from 10 A.M. to 5 P.M. all days except major holidays. There is a small entrance fee. School groups may make arrangements for guided tours of the mansion.

Access: The mansion is in Chico just south of the state college, on State 99E.

Lake Oroville State Recreation Area

The completion of the world's highest embankment dam in 1967 on the Feather River resulted in the creation of a lake with 167 miles of shoreline. Lake Oroville has become a mecca for boaters, even during the 100-degree weather common to this area in summer. In spring and fall the climate is more tolerable, and the park is not excessively cold in winter, although sometimes the area gets heavy winter rainstorms.

The lake is situated in rugged foothills forested with oak, digger pines, and toyon.

Activities: Camping, picnicking, swimming, boating, fishing, and water-skiing; there are 7½ miles of riding and hiking trails along the Feather River below the dam.

The Loafer Creek campground off the Oroville-Quincy road has 136 improved campsites (showers). There is a picnic area here and at the North Thermalito Forebay, the latter with beach facilities.

Altogether there are a dozen recreation areas along the lake, with many boat-in camps, marinas, and launching ramps. Currently, lifeguards are provided at swimming beaches.

The Kelly Ridge visitor and interpretation center on the south side of the lake above the dam is planned for

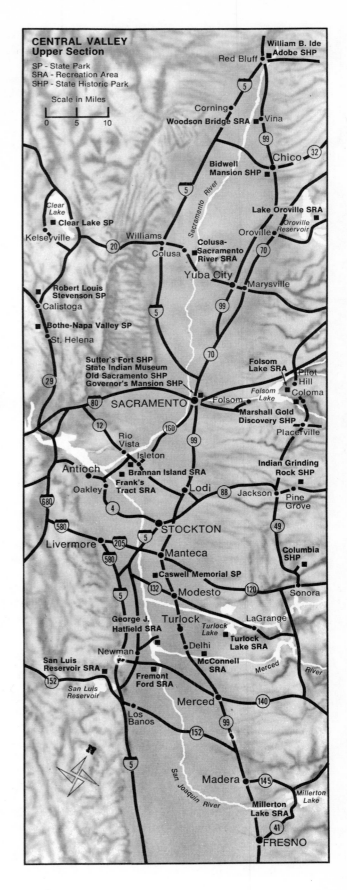

completion in 1972, with many displays of the dam engineering, an overlook of the lake, and historical exhibits.

When the lake was full, it was planted with a million fingerling rainbows, bass, German browns, catfish, and kokanee salmon. Fishermen are now catching these fish, which have grown to good size. Fishing is permitted the year around.

For further information: Area Manager, Lake Oroville Area State Parks, 400 Glen Drive, Oroville 95965.

Access: Drive through Oroville on State 70 and follow signs to the lake. Forebays are downstream and across river, west of town.

Supplies: Oroville.

Colusa-Sacramento River State Recreation Area

A delightful 67-acre park on the west shore of the Sacramento River, Colusa-Sacramento River is partly covered by dense groves of cottonwoods and willows.

Hot in summer, but cooler than the surrounding valley, the park is pleasant in spring and fall. It may be wet, damp, and foggy in winter, and portions are flooded if the river rises high.

Activities: Camping, picnicking, fishing, all boating sports. The campground in the groves has 24 unimproved sites, with fair privacy, close to the river. The park is open all year with a 30-day camping limit. Some campsites are removed in winter because of flooding.

A day-use area near the park entrance has 32 family picnic sites with ramadas, trees, and green lawns.

A small boat ramp is available, and in summer a 140-foot floating dock is anchored near the shore.

Some fishermen use the park for bank fishing, and many use it as a base for water-skiing and fishing exploration. From Colusa boaters can go upstream as far as Hamilton City, downstream to Sacramento (or all the way to San Francisco Bay if desired). This section of the river offers striped bass and shad fishing in spring, salmon, catfish, and black bass in the fall, and sometimes sturgeon and steelhead.

For further information: Area Manager, North Valley Area State Parks, 525 Esplanade, Chico 95926.

Access: Drive via State 20 to the city of Colusa; in the center of town, turn on 10th Street and go a short distance to the park entrance. A sign marks the turnoff. The park is 20 miles west of U.S. 99E at Yuba City, 9 miles east of Interstate 5 at Williams.

Supplies: Colusa.

Clear Lake State Park

Located along the largest natural body of water entirely within the state, Clear Lake State Park offers more than 500 acres with a wide diversity of terrain. About 2 miles of lake shoreline are included in the park.

The portion adjacent to the entrance is somewhat like a valley riverside park, with groves of large oaks and cottonwoods along Cole Creek. The lakeshore area is gently sloping, partially wooded, cut by several old channels and sloughs. Looping beyond the beach area, the road climbs up a hill overlooking Soda Bay.

Clear Lake is often hot in summer, but this does not deter the water-oriented people who use it. It has excellent weather in spring and fall but sometimes gets cold weather and heavy storms in winter.

Activities: Camping, picnicking, hiking, nature study, sunbathing, swimming, boating, water-skiing, fishing. Bayview Campground is on the hill, in scrub and other foothill vegetation, with 55 improved campsites affording semi-privacy; some give excellent views over the lake. Cole Creek has 25 improved sites in groves of trees along the creek. (Both campgrounds have showers.) Camping limit is 15 days in summer; the park is open all year.

Smoking is prohibited in some parts of the park, as are open fires, because of fire danger. A sanitation disposal unit for camping vehicles is available in the parking area near the boat moorings and launching ramp. Fish cleaning tables are provided.

The day-use area just across the mouth of Cole Creek has some small beaches and a shaded 28-unit picnic ground with its own parking apron. The main beach is below the Bayview campground near the old mouth of Kelsey Creek, but there are no lifeguards in the park.

In warm weather, water-skiing is a major sport at Clear Lake. There is good fishing at various times of the year for crappie, black bass, and catfish. Many fishermen use boats to work along the shores, but bank fishing is not unrewarding.

There are several hiking trails, including the Dorn self-guided nature trail. A self-guided loop trail on the slopes near the park entrance gives insight into the lives of the Pomo and Lili'ek Indians who once frequented the area.

For further information: Area Manager, Clear Lake Area State Parks, Route 1, Box 33, Kelseyville 95451.

Access: From Kelseyville on State 29, go east about 4 miles on the Soda Bay Road.

Supplies: Kelseyville, a recreation center.

Robert Louis Stevenson State Park

About 3,000 acres of wild area on the eastern slopes and around the summit of Mount St. Helena are designated as Robert Louis Stevenson State Park. There is a monument to the author, who spent his honeymoon here in 1880. Here he acquired the background for writing *Silverado Squatters*.

Completely undeveloped except for a rudimentary trail system, the park is suitable for hiking and rough picnicking, but fires are not allowed.

Access: The park is on the west side of State 29 between Calistoga and Middletown; parking is at the small bulldozed pullout near the top of the grade. The only sign is at the park boundary.

Bothe-Napa Valley State Park

About 1,100 acres of wooded valley flat and eastern slopes of Coast Range ridges make up Bothe-Napa Valley State Park. Generally heavily wooded with foothill-type vegetation, the park has some groves of large trees and a few redwood flats. Running along the park is Ritchie Creek.

Included in the park boundary are the old cemetery and the site of the first church in the Napa Valley. The Methodist Episcopal church, of which only the foundation remains, was built in the 1850's and became known as the "White Church" after its first minister, Asa White. The cemetery contains graves of Donner Party members.

The California Riding and Hiking Trail connects this park with Sugarloaf Ridge State Park to the west (see page 41). Climate may be warm in summer but is usually moderate much of the year, with some heavy rains and cold weather in winter.

Activities: Camping, picnicking, hiking, fishing (some small trout in creek), nature study, swimming. The campground has 35 improved sites in dense groves of large trees affording semi-privacy. The park is open all year, with a 15-day camping limit in summer.

A 35-unit picnic ground is available near the park entrance, there is a short self-guided nature trail, and campfire programs are presented on Friday and Saturday nights in the summer season. A swimming pool is operated by a concessionaire.

For further information: Area Manager, Bothe-Napa Area State Parks, 3601 St. Helena Highway North, Calistoga 94515.

Access: The park is on the west side of State 29 about 4 miles north of St. Helena.

Supplies: St. Helena, Calistoga.

Folsom Lake State Recreation Area

Closest to a major population center of all the state's big reservoir parks, Folsom has many developments which make it perhaps the best recreation area of all the reservoirs.

Situated in the lower foothills of the Sierra, Folsom Lake has 120 miles of shoreline, including the long and narrow afterbay, Lake Natoma. Since Folsom Dam was located virtually at the confluence of the North and South Forks of the American River, the lake has two long arms extending deep into the foothills with a peninsula between. The park land comprises almost all the shoreline at various widths. Oak-grass slopes surround the shores.

The little Folsom Powerhouse below the south abutment of the Folsom Bridge is part of the park. A pioneer facility in converting water to power electricity, it was a gift to the state from Pacific Gas and Electric. Some interpretive panels have been installed, and it is open daily except Wednesdays and Thursdays in summer, weekends only in winter.

Folsom Lake, *popular for boating, is most heavily used of state's reservoir parks, has well developed facilities.*

Statue *of James Marshall pointing to 1848 gold discovery site is on a hill above the town of Coloma in historic park.*

Climate here is hot in summer, mild in spring and fall; it may be damp and chilly in winter.

Activities: Camping, picnicking, hiking, riding, swimming, water-skiing, boating, fishing. Beal's Point on the main lake and Negro Bar on Lake Natoma have 120 improved sites, and there is a 30-unit unimproved campground on the peninsula. Many picnic areas offer a total of 700 family sites, most of them near beaches with

swimming (there are no lifeguards). The park is open all year, with 15-day camping limits. For detailed descriptions of facilities and locations, write for the park folder.

Folsom has about 50 miles of trails, some of them connecting to horsemen's trails outside the park. The Pioneer Express trail extends all the way from Beal's Point to Auburn along the shore and up the North Fork.

A concessionaire operates a massive marina at Brown's Ravine. The state also provides four paved launching ramps and nine unimproved ones at various points on the shoreline.

In addition to speedboating and water-skiing, sailboating is increasingly popular at Folsom. Fingerling fish planted when the lake was first filled, along with some from upstream, now offer the fisherman a chance at trout, catfish, large and small-mouth bass, perch, and kokanee salmon.

For further information: Area Manager, Folsom Lake State Recreation Area, 7806 Folsom-Auburn Road, Folsom 95630.

Access: For the newcomer, the various routes to different facilities along the lake are best reached from Folsom, where you should ask directions, or from park headquarters on the Folsom-Auburn Road just north of Folsom and below the west end of the dam.

Supplies: Folsom, Sacramento, Pilot Hill, and other nearby towns.

Marshall Gold Discovery State Historic Park

For Californians, the Marshall Gold Discovery park is in a sense the most important historic site in the state. It was here that James W. Marshall found gold in 1848 while digging the millrace for a sawmill on the American River. In less than a year, thousands of people were heading for California from all points of the globe, and the state was no longer a quiet cattle-ranching backwater.

Marshall was a business partner of Captain John Sutter when he found gold. He brought the gold samples to Sutter, who immediately realized the augury of the discovery and swore Marshall to secrecy. But the secret leaked out from workers at the mill site, and the rush was on.

The park now includes 70 per cent of the town of Coloma, which grew up after Marshall's discovery. On a high hill above the town stands a tall monument with a statue of Marshall pointing to the place where he found gold. You can drive up to the statue and pass the Marshall cabin on the way down. In the paved area near the monument are interpretive display cases, and among the trees just below are some king-sized picnic tables suitable for groups. The statue and cabin can also be reached by a stiff 1-mile hike up from Coloma.

There are plans for restoring many more of the Coloma buildings when funds are available, but at present restoration has been confined to two small stone structures, dating back to 1858, which were leased for many years by Chinese merchants. These are easily identified by their colorful signs written in Chinese characters. One building contains a mining and geological exhibit; the other is fitted out as a typical Chinese store.

A replica of the old sawmill has been built near its original site, with a parking apron nearby. The mill is operated several times on weekends for the benefit of visitors.

In the grove near the main picnic ground a handsome museum has many exhibits on gold rush days and associated history. Interpretive movies are shown here on weekends, and a ranger is on duty to answer questions.

In addition to the few large picnic tables on the hill, two picnic grounds provide a total of 143 family sites. The main picnic area at the north end of town is very pleasant, with big trees and green lawns; another area has been provided across the road near the river, northwest of the sawmill.

The outside buildings in the park are open from 8 A.M. to 5 P.M. daily, the museum from 10 A.M. to 5 P.M. with a 25-cent admission charge. The standard picnicking charge of $1 includes entrance to exhibits.

Access: The park is 8 miles north of Placerville and 19 miles south of Auburn on State 49. The highway passes through town as the main street.

Sacramento Historic Parks

Located at the juncture of two major rivers, once vital for transport into the interior of the state, Sacramento has been important in the history of California since before the gold rush. Four state historic parks here reflect that importance.

John Sutter, the eccentric Swiss who obtained a huge land grant here from the Mexican government in 1839 and set up a semi-military barony, appears again and again in the history of northern California during the decade before it became U.S. territory. One of Sacramento's historic parks is a restoration of the fort he built. It was a partner, James Marshall, who discovered gold on the American River and precipitated the gold rush which destroyed Sutter's hopes of empire. (See Marshall Gold Discovery State Historic Park, page 64.)

Before the influx of settlers, Indians in this area lived

THE CENTRAL VALLEY RIVERS

On a relief map of California, the Central Valley appears as a great, almost canoe-shaped depression, entirely walled by mountains except at one opening into San Francisco Bay through Carquinez Straits. The valley river system drains considerable portions of the Coast, Tehachapi, Sierra Nevada, Cascade, and Klamath ranges.

The Sacramento and San Joaquin rivers are like the main members of a fish backbone—with the tributaries joining at intervals like the sidebones, but almost all on one side. Drainage from the coast ranges on the west is only occasional, during heavy rains, and virtually all of the valley's water comes from the higher Sierra Nevada, Cascade, and Klamath ranges to the east and north. Here the heavy snow packs build up in winter and keep the rivers alive with the slow melt through spring and summer.

Before the state was settled, the flow was unchecked. When warm spring rains melted the snow pack on the mountain ridges, the valley was inundated almost from rim to rim. Early travelers tell of seeing it like a great inland sea. Today the rivers are confined by levee systems, and the many flood control dams of the Central Valley Project hold the water so it can be released slowly. The lakes created behind these dams have become popular parks and recreation areas.

The valley rivers have played an important role in California history. The Central Valley Indians lived prosperously along their shores, with huge salmon runs in season, oak groves for acorn meal, thousands of elk and antelope to hunt, waterfowl by the millions, and many seed-bearing plants. The Indians used the tule reeds for houses and even made quite adequate boats from them.

When gold was discovered in 1848 on the American River, a branch of the Sacramento system, the valley rivers took on new importance. For millions of years they had been washing gold out of the mountain gravels, and in places gold lay thick on their bottoms. Gold-seeking prospectors followed streams and dry water courses on both sides of the valley. Almost overnight hundreds of settlements sprang up along the valley rivers and deep in the mountains. Because water transport was fast and cheap, the major rivers became highways for a vast fleet of river steamers. Woodcutters along the rivers sold wood for fires, and riverside forests of great oaks rapidly disappeared into the steamer fireboxes.

Where the Sacramento and the San Joaquin Rivers join is a vast delta region—hundreds of square miles of flat terrain which flooded each spring and early summer, to drain more gradually through the Straits into San Francisco Bay and into the ocean through the Golden Gate. As a result of flooding, many new channels have been cut and old ones discarded, to remain as bypassed sloughs. These sloughs have created another kind of water-oriented recreation area, as at Brannan Island (see page 68).

Striking contrast *is presented by Sutter's Fort and modern city of Sacramento surrounding it. Fort was built in 1839.*

Mansion *built in 1870's served as home for 13 of California's governors over a period of 64 years; tours are conducted.*

quiet lives of relative prosperity. Annual floods provided an abundance of reeds for houses and boats, and sloughs and channels teemed with fish and birds. Huge herds of elk, antelope, and deer roamed the surrounding country.

Sutter's Fort State Historic Park: Carefully restored to its appearance when Sutter built it in 1839 as the commercial defense center of the vast empire he expected some day to control, the fort shows the self-sufficiency necessary for such an outpost of civilization. Sooner or later, all overland travelers to California touched here for vital supplies and rest.

Restoration of Sutter's Fort was based on historical research in Germany. In 1848 Sutter published a brochure there with a complete description of the fort to encourage German immigration.

The park is open every day from 10 A.M. to 5 P.M. except on Christmas, New Year's, and Thanksgiving. The

entrance fee includes a headset which can be used at each of 42 historical exhibits to play taped interpretive messages. Entrance fee is 50 cents for those 18 and over (age 17 and under are admitted free, with a 25-cent charge for the headset). Organized youth groups are admitted free if prior arrangement is made, at a group rate of 15 cents each for the headsets.

The fort entrance is at 27th and L streets; there is meter parking on the street.

State Indian Museum: Outstanding displays represent the six cultural regions of the California Indians (104 tribes in all) before the coming of Europeans. Artifacts range from objects hundreds of years old to those being made by Indians today. Beautifully organized exhibits include various cultural aspects, with examples of water craft, weapons, baskets, and religious objects.

The museum is in the same two-block parcel of land

which contains Sutter's Fort, diagonally opposite. It is open from 10 A.M. to 5 P.M., and admission to the fort covers the museum admission. The entrance is near 26th and K streets. There is meter parking.

Governor's Mansion: Originally constructed in 1877-78 as a residence for hardware dealer Albert Gallatin at a cost of more than $70,000, the Governor's Mansion was purchased by the state in 1903. The 15-room, five-bath building served as living quarters for 13 governors until 1967—although in 1941 the state fire marshall declared it unsafe.

The original furnishings have been retained in the building, and interpretive specialists conduct guided tours every half hour from 10 A.M. to 4:30 P.M. daily. Admission is 50 cents, and groups can make reservations up to six months in advance.

The mansion is at the corner of 16th and H streets. There is meter parking on the street.

Old Sacramento State Historic Park: This park is relatively undeveloped, but plans call for restoration of the old city area along the waterfront to its appearance in the 1850's and 1860's when it was the main supply point for the jumpoff to the northern mines. At present no funds have been allocated for further work, although the state has title to several old buildings. The area is along Front Street near the river ends of I and J streets.

For further information: Area Manager, Sacramento Area State Parks, 2701 L Street, Sacramento 95816.

Indian Grinding Rock State Historic Park

A great, flat limestone outcrop marked by hundreds of mortar holes, once used by Miwok Indians for grinding acorns into flour, is now a state historic park. A self-guided trail takes you along the rock—you are not allowed to walk on the rock itself.

According to the trail guide sheet, there are 1,185 mortar holes in the rock. If you look closely you can also see petroglyphs.

Hundreds of Miwok women and children must have worked industriously in this pleasant meadow when the acorns were ripe. Nearby are some magnificent oaks to enhance the scene. This is a small park, only 48 acres, with a large open oak-grass area near the rock and some upland with scrub oak and other foothill vegetation.

Park altitude is about 2,500 feet. It can be hot here in summer. Spring and fall days are usually fine, but winter may be cold, and there may even be light snowfall.

Activities: Camping, picnicking, and day use for visiting the Grinding Rock trail. A parking apron is provided at the trail head, and there are interpretive displays. A campground has 21 unimproved sites which may be used for picnics when unoccupied; sites are semi-secluded. The park is open all year, and camping limit is 15 days.

For further information: Area Manager, Sacramento Area State Parks, 2701 L Street, Sacramento 95816.

Access: Take State 88 from Jackson and go east 6 miles to Pine Grove; turn north on Volcano Road. From here it is 1 mile to the park entrance on the left of the road. The sign identifies the spot as "Chaw'se," its Indian name. The road drops steeply from Pine Grove and is difficult for heavy trailers.

Supplies: Pine Grove or Jackson.

Hundreds *of mortar holes in Indian Grinding Rock were used by Miwok Indians to grind acorns into flour.*

Brannan Island State Recreation Area

Gradually developing into one of the state's best water sport parks, Brannan Island covers more than 300 acres of flat Delta land almost completely surrounded by sloughs and the Sacramento River. A continuing tree planting program and facility development are making this an attractive center for access to the various Delta region waterways.

Climate at the park is hot in summer, variable in other seasons. Often it is windy here, as the island lies across the air channel from the San Francisco Bay Area into the interior valley. Brannan Island is usable most of the year, but it can be cold, damp, and foggy during the winter season.

The island was formed in the late 1920's from debris moved from Sacramento Channel by U.S. Army Engineer dredging. The state took title in 1954.

Activities: Camping, picnicking, sunbathing, swimming, all boating activities, fishing. The campground on Three Mile Slough has 100 unimproved campsites, heavily used by vehicle campers with boats. A sanitation station is provided. The park is open all year, with 15-day camping limits. Reservations are important from Memorial Day through Labor Day.

A day-use area on Seven Mile Slough has a swimming beach with lifeguards, and the slough is closed to boats.

Nearby dunes are good for sunbathing. This area has a separate large parking apron, windbreaks, and 75 family picnic units. A group camping area and a group picnic area are available on reservation.

Between the campground and the day-use area there is a sizable boat launching ramp. An adjacent parking apron has spaces for 200 cars and boat trailers.

Bank fishing is productive at one or two spots, but most fishermen launch boats and explore the various waterways in their quest for salmon, stripers, bluegill, crappie, sturgeon, and catfish.

For further information: Area Manager, Delta Area State Parks, Star Route Box 75A, Rio Vista 94571.

Access: The park entrance is on the east side of State 160, east of the Sacramento River, 4 miles below Rio Vista bridge or 10 miles upstream from Antioch.

Supplies: Rio Vista, Isleton, Antioch.

Frank's Tract State Recreation Area

About 300 acres of land in the San Joaquin-Sacramento Delta region, Frank's Tract is accessible only by boat. Fishermen and water-ski boaters use the recreation area for occasional landings. The park is completely undeveloped except for chemical toilets.

Access: From State 4 at the south end of Oakley, follow Bethel Island signs. There are commercial launching facilities at Bethel Island; the state area is opposite Bethel Island across Piper Slough.

Columbia State Historic Park

Best known of all the state's historic parks, the preserved and restored section of the town of Columbia takes in the heart of one of the most important gold rush centers. During the 1850's some 10,000 miners gleaned $87 million in gold from the placers in the surrounding area.

Here you can easily imagine yourself a miner striding the wooden sidewalks. Restoration has been extensive, and today several city blocks look almost exactly as they did when gold dust was the only medium of exchange. There is a great deal to see—allow a full day for a tour of Columbia. The historic buildings are open from 8 A.M. to 5 P.M.

After the town was virtually wiped out several times by fire, the townspeople finally rebuilt it with brick and fitted the building openings with iron shutters for fire resistance. (The iron shutters were not, as commonly supposed, to keep out badmen.) The result was that many of the buildings were in reasonably good repair at the time Columbia became a historic park.

In the center of town, at the corner of Main and State streets, the restored Knapp's Corner building functions as park headquarters and houses an extensive museum collection. A ranger-interpretive specialist is on duty.

The park folder, which lists 42 points of interest and

includes a map, is an excellent interpretive guide; you should get a copy before you tour the park. For 25 cents you can also buy a privately printed souvenir tabloid which gives detailed descriptions of the town and concessions. The state's property does not take in all of the historic sections, and the streets belong to the county.

The handsome old Wells Fargo building is a center of interest and a favorite of photographers (morning light is best for taking pictures of it). Diagonally across the street from park headquarters is the Columbia House, carefully reconstructed in the style of a restaurant which once stood there but burned. The restaurant includes 49er specialties on its menu.

Columbia has never been a ghost town, and even today it has permanent residents. Downtown you will find many places to shop for antique objects of art, souvenirs, and home-made candy and bakery goods. There are saloons where you can get a glass of beer—or sarsaparilla—and dance on the bare wooden floors. Stagecoach rides for children are popular attractions; fare is 75 cents, or $1 for the shotgun seat.

When the state restored the old firehouse, local citizens made a charming restoration of *Papeete*, the hand pumper built in 1852 on the east coast for the King of the Sandwich Islands. The state keeps a modern pumper at the park, but with a dozen husky men working the pump bars, *Papeete* can throw a stream about as far as the modern contrivance. *Papeete* figures strongly each year, along with other ancient units from Mother Lode towns, in the Firemen's Muster held the first weekend in May.

The Fallon House Theatre offers stage performances by the University of the Pacific drama department during July and August. The Columbia Grammar School, its restoration aided by the pennies of thousands of children, is an authentic school of the 1860's, even to the old tobacco can lunch boxes—a supply of them was found beneath the floors.

Private development has grown up around the park, and there are two private campgrounds and a 35-unit picnic ground. Many additional curio shops are open outside the park, and motels and restaurants are nearby.

Access: From State 49 turn northeast 2 miles north of Sonora; follow 2 miles of access road, well marked. Another way to reach the town is by the Columbia-to-Vallecito road which connects with State 4 about 9 miles away. Steep and winding but scenic, this paved road takes you through Stanislaus River canyon.

Main street in Columbia recreates feeling of gold rush days. Wells Fargo building is at left. Several blocks of the old mining town have been restored as a state historic park, and vehicles are kept out during busy hours.

Caswell Memorial State Park

A wild, dense forest covering about 250 acres along the San Joaquin River, the area designated as Caswell Memorial State Park is unchanged from its state before civilization came to California.

Sizable groves of valley oaks include many large, old specimens. In some areas the park is a dense jungle of smaller trees with an impassable undergrowth of wild blackberry, grape, wild rose, elderberry, and other shrubs (but no poison oak). Several miles of trails have literally been chopped through. Cottonwoods and box elder give good color displays in autumn.

The park is hot in summer but still cooler than surrounding farm land. Mild climate is usual in spring and fall, and the park may be damp, cold, and foggy in the winter.

Activities: Camping, picnicking, sunbathing, limited hiking and nature study. The campground has 66 improved sites (showers) cut into dense growth—shaded and private. The park is open all year, with 15-day camping limits. There are a number of small, scattered enclaves

---

THE PACIFIC FLYWAY

The major path of migrating waterfowl in the West is directly down the central valleys of Washington, Oregon, and California. This route is known as the Pacific Flyway, and it is the most important of four flyways on the continent (the others are the Central, the Mississippi, and the Atlantic flyways). The Klamath-Tule Lake region on the Oregon-California border gets the greatest concentration of migrating waterfowl in the country.

Depending upon summer weather in Canada and Alaska, between 8 and 15 million waterfowl come down the Pacific Flyway each fall. Almost all of these breed and nest in the far north; if the season is wet there, breeding conditions are good. As cold weather approaches, the parents and young birds head south to winter in California and Mexico.

When there were no dams, no drainage canals, and no levees in California, flooding river waters created about 5 million acres of permanent wetlands. Today much of this land has been drained and is producing tomatoes, sugar beets, cotton, rice, fruit, and other crops—but also reducing the wetlands to a tenth of their original size. Both federal and state governments have become increasingly aware of the necessity for resting and habitat areas for the migrating birds. The state now has about two dozen federal and state refuges, and more are being added as possible. Funds come from the California parimutuel horseracing fund, federal cooperative provisions, Duck Stamp money, and other sources including private groups.

---

of picnic sites, with six to eight family units in each, totaling 50.

The river beaches are usable for sunbathing, but the bacterial pollution in the San Joaquin River during low water makes it inadvisable to swim there. It has no effect on fish, and bank fishing is possible for bass, crappie and bluegill, and sometimes stripers.

For further information: Area Manager, Four Rivers Area State Parks, P.O. Box 991, Los Banos 93635.

Access: There are several possible routes, but the best approach for newcomers is to turn south on Austin Road from U.S. 99 about a mile south of Manteca and drive straight to the park entrance.

Supplies: Manteca.

Turlock Lake State Recreation Area

Turlock Lake State Recreation Area almost amounts to two parks—one section at Turlock Lake oriented to boating sports and another along the Tuolumne River similar to several other valley river parks. The two parts are divided by a county road.

Except for the now-mature tree plantings in the day-use areas near the reservoir, the park's upper landscape is barren, with low grass-covered hills. The section along the river lies beneath low bluffs and has dense growths of native trees.

Climate is typical of the Central Valley—hot in summer, pleasant in spring and fall, sometimes chilly, wet, and foggy in winter.

Activities: Camping, picnicking, swimming and sunbathing, boating and water-skiing, lake and stream fishing. The campground lies along the river, about a half mile east of the water sports area, with a separate contact station and 65 improved campsites in groves of native oak, elder, and sycamore (showers). The park is open all year, with 15-day camping limits.

At the lake there are two picnic grounds in deep shade with green lawns on low bluffs above the northern shoreline, providing about 35 family units. A small, sandy beach in a nearby cove has a buoyed area to protect swimmers from boats, but there are no lifeguards.

Boating facilities are excellent, with a sizable launching ramp and a large parking apron for cars and boat-trailers in addition to parking space at picnic areas. The large Modesto Reservoir recreation area is a few miles away to the north, and there are many others within a distance of 25 miles.

Lake fishing offers black bass, crappie, some catfish and bluegill; the river has catfish, large and smallmouth bass, and some salmon and steelhead in winter.

For further information: Area Manager, Four Rivers Area State Parks, P.O. Box 991, Los Banos 93635.

Access: The lake is about 25 miles east of Modesto. Take State 132 from U.S. 99 (or Interstate 5 to the west)

Trees planted *near launching ramps at Turlock Lake provide shade for picnicking. An adjacent cove has a roped-off area for swimming. Part of park is along Tuolumne River, and a campground is situated there in groves of trees.*

and continue east about 23 miles to Robert's Ferry School. Turn south and follow signs about 2 miles. You also can approach by a good but winding road from State 108-120 some 13 miles south of Sonora, via La Grange.

Supplies: Concessionaire-operated snack bar and small general store within park; otherwise La Grange or Modesto.

McConnell State Recreation Area

A small oasis along the Merced River, McConnell gets heavy use by local residents. The park has watered green lawns shaded by large trees.

Climate is hot here in summer but cooler than the surrounding valley, and it is moderate in spring and fall; it may be damp, chilly, and foggy in winter. Mosquitoes sometimes are a nuisance.

Activities: Camping, picnicking, water play and sunbathing, fishing. McConnell has a small campground with 17 improved sites for which reservations are necessary. The park is open all year, with a summer camping limit of 15 days. A group campground with a capacity of 40 persons is available on reservation. The 25-unit family picnic area is near the river, and there is a small group area with a huge barbecue pit (reservations required).

An oasis *in the Central Valley, McConnell State Recreation Area has Merced River for cooling off in summer.*

Both camps and picnic areas are in groves of oak and box elder.

Several sand beaches along the river are good for sunbathing. Swimming is possible when there is enough water in the river, but the park does not furnish lifeguard service.

Bank fishing for catfish, crappie, bluegill, and bass is popular here.

For further information: Area Manager, Four Rivers Area State Parks, P.O. Box 991, Los Banos 93635.

Access: From Delhi on U.S. 99, turn east on El Capitan and drive 3 miles, then turn south on Pepper and follow the road a few miles until it ends at the park at McConnell Road. There are signs at Pepper and on U.S. 99.

Supplies: Delhi or other towns on U.S. 99.

George J. Hatfield State Recreation Area

A heavily used river park of 47 acres, George J. Hatfield has many big trees and watered green lawns, impeccably

Swimming and fishing in Merced River are among activities enjoyed at George J. Hatfield State Recreation Area.

maintained, with more than a mile of frontage on the Merced River. A 14-acre portion of this recreation area is developed and intensely used.

Climate is hot in summer, but cooler than the surrounding valley. Mild weather can be expected in spring and fall, but the park may be wet, chilly, and foggy in the winter.

Activities: Camping, picnicking, swimming, fishing, limited hiking, canoeing. There are seven unimproved campsites, but campers often use the 33 family picnic sites and also overflow areas. A small group camp is available on reservation. Many campers pitch tents on the lawns adjacent to the parking area or use the apron for camping vehicles. The campground lacks privacy.

There is a 2-mile hiking trail along the river. Some canoeing is done between Hatfield and Haagaman County Park 8 miles upstream. Catfish provide the best fishing, with some striped bass when the river is high enough.

There are one or two small beaches, where swimming is relatively safe in summer because of low water, but no lifeguards are provided.

For further information: Area Manager, Four Rivers Area State Parks, P.O. Box 991, Los Banos 93635.

Access: From Newman on State 33 turn east onto Merced Avenue and drive 5 miles; at the old bridge, turn north and follow Kelly Road to the park entrance.

Supplies: Newman.

Fremont Ford State Recreation Area

A shaded 100-acre park on the San Joaquin River about 10 miles south of Hatfield State Recreation Area, Fremont Ford is an undeveloped day-use area. Camping is not permitted, nor are fires.

Sometimes the park is used by fishermen after catfish and striped bass. There is bacterial pollution in the river at low water. The park gets hot weather in summer and may be cold and damp in winter, but spring and fall are mild here.

Access: The park is south of the bridge crossing the San Joaquin River on State 140, on the west side of river. There are no signs.

San Luis Reservoir State Recreation Area

Newest of the reservoir recreation areas, San Luis is still under development. The lake filled sooner than expected, so improvements are somewhat behind schedule. The surrounding area, in the Coast Range rain shadow, is dry and barren, with grass its only vegetation. Trees are being planted, beaches and use areas provided, and roads constructed.

This area is hot and dry in summer, and fire control

THE LAKEVIEW GUSHER

In the barren Kettleman Hills country of the southwestern San Joaquin Valley, an under-capitalized and trouble-ridden oil company in 1910 found the country's greatest gusher.

The Lakeview Oil Company had decided to shoot the works on a 100-acre tract for which it held a lease. The Union Oil Company was drilling on adjacent properties, and several times its crews helped the Lakeview through difficulties. Finally, down to 1,800 feet in a dry hole, Lakeview offered Union a 51 percent interest to take over the job. Union already had four dry holes in the area and was not enthusiastic, but the property had advantages as a storage area if and when any oil was found. Union agreed to continue drilling when crews could be spared.

A drilling foreman nicknamed "Dry Hole Charlie" Woods was assigned to the job. He was competent but unlucky; of 15 wells he had supervised, none had produced oil. In an intermittent fashion, drilling continued at Lakeview, and at about 2 A.M. on March 15, 1910, at 2,200 feet, oil unexpectedly appeared in the baler.

By dawn the next day a mixture of water, oil, and gas was bubbling out of the top of the well, and when "Dry Hole Charlie" came on the scene at 8 A.M. he saw gas and oil roaring hundreds of feet into the air.

The cataclysmic explosion terrified residents for miles around. Ministers even prayed from their pulpits for deliverance from God's wrath.

Much of the oil was saved. Working in a dense petroleum rain, crews dammed nearby arroyos as emergency reservoirs. After months of perilous work, the well was capped and connected into the pipelines to the seaport at Avila near Morro Bay.

It is estimated the first day's flow was 125,000 barrels, and recorded flow over the first 30 days was 90,000 barrels per day. Total production was 9 million barrels, of which 4 million were lost from evaporation and seepage.

On September 9, 1911—18 months after it blew so tempestuously—Lakeview just as abruptly went dry. A later redrilling of the well never produced more than 35 barrels a day.

---

measures are vital. The surrounding hills are green and the park is at its best in spring or after the fall rains have started. Winter weather is often cool and pleasant, but the ground may be muddy.

Activities: Camping, picnicking, hiking, swimming, boating activities within restrictions of park rules, fishing, migratory wildfowl hunting in season.

The recreation area includes three different bodies of water—the main reservoir, O'Neill Forebay, and Los Banos Reservoir. A campground in the Medeiros Area with 20 unimproved sites has been provided in the open on the south shore of the Forebay off State 207 with a sandy beach nearby. The park is open all year, and camping limit is 15 days. A joint picnic-camping area is available at Los Banos Reservoir, with limited facilities that include ramadas and piped water.

Although there are plans for development at several points on the main reservoir, funds are not yet available and emphasis is on improvement of the San Luis Creek Area. Here there are picnic sites, a planted grove of young trees, a beach, lifeguards, a buoyed swimming area, a boat launching ramp, and other facilities. Development will continue through the early 1970's, with better access roads, turf, dressing rooms, and permanent restrooms planned.

Boating and fishing regulations are complex. Water-skiing is allowed only on O'Neill Forebay, and boat speeds on the main reservoir must be kept down to 10 m.p.h. No boating on any of the reservoirs is permitted between sunset and an hour before sunrise.

Fishermen report surprisingly good catches of several varieties of fish—striped and black bass, white and channel catfish, crappie and bluegill. Not only have planted fish done well, but many come in through the pumping system. Night fishing is allowed in certain areas from the reservoir banks.

A portion of the main reservoir is set off as a reserve for migratory water fowl, but hunting is allowed accordance with Fish and Game regulations.

The park folder includes maps, and information is available from park headquarters at the pumping and generating plant just below the main dam.

For further information: Area Manager, Four Rivers Area State Parks, P.O. Box 991, Los Banos 93635.

Access: The park is on both sides of State 152 on the east side of Pacheco Pass, about 15 miles west of the town of Los Banos.

Supplies: Los Banos.

Millerton Lake State Recreation Area

Millerton is a very popular boating lake for residents of the lower Central Valley. Here Friant Dam holds San Joaquin River water, and the resulting lake backs up 15 miles into the foothills and precipitous river canyon. Some upstream locations are accessible only by boat.

Vegetation downstream is spotty, with much of it oak-grass combinations. The shoreline is rocky, particularly since the lake level changes considerably from spring flood to late season drawoff.

Climate here is hot and dry in summer, cooler in spring and fall; the park may be wet, chilly, and foggy in winter.

Activities: Camping, picnicking, hiking, nature study, swimming and sunbathing, water-skiing and other boat sports including boat camping and fishing.

The major campground has 92 improved sites. An additional 46 unimproved sites are located at several points upstream, some accessible only by boat—they may be unapproachable in times of low water. A riding and hiking trail is being constructed around the entire lake perimeter. Rangers give nature talks in summer.

Most days there are tours from 1 to 4 P.M. through the old Fresno Courthouse, which has been restored. The courthouse is on the south side of the lake near the dam; it contains exhibits relating to local history—Millerton was the original county seat, and the courthouse was built in 1866. It is closed on Mondays and Tuesdays.

Because of its location the park has a wide variety of wildlife, especially rabbits. Golden and bald eagles may be seen in late fall and early spring, and blue heron frequent some areas.

Both boat and bank fishermen catch crappie, large and smallmouth bass, bluegill, green sunfish, catfish, and striped bass. The latter are something of an ecological oddity in a closed water system—they are normally anadromous, but it has been discovered they spawn in the live water just above the lake.

On the south shore near the dam there is a two-level boat launching apron which accommodates 15 to 20 boats simultaneously, and there is parking for 750 cars and boat trailers. The north shore has a two-lane launching ramp and a smaller parking area.

Tule elk *herd is protected at state reserve. Bulls in foreground are in "velvet" stage of new antler growth.*

A concessionaire operates a marina in Winchell Cove, providing skiff rentals and mooring, gas and oil.

For further information: Area Manager, Millerton Lake State Recreation Area, P.O. Box 205, Friant 93626.

Access: On U.S. 99 at Madera, turn east at park signs onto State 145 and drive about 20 miles; from Fresno, take State 41 north to its junction with State 145.

Supplies: Madera or Fresno.

Kern River State Recreation Area

Operated by Kern County and locally named Hart Memorial Park, the Kern River State Recreation Area has been intensively developed for day use. This small, shaded acreage on the Kern River includes two small lakes (ancient river channels), two subsidiary river channels, a swimming pool, and huge picnic facilities with 900 tables and 200 barbecue pits.

Hart Memorial Park also offers sailing and rowboating, a playground, concession rides, piped water, a softball diamond, a bandstand, boat rental, snack bars, fishing, and swimming in the river.

Access: The park is 9 miles east of Bakersfield via the Alfred Harrell highway.

CENTRAL VALLEY
Lower Section

SRA - State Recreation Area
SR - State Reserve
SHP - State Historic Park

Scale in Miles
0 5 10

Fort Tejon *was noted for its experiments in using camels for cavalry pack animals from late 1850's until the time of the Civil War. Contrary to common supposition, the fort's function was not to fight Indians but to protect them.*

Tule Elk State Reserve

Tule elk once roamed in great herds over the entire Central Valley and foothills. Today a small herd of this almost extinct animal is protected at Tule Elk State Reserve.

Although Tule elk were thought to be completely extinct by 1880, a herd of about 400 had been protected on the Henry Miller Ranch in the San Joaquin Valley. Many of these animals were distributed to other points to reestablish the species, and in 1934 the state set aside the reserve to protect a portion of this herd.

The Tule elk is the smallest kind of American elk, and even large bulls reach only about 600 pounds—the Roosevelt elk of the more northern areas grow to twice that size. (See Prairie Creek Redwoods, page 12.)

The fenced reserve is on dry lake bottom surrounded by ranchland. The animals are shy and hard to see even with binoculars; best time to see them is in early morning or late afternoon, when they come to the headquarters area for food.

Park headquarters is a little oasis in the great dry expanse, excessively hot in summer. Three picnic ramadas on green lawns are available, with piped water, and there are Tule elk interpretive display cases nearby.

Access: Turn west 8 miles south of Bakersfield on State 119 (through Pumpkin Center); drive 17 miles to a canal and take the fork to Tupman. Follow the road through Tupman and watch for signs, as you must turn east again a short distance on park access road.

Fort Tejon State Historic Park

In 1854 Fort Tejon was established in the Tehachapi Range near the summit of the old Grapevine Grade as headquarters for the First U.S. Dragoons. Now the state maintains it as an historic site.

The Dragoons ranged over many miles of the Southwest from the fort, though their primary function was to protect the San Joaquin Indians and to discourage rustlers. The Butterfield Stage (see page 122) began using the fort for a station in 1858—the same year the Dragoons started their famous experiment of using camels as pack animals. The camels proved to be of limited value in the broken western terrain, and their use was discontinued at the outbreak of the Civil War. The fort was abandoned in 1864. Restoration as an historic park began in 1948. The barracks building, the officers' quarters, and the orderly quarters have been restored. A small, handsome museum near the park entrance interprets the fort's history. A number of picnic tables are scattered beneath the big oaks on grassy lawns.

Access: The park is on the west side of Interstate 5 about 36 miles south of Bakersfield.

Central Coast Region

In the central coastal section of California, from Santa Cruz southward to Pismo Beach, almost all of the state parks are within sight and sound of the surf. State Highway 1 gives access to most of these parks.

Three bowl-shaped indentations break the otherwise almost straight coastline in this part of the state—Monterey, Estero, and San Luis Obispo bays, all named by Spanish navigators long before California was colonized. Along these three bays are excellent beach parks where the water is warmer than at the north coast beaches and the surf usually is gentler. Monterey Bay's several parks offer wide beaches, often with sand dunes and sometimes backed by high cliffs. At Estero Bay are the fine Morro Bay park and several other nearby parks, and at San Luis Obispo Bay is Pismo Beach. Swimming may be safe at many of these beaches, but the sensible visitor will learn about them first—some do have riptides and bad surf conditions.

Between Monterey and Estero bays the Santa Lucia mountains thrust directly from the ocean. The ceaseless waves have undercut them to create great dramatic cliffs and headlands. The scenery often is spectacular, though there are relatively few beaches usable except for casual beachcombing (even in this pastime you should be alert lest the incoming tide cut off your return route).

Rainfall is not heavy along this section of the coast, so vegetation is more sparse than in the northern coastal regions, except in canyons which get more water. You may see a few redwoods, but the Big Sur country marks the southern end of their range. Fishing is generally not so good as at some of the northern parks with their cold water; this is a transition zone between northern and southern species. You may find it necessary to go to sea in a charter boat to catch fish. On the other hand, abalone hunting can be rewarding if you know where to go, and even novices manage sometimes to get the limit of Pismo clams.

In addition to its good beaches, the central coast has three important historic parks. San Juan Bautista dates from the founding of the mission by the Franciscans in 1797. The city of Monterey, capital during the Spanish-Mexican period, has a number of fine old adobes which have been designated a state park. Farther south along the coast is the fantastic Hearst Castle.

Santa Cruz Mission State Historic Park

The state does not own the Santa Cruz Mission building for which the historic park is named, but it does own the Neary Adobe on the square, with its acre of garden. This is the only structure that survives from the original mission complex. It was built as headquarters for the mission guard.

The mission you see nearby is a half-scale replica of the original, built in 1931 near the original site, but it

Monterey *history is chronicled in old buildings scattered around the city; nine sites are part of a state historic park here (see page 83).*

Tucked *below cliffs at south end of Point Lobos State Reserve (see page 85) is white sand crescent of small but beautiful Gibson Beach, opposite photo.*

Sea action *on soft sandstone created rock formation at Natural Bridges State Beach, a popular day-use park where you can picnic, fish, or enjoy the surf against the dramatic background of the stone arch.*

houses many artifacts from the old mission. Both the Neary Adobe and the mission buildings are open to visitors from 9 A.M. to 5 P.M. daily, and you can absorb from them a great amount of history of the early days in Santa Cruz.

The quiet, old-fashioned quality of the square seems incongruous in the bustling resort center which Santa Cruz has become since the square was the center of the settlement's life and was ringed by the many buildings of the Franciscan establishment. The mission was never a very successful one. Santa Cruz was somewhat off the beaten track, and the great redwood forests which shouldered close to it in those days made difficult the type of agrarian prosperity which helped develop the better known missions. Government support with funds was meager, despite great plans, while the decision to set up a military colony and presidio at nearby Branciforte was fatal. Many of the soldier-colonists selected disrupted mission administration. At the time of secularization the original mission buildings were already falling down. An earthquake in 1857 completed the devastation.

Access: You reach the mission plaza by going north on Mission Street from downtown Santa Cruz and turning right at the school. The buildings are on the hill above the city at the corner of High and Emmet Streets, but the entire Mission Square has been kept as a park.

Natural Bridges State Beach

Although it is a highly popular day-use park, a major function of Natural Bridges State Beach is to preserve the natural arches which have been cut by wave action in a thin promontory of rock jutting out from the bluffs. Except in times of heavy surf, visitors delight in running the gauntlet between waves to make the passage beneath the main arch.

The rock is soft and fragile, and inevitably the sea will someday complete its work and cut away the arches entirely—but to keep this from happening for as long as possible, climbing the arch rock top is prohibited.

In October and November, Monarch butterflies migrate to the park's eucalyptus groves in great numbers; they come again in March when the milkweed begins to grow tall. This plant, cursed by most gardeners, is an important ecological factor for the Monarch. Ask for the mimeographed information sheet on the insects; it is available at park headquarters. Other inhabitants of the park include about 150 species of birds.

This 35-acre unit is the northernmost of the state parks strung along the big coastal indentation of Monterey Bay. It enjoys the same climatic advantages as the other beach parks in this area—less summer fog, warmer days, gentler surf, warmer water.

Activities: Picnicking, surf play, surf and rock fishing. No lifeguards are provided, and the rangers warn that swimming is unsafe. Fishing may be productive in the off season, but the great amount of activity and the number of people discourage this sport in summer.

The large parking lot is tree-encircled, with 25 picnic tables and stoves on the perimeter beneath tall eucalyptus and half-grown Monterey pines.

Access: The park is off State 1 just south of the northern city limits of Santa Cruz. A sign marks the turn-off. You turn west, and then turn again onto Natural Bridges Road, which leads to the park.

Twin Lakes State Beach

The "twin lakes" are coastal lagoons just in from the beach, within the city limits of Santa Cruz. A day-use-only park, Twin Lakes State Beach has 3,500 feet of ocean front and about 20 fire rings for picnics. The lagoons are waterfowl refuges, and Woods Lagoon has been developed as a small craft harbor.

Access: The park is on East Cliff Drive at the south end of the city near the yacht harbor.

New Brighton State Beach

A high-and-low park, New Brighton State Beach has campsites and some picnic sites on bluffs 135 feet above the beach. The bluffs afford an excellent view of Monterey Bay in both directions.

Mild coastal weather in the vicinity provides a long use season, with occasional fog in summer. Often the area is usable in winter.

Activities: Camping, picnicking, surf play, fishing (usually poor), bird watching. Planted pines and cypress in the camp and picnic sites on the bluffs are now mature and provide shade and protection for the 100 improved campsites (showers) and 35 picnic sites. Camping limit is 7 days in summer.

The beach is reached by stairs, and there are adequate parking areas at several points. The big attraction is the beach, which is 3,200 feet long and heavily used. A wide variety of migratory waterfowl in the fall and spring attracts many bird watchers.

For further information: Area Manager, Santa Cruz Coast State Parks, 120 Ninth Avenue, Santa Cruz 95060.

Access: From State 1, about 5 miles south of Santa Cruz, turn west on Park Avenue and follow park signs.

Supplies: Santa Cruz or many other sources.

Seacliff State Beach

At Seacliff State Beach, you can fish from the side of a ship without leaving the shore. Seacliff is northern California's most popular beach park, with over a million

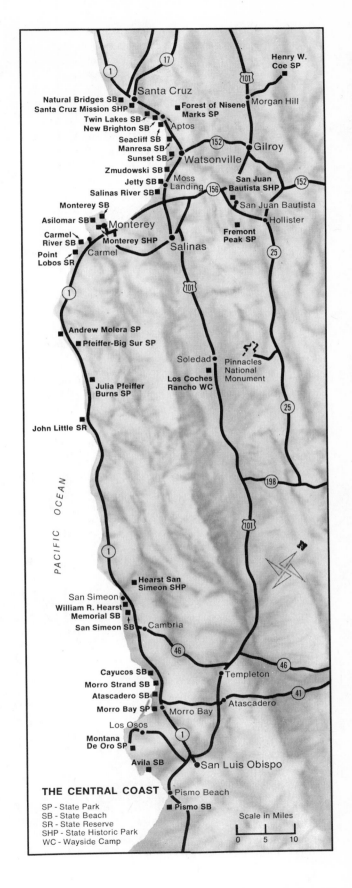

THE CENTRAL COAST

SP - State Park
SB - State Beach
SR - State Reserve
SHP - State Historic Park
WC - Wayside Camp

Scale in Miles

0   5   10

visitors a year. One of its attractions is an old ship's hull with its stern high and dry and its bow in the ocean. Storms have broken up the old hull somewhat, so you are only allowed to fish from the stern portion—if you can find an unoccupied place.

The climate is mild, with morning and evening fog in summer.

Activities: Vehicle camping, picnicking, swimming, surf and beach play, surf fishing. There are 26 campsites with hookups for camping vehicles on the upper rim of the beach at the north end for one-night use only (showers). They are close together with no privacy, but facilities are good. The park also has 115 picnic sites at various points, some with ramadas.

Seacliff is considered the safest northern California swimming beach, with warm water, but it is not danger-free; there are no lifeguards. Day-use hours vary with the season but start at 8 A.M. and last until one or two hours after sunset. Check the hours at the entrance.

Surf fishing is popular when the beach is not too crowded.

For further information: Area Manager, Santa Cruz Coast State Parks, 120 Ninth Avenue, Santa Cruz 95060.

Access: Take the Seacliff Drive offramp from State 1 west and follow the signs to the park.

Forest of Nisene Marks State Park

A very large wild area of nearly 10,000 acres, the Forest of Nisene Marks is rugged and heavily wooded, with several creeks in which you may find native trout. An access road along Aptos Creek Canyon penetrates the park about 2 miles, but it is narrow and winding and lacks bridges. There are no facilities except for occasional unpaved pullouts.

A ranger patrols the park daily. No fires are allowed. Horseback riding is prohibited. Shady and cool in summer, the forest is cold and damp in winter with high water in creeks.

Access: From Soquel Road in Aptos, turn left about a block past Pop Inn across a private railroad track and through an old stone gateway marked "Aptos Creek Road." About 2½ miles of unpaved road lead to the park boundary, where there is a sign.

Henry W. Coe State Park

Though it is within easy driving distance of the San Francisco Bay Area, Henry W. Coe State Park is still little known and usually uncrowded. This coast-range park includes more than 13,000 acres. Relatively new in the system, it is gradually being developed. Much of

Fallen tree trunk *provides platform for optimistic fishermen in Forest of Nisene Marks. This park is wild and little developed, but sometimes anglers catch native trout in the fern-bordered streams.*

it consists of oak-grass hillsides, and its great rolling ridges slope down to sequestered canyons. There are 30 miles of riding and hiking trails.

Henry Coe has good wildflower displays in spring. A new visitor center opened in 1972 has offices, museum, interpretive services, and tack room.

Altitudes are 2,000 to 3,000 feet, and the park may be cold in winter; best weather is in spring and in fall after the first rains. The park is apt to be hot and dry in late summer and early fall.

Activities: Camping, picnicking, hiking, riding, fishing. The main campground is accessible by car and has 20 unimproved campsites with ramadas which may be used by picnickers if unoccupied. Camping limit is 15 days.

Coe has primitive backpack camps at Upper Camp and Meadow Camp on the middle fork of Coyote Creek and at four other points. The Manzanita group camping area is divided into ten sections, portions or all of which may be reserved for riding, hiking, or recreation vehicle groups. Total capacity at Manzanita camping area is about 500 persons.

Horses may be brought into the park, and four-wheel-drive vehicles are permitted on many of the trails.

Fishing is good for those willing to hike in about 4 miles. Three streams furnish trout fishing into early summer, and Frog Lake also has fish.

Henry Coe *offers a large expanse of rolling, grass-covered hills with many oak trees, some wooded canyons.*

For further information: Henry W. Coe State Park, c/o Area Manager, P.O. Box 258, Diablo 94528.

Access: On U.S. 101 at Morgan Hill, turn east on East Dunne Avenue—there are signs. Most of the road is a steep and winding climb, but it is paved and passable with heavy trailers. Total distance from Morgan Hill is 14 miles.

Supplies: Morgan Hill.

Manresa State Beach

A 21-acre beach with bluffs behind, Manresa is used for beach activities, surf fishing, and clamming. There is an unpaved parking area, but there are no facilities.

Access: The beach is about 8 miles west of State 1 on San Andreas Road, about 4 miles north of Sunset Beach.

Sunset State Beach

Four miles of coastal frontage make Sunset a very popular beach. Considerable acreage on the bluffs behind the beach has been developed for camping and picnicking, and plantings by park personnel over the years have made a natural-looking forest cover on the uplands.

Palm Beach was added to the park in the 1960's, extending it to the mouth of the Pajaro River.

The climate is mild, and the park is usable much of the year. Morning and evening fog may be expected in summer.

Activities: Camping, picnicking, beachcombing, surf fishing, clamming, surf play. Swimming is hazardous because of riptides and the absence of lifeguards.

Trails lead down to the beach from the three campgrounds above—Pine Hollow, Dunes, and South Campsite. There is a total of 90 improved campsites (showers), mostly with trees or behind dunes. Camping limit is 7 days in summer. In addition there are 55 picnic sites (some with ramadas), including one picnic area on the beach behind low dunes. Day use is permitted from 8 A.M. to 11 P.M.

The beach is long enough to allow room for surf fishermen. Clammers often take limits of Pismo clams during the September-to-April season. (Limit is 10 clams, with 5 inches the minimum size.) A fishing license is required.

For further information: Area Manager, Santa Cruz Coast State Parks, 120 Ninth Avenue, Santa Cruz 95060.

Access: From State 1, take the Aptos turnoff west 1½ miles south of Seacliff State Beach; follow the signs.

Supplies: Aptos, about 3 miles away.

Zmudowski State Beach

Zmudowski State Beach is a favorite of fishermen. The park is completely undeveloped and has dangerous surf

Across the Plaza *at San Juan Bautista are buildings from Mexican period of California history. Building at right was stable when town was an important transportation center in horse and wagon days; it contains old vehicles.*

and no lifeguards, but it offers good surf fishing. Open for day use only, it is just south of the Pajaro River and west of State 1 about 3 miles above Moss Landing. Inquire locally for directions; there is no sign.

Jetty State Beach

Jetty State Beach, on the strand on the north side of the harbor entrance at Moss Landing, has much to offer the fisherman. Just opened in 1972, the park is still undeveloped, but you can dig for Pismo clams, surf-fish for perch, and net for night smelt. There are gaper and Washington clams on the shores of Elkhorn Slough above the harbor; jetty and harbor fishing produces jacksmelt, surfperch, striped bass, and California halibut.

Local establishments rent boats and tackle, sell bait, and provide launching facilities.

Access: About 1¼ miles north of Moss Landing, turn west at Paul's Island onto Jetty Road and continue about a half mile.

Salinas River State Beach

Big dunes back Salinas River State Beach, a day-use park where there is surf fishing. No facilities have been developed. The surf is dangerous, and there are no lifeguards. There is an unpaved parking area. Salinas River Beach is similar to Zmudowski (see above) but is longer. Access is via Moss Landing, but inquire locally for directions.

San Juan Bautista State Historic Park

San Juan Bautista offers a chance to investigate three periods of California history. The Plaza, once the social center for the San Juan Valley during the Mexican period, still looks much as it did a hundred and more years ago when Spanish and Mexican soldiers used it for drill and the community held its dances, bear baitings, and rodeos here.

With one side of the Plaza open to the valley below, the other three sides reflect the Mission times, the Spanish-Mexican period, and the bustling transportation center which later catered to the Yankee "drummer."

Extending along one side of the Plaza is San Juan Bautista Mission (St. John the Baptist), which goes back to 1797 and still functions as the local parish church. On an adjacent side stand the Castro House and the Plaza Hotel, made famous for its food and hospitality by Angelo Zanetta in the 1860's and 1870's. Before he remodeled it, this was a one-story adobe building which served as a barracks for the mission guard. On the third side is Zanetta's own house, built in the 1870's, and next to it the old stables crammed with all sorts of contrivances from the horse era.

Visiting hours are 8 A.M. to 5 P.M. normally, but under Daylight Saving Time you may stay until 6 P.M. All of the buildings are open to visitors and have been completely restored inside and out. Even the gardens are planted with shrubs and trees of the period. There are a few picnic tables in the gardens.

Access: Take the San Juan Bautista turnoff from U.S. 101 about 9 miles south of Gilroy and go east about 3 miles on State 156 to the town of San Juan Bautista. Follow the signs to the historic park. (You can also reach it from Hollister 7 miles east on State 156.)

Fremont Peak State Park

Imagine yourself with Captain John Fremont and Kit Carson in 1846, defying Mexican government orders to leave the territory. The historic setting of that event is Fremont Peak State Park, the highest point (3,169 feet) in the Gabilan Range.

Aside from its historical significance, this park has some unusual botanical specimens and wildflowers. Heavier rainfall around the summit has nurtured many big oaks of several species. There are also Coulter (big cone) pines, which are rare in this part of the state. Wildflowers in spring make a colorful show and attract hundreds of hummingbirds.

Climate may be cold in winter, on rare occasions with light snowfall, but in spring and autumn the weather is excellent. It is dry in summer here, with occasional hot days into the 90's but normally in the 70's and 80's. Spring is the most popular season.

Activities: Camping, picnicking, climbing and hiking, nature study. A campground under big trees has 12 unimproved sites; a 30-day limit is in effect year-round. Two picnic areas have a total of 23 sites, which are available for overflow camping, and there is a 50-person group picnic area available on reservation.

There is a trail to the summit of the peak, with outstanding views of adjacent valleys for many miles, and a 1-mile nature trail.

For further information: Fremont Peak State Park, c/o Area Manager, 10 Custom House Plaza, Pacific Building Annex, Monterey 93940.

Access: Turn southeast off State 156 at San Juan Bautista onto county road G-1. Go a half mile to San Juan Canyon Road on the left (the route is clearly marked). The park is 11 miles from San Juan Bautista, mostly over a paved but winding and sharply ascending road that is narrow in many places with poor visibility on curves.

Supplies: San Juan Bautista.

Monterey State Historic Park

To visualize Monterey as it was in the 1840's when it was the Mexican capital of the territory, visit the buildings which have been set aside as Monterey State Historic Park. The state owns nine sites scattered over the older part of the city, so the park is really a sizable part of downtown Monterey.

Except for a few wooden buildings which have been burned and some barns and stables, the town of Old Monterey consisted of the historic buildings you can

ABALONE AND SEA OTTERS

Abalone have been an important part of the California scene since prehistoric times. Great piles of shells have been found at many places where coastal Indian groups lived. As early as 1850, Chinese fishermen were taking about 1,000 tons a year from the shallow waters along the coast, and by the 1880's the annual harvest was 2,000 tons. In 1900 new laws on abalone fishing were passed, reserving the shallow waters for sport fishermen, but commercial fishing continued in deeper waters offshore. Commercial fishing has continued to provide fairly close to the same 2,000 tons annually, while individuals now also harvest about the same amount. With more popular demand, in the past few years production has shown signs of faltering.

Abalone fishermen point to the sea otter as the villain—with perhaps some justification. Most recent studies by the Department of Fish and Game indicate the sea otter does eat a great many abalone. An accomplished diver and swimmer, he clutches a rock as big as a softball in his forepaws, goes to the bottom, and either smashes the abalone's shell with the rock or knocks it free.

Once very numerous along the entire Pacific Coast, the sea otter was hunted in the early decades of the nineteenth century for his fur—one pelt was worth up to a hundred dollars in the China trade, and in 1910 a single skin sold for $1703 in London. So numerous were the animals that in the early 1800's, 10,000 a year were taken in San Francisco Bay alone for five years, then about 5,000 a year until 1831. Close to half a million sea otter furs were taken altogether on the Pacific Coast from the beginnings of the trade in the eighteenth century until it was brought to an end by international agreement in 1911.

By 1900 the sea otter was thought to be extinct in California. But biologists knew a small herd survived along the Monterey coast; when the new highway through Big Sur was opened in 1938, the secret was out. Estimates of the size of this residual herd run from 150 to 300. Although the otters bear only a single young about every two years, the small herd has slowly expanded to perhaps 1,000 animals today and has spread as far south as Cambria, as far north as southern Monterey Bay.

Even assuming an abalone a day for each sea otter, and allowing about two pounds of meat for each, the present otter population of 1,000 individuals would at most seem capable of consuming only about 350 tons of abalone per year. This figure is probably very high. Also, the sea otter eats great quantities of sea urchins, which have become a nuisance in recent years.

Other factors must be considered. The sea otter is not yet reestablished in the important abalone fishing areas. Both abalone and sea otters existed in great numbers along the coast in the past. The sea otter leaves many abalone he cannot reach in crevices. These spawn heavily, but great numbers of abalone young are eaten by the cabezon, a rock fish.

see now. A few others are still standing which have not been turned over to the state. Built of adobe and built well, much of the old city survives.

The historic sites are as follows:

California's First Theatre: Built in 1846-47 and first opened to public performances in 1848. New York volunteers who served in the Stevenson battalion during the Mexican war produced several of the early programs.

Casa del Oro: An early general merchandise store operated by Joseph Boston & Company in the 1850's.

Casa Gutierrez: Typical adobe home of the period on a homesite granted to Joaquin Gutierrez and his wife Josefa by the city in 1841.

Thomas Oliver Larkin House: Built in the 1830's by the energetic young American immigrant who became the first and only U.S. Consul while Monterey was under Mexican rule.

The Larkin House is considered the prototype of the Monterey style of architecture now so widely copied. It can be seen by guided tour only.

Robert Louis Stevenson House: This house was occupied by the famous English author for a few months in the 1870's, but the original portion dates from the 1830's. Then it was the home of Don Rafael Gonzales, first administrator of customs for Alta California.

Custom House: The north end of the building dates from about 1827; it was then enlarged to its present form in the 1840's at about the time of the American occupation. It is the oldest government building on the Pacific coast, and custom duties collected here from foreign shipping were the main source of government revenue for California under the Mexicans. Recently the interior was authentically redone.

Casa Soberanes: Originally constructed in 1830 by Don Jose Rafael Estrada, this building has been in continuous use as a dwelling ever since. It is a delicate example of Monterey architecture which may be viewed from the street but is not open to the public.

Pacific House: This structure was originally built in 1847 for Thomas Larkin, who rented it to the U.S. Army for an office and supply center with the beginning of American occupation. Since then it has been a tavern, a courthouse, a church, and a ballroom. The first floor has a museum, and upstairs is an extensive collection of Indian artifacts.

Serra Landing: This location should really be called the Vizcaino landing site—a monument in a small park marks the spot where Vizcaino landed in 1602 and where 168 years later Father Serra and Portola held services to found Monterey. Serra did not land here but journeyed overland.

Colton Hall: Not part of the state's holdings (it was turned over to the city in 1903), this building is still worth a visit. The Reverend Walter Colton built it in 1847; Colton was chaplain of the U.S. Frigate *Congress* and at the beginning of the occupation was appointed alcalde by Commodore Stockton. Colton ignored the local style and built the structure in the style of a New England academy. In 1849 California's Constitutional Convention met on the second floor.

Carmel Mission: Considered the most beautiful of all the California missions, this should be included in any tour of the vicinity by the history enthusiast. It is not part of the state historic park, but it is normally open to the public during the day. This was Father Serra's headquarters, and his body lies in the sanctuary.

Access: The park rangers recommend starting your tour at the Pacific House on the Custom House Plaza on Calle Principal near Fishermans Wharf. Here you can pick up the park folder with descriptions of the various exhibits and a detailed map showing their locations. A 25-cent fee covers all admissions for adults; those under 18 are admitted free of charge.

The best way to make the complete tour is on foot, with perhaps a stop for lunch at one of the restaurants along the way; or you can follow the red line through the city streets in your car past the historic buildings.

Monterey State Beach

Fourteen acres of beach and coastline at Monterey have been set aside as Monterey State Beach. The area is used mostly by local people, for sunbathing and some fishing. There are no facilities, and the beach is for day use only.

Access: The beach is on the approach to the 17-Mile Drive. It is not marked.

Asilomar State Beach

Although Asilomar State Beach on the north side of Pacific Grove has a small and rocky beach, its primary function is as a conference ground. Set aside by the city of Pacific Grove back in 1913 as a religious meeting place, it was later acquired by the Y.M.C.A. and operated in the same general manner for several decades. In 1956 the property was sold to the state.

The 60 acres of grounds have dormitories and dining halls, meeting rooms, chapel, tennis courts, a swimming pool, and a barbecue area. Asilomar is much in demand for conferences today—often by state and federal workers for annual meetings and training sessions. Individuals can make reservations on a space-available basis, and the beach is open to the public. The entire unit is operated by a concessionaire. A park ranger is on duty.

For further information: Manager, Hotel and Conference Grounds, 800 Asilomar Boulevard, Pacific Grove 93950.

Access: The park is off the 17-Mile Drive, just west of Pacific Grove.

Carmel River State Beach

A beautiful little crescent-shaped, sandy beach backed by cypress and eucalyptus, Carmel River State Beach is about midway along the shore of Carmel Bay, close to the highway. This is a day-use park for sunbathing, beach activities, scuba diving, and picnicking, with no facilities. The beach is dangerous when the surf is up.

The area is closed between 11 P.M. and 7 A.M.

Access: The beach is on the ocean side of State 1 just south of Carmel River bridge. It is not marked.

Point Lobos State Reserve

For the nature experience it provides and for its panorama of scenic beauty, Point Lobos is unique among California's parks. The sea, driving unimpeded for millions of years, has penetrated deeply in places along the shoreline, and in others it has been foiled by sturdier rocks. The result is a shimmering interplay of surf and headland and deep blue ocean relieved by aquamarine shallows in the coves.

Almost completely protected from the onslaught of man's technology, the reserve has many wild animals, teeming bird life, rare wildflowers and trees. More than 250 species of plants and 300 of birds have been identified here.

"Bluff lettuce"—the native succulent which thrives virtually to the water's edge—adds touches of pale blue accent against the dark cliffs, and sea lions may be seen offshore working in the surf for their food. If you are very lucky you may catch a glimpse of a sea otter, for they are slowly increasing their numbers again under strict protection.

Lobos is more than just one point. Its broken coastline is 6 miles long and encompasses many points— Granite and Coal Chute and Pinnacle, Pelican and, most famous of all, Lobos itself with its magnificent meeting of land and sea.

The park's more than 1,200 acres are traversed by several trails which connect the various points and wind along the coves, leading from the Whaler's Cottage to fascinating views of Bird Island, through meadows of wildflowers and beneath wind-distorted cypress.

The weather is typical of the central coast, generally mild, with fog in summer. You will get many sparkling days in spring and fall—and often in summer and winter as well.

Activities: Nature study, hiking, picnicking, controlled skin-diving and fishing, swimming, guided tours. Rangers conduct tours twice daily in summer, less often in winter; when tide conditions permit, tide-pool walks are conducted early on summer mornings.

Trails lead to all the park's features, but Lobos is a carefully protected reserve. You may not go off the marked trails, and you may smoke only in your auto-

Small crescent of Carmel Beach is south of the town of Carmel near the mouth of the Carmel River. Facilities are limited, but the park generally is uncrowded and makes a good spot to picnic or just enjoy the sun.

mobile; you may picnic, but fires are not permitted.

Use has become so heavy in recent years that you may have to wait to get into the park on summer weekends and holidays. At such times, buses and large motor homes are not allowed to enter.

Swimming is permitted at China Cove, but there are no lifeguards. A section of the ocean has been set aside as an underwater preserve, with divers permitted to enter only at Whaler's Cove. Marine life may not be disturbed, but skin-divers are allowed to study the sea bottom here if they obtain a permit at the park entrance.

Fishing is permissible in certain areas and for certain kinds of fish, but these vary with the season. You must first check with the park ranger.

Pick up the folder with its excellent map at the park entrance; other interpretive books are sold.

Picnic tables, drinking fountains, and restrooms are provided near parking along the ocean shore and at Whaler's Cove beneath the bluff. The park is open from 9 A.M. to 7 P.M. in summer, 9 A.M. to 5 P.M. in winter.

Access: The entrance is a short distance south of Carmel River on the west side of State 1.

Los Coches Rancho Wayside Camp

The primary function of Los Coches Rancho is the preservation of the Richardson adobe and ranch house. The adobe portion was built in 1843 as the center of a 115,000-acre ranch. Wooden additions were made in 1848 at about the time the building was converted to a stage stop, which it remained for 20 years.

The building and 10 acres were donated to the state in 1958 as an historic monument and museum. Although

THE SURVIVAL OF POINT LOBOS

One of the miracles of Point Lobos is that it has survived at all for public enjoyment. It was grazing ground for herds of cattle for decades, and at least some parts were plowed for farming. Once lost in a wager in a Monterey card game, title to the land was under litigation for many years after American occupation because of this unconventional land transfer.

The parking and picnic space at Whaler's Cove was a granite quarry in the mid-1800's, after which the site was occupied by an abalone cannery until the early 1930's. Because of the great numbers of shellfish on the rocky reefs offshore, abalone fishing had long been an important industry. Prior to the building of the cannery, many acres of the Point were covered with great drying racks.

In the 1870's and 1880's, Whaler's Cove was used for flensing whales and rendering their blubber into oil in great pots. A Portuguese lookout watched from

California *gull in Point Lobos Reserve is one of 300 kinds of birds that have been identified here.*

the peak above the Point and shouted when he saw whales offshore. Crews then launched boats from the cove and rowed out to kill the whales.

In 1933 the efforts of conservationists, led by the Save-the-Redwoods League, finally resulted in the state government's setting aside Point Lobos as a nature preserve. Luckily, none of the important natural features had been destroyed. The infinite variations in the views of rocky shore and sea were unspoiled. The Monterey cypress and pine—both exceedingly rare—were untouched. The Monterey cypress has been planted widely, but it is native to an area of only about 100 acres—at Point Lobos and at Cypress Point between Carmel and Monterey. Almost as scarce are the Monterey pines, although they are still native to an area of square miles. The gnarled trunks of Monterey pines frame superb vistas from Vizcaino Hill.

On the rocks offshore, the Steller and California sea lions have survived. The Steller is the larger and more numerous—the old bulls sometimes reach 1,400 pounds—and can be distinguished by a more deep-throated barking. The California species is smaller and more agile and has a higher pitched voice.

Today at Point Lobos Reserve, fishing is limited to rod and reel, to specified times, and normally to Whaler's Cove. The vast abalone beds, which once provided thousands of tons of the food fish, are slowly increasing again. Since 1959, some 775 acres of sea bottom offshore have been set aside as a protected marine reserve. Experienced skin-divers who obtain a permit can explore the reserve but are not allowed to disturb any of the under-water life. In addition to a richly varied marine life, this portion of the reserve offers kelp forests with "trees" 70 feet tall, fascinating underwater caves, and even access to a branch of the Carmel submarine canyon.

an effort was made to set up a museum here a few years ago, the property functioned as a roadside rest until recently, when it was turned over to a concessionaire. He has provided 89 trailer sites in the grove of trees west of the building, with hookups, and charges $3.50 per day.

Access: Los Coches is on the west side of U.S. 101 at the Arroyo Seco interchange 2½ miles south of Soledad.

Andrew Molera State Park

Small groves of redwoods, rocky bluffs, the Big Sur River, open meadows, and 3 miles of beach make Andrew Molera a potentially-fine park. Just opened for limited public use in 1972, this park covers more than 2,000 acres. Currently visitors are restricted to the beach and river areas.

Climate is moderate much of the year but may be stormy and chilly in winter. Fog may be expected along this section of coast in summer.

Activities: Currently limited to basket picnicking, hiking, beachcombing, and fishing—both stream and ocean. There are no facilities, and visitors must carry away their own litter.

Ocean fishing is both surf and rock, with catches including perch and rockfish. The Big Sur River offers trout fishing, and steelhead in season. When fishing or otherwise using the beaches, be aware of the tide schedules, as high tides come right up to the bottom of the cliffs. Also remember that all tide-pool life is protected except as authorized in the State Fish and Game Code.

The area around the lagoon at the mouth of the Big Sur River has a profusion of birds, and from the coast you can sometimes observe sea otters at play. During seasonal migrations gray whales come close to shore.

Trails lead into the Ventana Wilderness Area of the Los Padres National Forest, and permits to enter may be obtained from the national forest office 1 mile south of the Pfeiffer-Big Sur State Park turnoff (see below).

Access: The park is off State 1 about 30 miles south of Monterey and 3 miles north of Pfeiffer-Big Sur.

Pfeiffer-Big Sur State Park

Most popular of all the state's non-beach parks is Pfeiffer-Big Sur, surrounded by the ridges of the Santa Lucia Range. Although the park is somewhat small—covering only about 800 acres—its trails give access to 300,000 acres of back country in Los Padres National Forest and to the Ventana Wilderness.

The park road winds upgrade slightly through the river canyon to a broad bowl called Sawmill Flat, where the park facilities are located. Vegetation is heavy, with dense shade and shrubbery for the picnic and camping areas. The mouth of the canyon has a few mature redwoods, but the majority of the vegetation is foothill hardwood.

One reason for Pfeiffer-Big Sur's popularity is its protected location, just on the edge of the fog belt. It is relatively cool in summer, yet often warm and sunny in winter.

With the great national forest area around it, the park abounds in wildlife. There are many deer which are remarkably tame, but the wild boars are not, and they should be avoided. Cougars range the ridges, and raccoons can be camp pests if allowed to get at supplies.

More than 600,000 visitors come here annually, and the park is showing some signs of overuse. The big swimming pool was a casualty a few years back because the flow of Big Sur River was inadequate to flush out the pollution from heavy summer use; it has been filled in and converted to a parking area.

Activities: Camping, picnicking, hiking, nature study, fishing, swimming in the river. Trout are planted in the river, with best fishing in spring and fall. Horses are not permitted on the park trails, but they are allowed on the adjacent national forest trails.

The main campground has 198 improved campsites (showers) which get heavy use. Reservations are a must in summer and even on many weekends off-season. Summer camping limit is 7 days. There are three group camp areas which should also be reserved well ahead of time, and there is a 200-person group picnic area. Normally there is space available in the 92-unit family picnic ground.

The park's 8 miles of trails go to Pfeiffer Falls and several viewpoints and also connect with forest service trails at the park boundary. There is a park amphitheatre; campfire programs and nature walks are conducted in summer.

For further information: Area Manager, Big Sur Area State Parks, c/o Pfeiffer-Big Sur State Park, Big Sur 93920.

Access: The park entrance is on the east side of State 1, about 27 miles south of Carmel.

Supplies: Camp store and laundromat. Big Sur Lodge provides cabins and grocery store on private land near the park entrance.

Julia Pfeiffer Burns State Park

A dramatic waterfall, redwood groves, and vantage points for viewing gray whale migrations are all offered by Julia Pfeiffer Burns State Park. The park includes 2 miles of scenic coast and extends upward into the Santa Lucia Range to about the 1,500-foot level, taking in Anderson, Partington, and McWay Canyons. The latter two have live creeks.

This park was created by Lathrop and Helen Hooper Brown's 1961 gift of almost 1,800 acres of land in memory of one of the Big Sur country's pioneer women. The canyons also take their name from pioneer families who settled in this remote, incredibly rugged coast when

Hearst Castle's *twin towers rise against backdrop of Santa Lucia Range. Elaborate structure was begun in 1922.*

the canyons, meager on the slopes. The park is often wet and stormy in winter, and fog may be encountered in all seasons. The middle hours of most days are sunny and clear, or moderately hazy.

Activities: Picnicking, hiking, beachcombing. The park has a small picnic area near the entrance with 12 units accommodating about 75 people.

There is a trail to the beach and to the falls overlook. Rudimentary trails give access to the canyons and to adjacent Los Padres National Forest, which extends the hiking possibilities for many miles.

The park is open only during summer months and some weekends in spring and fall if rangers are available.

Access: A handsome stone marker marks the entrance on the east side of State 1 about 7 miles south of Nepenthe, 40 miles south of Monterey.

John Little State Reserve

A small coastal reserve park on State 1 about 50 miles south of Monterey, John Little State Reserve has a very delicate ecology and cannot support any facilities. It is closed to the public, and there is no sign to mark its location.

Hearst San Simeon State Historic Park

Once you could only see the famous Hearst Castle from a coin-operated telescope on the road below. Since 1958, seven years after the death of the famous publisher, it has been an historic unit of the state park system, donated by the descendants of William Randolph Hearst. Millions of visitors have toured the remarkable castle since it was opened to the public.

Hearst inherited wealth from his father and increased his holding many times during his lifetime to become one of the country's most wealthy and influential men. He became interested in artifacts from all over the world, and it has been estimated that he spent a million dollars a year on his collections for a period of 50 years. Today their value is almost incalculable, and a great many of them are preserved either in or as a part of the baronial estate he built.

His "castle" would have made many an absolute monarch of the sixteenth and seventeenth centuries gasp at its magnificence. He kept an architect employed full-time to blend the Greek gardens and temples, the facade from a South American grandee's home, and the baroque towers from Renaissance Europe into a structure which is, to say the least, striking. The gardens are breathtaking with their hundreds of statues, the great swimming pool where movie stars of a long-ago era played in the moonlight, and a constantly varying mixture of art from all periods of man's history.

Inside there is even greater richness of detail, with hardly a change made since the days when Hearst descended in his private elevator to greet his dinner guests.

their only connection with civilization was a horse trail to Monterey, over 40 miles distant. They eked out a living mostly by sale of tanbark, which was collected by "doghole" schooners from Partington Landing at the foot of the canyon.

The park's 50-foot waterfall comes down over a sheer precipice where McWay Creek reaches the ocean—the only such fall directly into salt water found in the state park system. The finest redwood groves south of Henry Cowell Redwoods State Park also are found here, though this is near the southern extremity of the redwood belt.

The park provides scenic overlooks up and down the precipitous and rocky coast for viewing gray whale migrations and sometimes for observing at fairly close range the antics of sea otters. The sea otters survived here after most people thought they were extinct.

Terrain in the park is mostly steep, with a few level spots near the canyon mouths. Forestation is heavy in

FOUR CENTRAL COAST MISSIONS

Four missions located some miles in from the sea in the Central Coast section of the state are Soledad, San Antonio, San Miguel, and San Luis Obispo. These old churches are all close to U.S. 101, and a visit to one or more of them can easily be included in a trip through this country. All are active parish churches.

Northernmost of the four is the site of Nuestra Senora de la Soledad Mission, one of four founded by the energetic Padre Lasuen in 1771 alone. Most of the buildings are in ruins, but the chapel was restored in the 1950's, under the auspices of the Native Daughters of the Golden West. The mission is reached by turning west off U.S. 101 about 3 miles south of the town of Soledad and going a mile farther.

The thirteenth in the California chain, Soledad was beset by problems. It was virtually destroyed several times by floods from the Salinas River, epidemics killed off many Indians, and rheumatism and other afflictions plagued the priests. During its brief span more than 30 padres served there.

About 65 miles south of the Soledad mission is San Antonio de Padua, which rivals La Purisima (see page 96) in the completeness of its restoration. Once reduced to desolate and crumbling ruin, the church was restored by the California Historical Landmarks League in 1907, and complete restoration of the entire complex was begun in 1948 with funds from The Hearst Foundation and The Franciscan Fathers of California.

San Antonio was founded by Father Serra in 1771 —third in California. On the day of his arrival at the site, Serra hung a bell on an oak tree branch and began ringing it. "Oh, ye gentiles! Come, come to the holy Church," he cried, while the rest of the party stood by in amazement at his enthusiasm.

You can spend several hours touring the buildings, all of which are open to visitors except for those areas set aside for the resident staff. The church itself is beautiful, and you can visit the old music room with its colorful murals; see the olive press; and wander the grounds to see the uncovered water system, the grinding mill, and the apron where grain was threshed by donkey power. San Antonio is on a pleasant detour off today's El Camino Real. A good secondary highway leaves U.S. 101 just north of King City, passes through the old town of Jolon, and rejoins U.S. 101 again 33 miles south of King City, adding only a half dozen miles to your trip.

About 40 miles to the south, easily identified from the highway and by signs, is San Miguel Arcangel, founded by Father Lasuen in 1797. This was one of the most successful missions of all, with a very loyal Indian congregation which bitterly resisted secularization. Extensive restoration has recreated the charm of the old courtyards, and there is a museum. The church interior is considered one of the finest in the system. The roof has stood up through the years, preserving the fascinating murals of Estevan Munras and his Indian assistants.

Most southerly of this group is San Luis Obispo de Tolosa. It was fifth in the system, founded in 1772 by Father Serra. In the mission's first years, hostile Indians several times attacked the buildings with flaming arrows, causing disastrous fires. Thereafter the priests duplicated the tiles of Spain for their roofs—a technique soon copied by all the others.

The mission is located right in the town of San Luis Obispo, a few blocks off the freeway and some 40 miles south of San Miguel. It sits high above the land in front of it because the city once lowered the street before it by 10 feet. In recent years this street has been closed, and a small historic mall has been developed. Museum exhibits in the old priests' quarters are particularly interesting.

It is unwise to attempt to visit the Hearst monument without reservations, particularly in the tourist season. There are several tours, some not available every day; prices are $3 to $4, depending upon the tour, with half price for children 6 through 12. Reservations must be requested in writing; send requests to Hearst Reservation Office, Department of Parks and Recreation, P.O. Box 2390, Sacramento 95811. Reservations can also be handled through Ticketron at a slight extra fee.

You may carry a camera and take pictures on the tours, but to avoid delays and prevent damage to the artifacts, gadget bags, flash equipment, or tripods are not allowed. Food and beverages are not allowed on tour buses or along the tour route; smoking is prohibited on the tours. Pets must be left at the parking lot.

Access: Entrance to the park is on State 1 near the village of San Simeon and is very well marked. You must leave your car in a large parking area at the highway and go to the castle by bus.

William R. Hearst Memorial State Beach

At the inland side of the small harbor at the town of San Simeon is Hearst Memorial beach. Until 1971 this was a county park administered by San Luis Obispo County, but the 4-acre park is now in the state system.

The county built a small fishing pier here in 1959, and this was extended another 300 feet into the harbor in 1969 by county and state cooperative funding. The harbor sometimes serves as a small-craft refuge but is unprotected from south and southeast gales.

Climate is normally mild, often foggy in summer, sometimes wet and stormy in winter, but the park is usable much of the year.

Activities: Shore and pier fishing, beachcombing, and picnicking. Although campsites were available under the county administration, these have been removed to provide a better day-use park.

The park now has 30 picnic sites, with standard day-use fees charged. Beach and rock fishing are sometimes productive, but most fishermen prefer the public fishing pier, from which you may catch rockfish, halibut, and greenling.

Access: The beach is adjacent to State 1 at San Simeon.

San Simeon State Beach

A strip of rocky and dramatic coast with small beaches, coves, and inlets comprises San Simeon State Beach, an area of about 500 acres.

Vegetation on the coastal shelves is sparse. Although the climate generally is mild, fog is common in summer, and there may be strong, cold winds coming from the ocean at times.

Activities: Camping, picnicking, hiking, beachcombing, fishing. The two units offer a total of 80 unimproved campsites and 10 scattered picnic sites.

The water is cold and dangerous for swimming. A variety of fish may be sought in San Simeon Creek and in the surf and rocks along the wild shoreline.

For further information: Area Manager, c/o Hearst San Simeon State Historic Park, P.O. Box 8, San Simeon 93452.

Access: Watch for signs a short distance north of Cambria on State 1.

Supplies: Cambria.

Cayucos State Beach

Cayucos State Beach, operated by San Luis Obispo County, is a day-use area where you can picnic and enjoy warm water and mild surf. A concession rents beach equipment, and the county furnishes lifeguards in summer. There are charter boats, a boat launching ramp, and open berthing facilities.

Access: You can reach the park either by State 46 from U.S. 101 some 4 miles north of Templeton and then a county road; or via State 41 from U.S. 101 at Atascadero, then north about 6 miles on State 1.

Morro Strand State Beach

A small strip of shoreline just south of Cayucos is called Morro Strand State Beach. The park is some miles north of Morro Bay—don't confuse this one with the strand at Morro Bay State Park. The park has modern restrooms, a small parking apron, and several picnic tables. It offers beach play and surf fishing. A sign on State 1 marks the location.

Atascadero State Beach

A mile of broad, usually uncrowded beach is designated as part of Atascadero State Beach. This 75-acre park gets a great deal of use as a base camp for those who want to enjoy the surrounding region. Despite the name, this park is about 20 miles west of Atascadero and is actually much closer to the city of Morro Bay.

The park is mostly open beach and small dunes with very little vegetation, between the highway and the ocean. Climate is usually mild, with overcast mornings and evenings in summer. It may sometimes be breezy because of the unprotected location.

Activities: Camping, picnicking, beachcombing, surf play (no lifeguards), clamming, and surf fishing. The beach is broad and usually uncrowded.

Facilities are modern, with 104 improved campsites (showers) heavily used by vehicle campers. Camping limit is 7 days in summer, 30 in winter. Picnickers may use unoccupied campsites.

Rock fishing *at San Simeon Beach is typical of many places along the central and northern California coast.*

For further information: Area Manager, c/o Morro Bay State Park, State Park Road, Morro Bay 93442.

Access: The park is just north of Morro Bay city limits west of State 1.

Supplies: Morro Bay.

Morro Bay State Park

Dramatic Morro Rock dominates the coastline around Morro Bay. The state now owns the rock, the most seaward of a chain of volcanic necks—old hardened volcano throats—which may be seen all along the highway between Morro Bay and San Luis Obispo. The major portion of Morro Bay State Park is located on the slopes of another—Black Hill—which is not so dramatic.

The quarrying which was nibbling away the south side of Morro Rock has been stopped, now that the state owns it, although you can still see the scars. The rock is said to have been named by Cabrillo on his 1542 voyage of exploration. From seaward the rock does have a resemblance to a Moorish turban, and the Moors were still important in Spanish affairs at that time. If Cabrillo did name the rock, it would be one of the oldest European place names on the West Coast. At the rock there is parking and a small picnic area furnished by the city of Morro Bay, with play equipment for children.

A big attraction here is the fine golf course on the side of Black Hill within the park boundaries. The course is operated by San Luis Obispo County. Lower down, on the bluffs above the bay and along the estuary, there are a fine campground, several trails, a small boat harbor, and an outstanding nature museum.

Morro Bay museum is one of the finest in the park system. Hung on the side of the cliff overlooking the bay, it features central coast wildlife, with emphasis on birds, in view of the natural marshland in the southern part of the park. More than 250 species of birds have been seen in Morro Bay area. A hiker's trail winds through the preserve.

The strand which separates the bay from the ocean with its strip of high dunes is part of the park, and it can be reached by boat or a circuitous route over land from the south. It offers surf fishing, clamming, and bird watching.

The city of Morro Bay itself is a major recreation area—centered among a number of state and local parks along Estero Bay. There is party-boat fishing, particularly during seasonal runs of salt-water steelhead.

Climate at the park is moderate all year, often foggy in summer, with some winter rain and storms—but you may have to reserve a campsite even in winter on a holiday weekend.

Activities: Camping, picnicking, swimming, beachcombing, pleasure boating, boat and surf fishing, clamming, nature study (especially bird life). In summer there are nature walks and campfire programs.

The campground has 115 improved campsites (showers), including 20 trailer hookups. You have to reserve the latter at any season. Camping limit is 7 days in summer, 30 in winter. A group area may be reserved for picnics or camping. The picnic area has 15 family sites, and there is a city-operated area on the road to the park.

Fishing is mostly from boats in the bay or from party boats based in the fishing harbor; but surf fishing is sometimes good on the ocean side of the strand. Fishermen have many favorite spots around Morro Rock and the isthmus.

A concessionaire operates the boat launching and mooring facilities at the inlet.

For further information: Area Manager, c/o Morro Bay State Park, State Park Road, Morro Bay 93442.

Access: The park is south of the city of Morro Bay on State Park Road.

Supplies: Morro Bay.

Pier fishermen *try luck in Morro Bay; commercial fishing boats are in foreground, Morro Rock looms in background.*

Montana de Oro State Park

At an unspoiled area just north of wild Point Buchon, you can get an idea of what this country must have looked like to the first Spanish explorers. Montana de Oro State Park is 9,000 acres of rugged headlands, small beaches and coves, and coastal ridges rising to 1,500 feet.

For those who do not demand all the niceties of civilization, this is a place to camp for peace and quiet, except for the faint booming of the surf. Opened in 1965, it is relatively undeveloped, and facilities are primitive. It has 3 miles of coastline. The name "Montana de Oro" is an old rancho name which comes from the many golden wildflowers on the mountain in spring and summer.

Climate is mild year-round, rainy and wet sometimes in winter; there is often fog, particularly at night and in the mornings, in summer.

Activities: Camping, picnicking, hiking, beachcombing, fishing, nature study. The 50 campsites are unimproved, generally in the open in a valley a short distance back from the ocean, but trees have been planted and are growing. The beach near park headquarters has a separate picnic area. The park is open all year. Camping limit is 7 days in summer, 30 in winter.

Several old roads cross the area, and trails have been developed along the coastline and to the summit of Valencia Peak. On a clear day this vantage point gives a view of the coast from Point Sal to the south to Piedras Blancas in the north.

The persistent fisherman may catch surf and rock fish. Stream fishing is closed. The park has many herds of deer and a profusion of smaller wildlife. Over 100 species of birds were recorded during one 12-hour count.

Horsemen and horses in trailers are permitted in the park.

For further information: Area Manager, c/o Morro Bay State Park, State Park Road, Morro Bay 93442.

Access: From U.S. 101 south of San Luis Obispo, take the Los Osos offramp to the town of Los Osos; follow Pecho Road 5 miles south to the park entrance.

Supplies: Los Osos, Morro Bay, San Luis Obispo.

Avila State Beach

A small day-use area covering 10 acres, Avila State Beach includes a half mile of excellent beach. The water

Dramatic dunes *at both ends of Pismo State Beach attract horseback riders, hikers. Broad expanse at the north end of the park is typically crescent shaped, while the dunes at the south end are higher and more massive.*

is warm here and the surf mild. Lifeguards are on duty during the summer months.

Avila is locally operated by San Luis Obispo County, and its major use is by local people. Facilities include dressing rooms, picnic tables, fire rings, a playground, charter boats, a boat launching ramp, open water berthing facilities, and a concession in summer which rents surfboards, beach equipment, and crab nets.

Access: Turn northwest on county road 4 miles north of Pismo Beach.

Pismo State Beach

Long famous for its Pismo clams, Pismo State Beach is one of the older units of the park system. In the early years of this century, commercial operators turned the clams out with horsedrawn plows, and the beds were rapidly exhausted. Under control of both the state rangers and Fish and Game wardens, beds are slowly being replenished. Clam diggers must have a fishing license, and no clams smaller than 5 inches may be taken.

But Pismo has much more to offer than clams. Its dunes are dramatic and extensive, the beach is excellent, good landscaping has developed tree cover in both campgrounds, and vehicles can use part of the beach. The inward curve of the coast here is framed on the north by the Santa Lucia range.

Climate is equable most of the year, with summer mornings and evenings overcast at times and storms occasionally in winter. Weather may be windy in spring.

Activities: Camping, picnicking, surf play, surf and lake fishing, dune hiking, nature study, riding, beach buggies, swimming in season when lifeguards are present.

The two campgrounds have a combined total of 143 improved sites (showers), with 42 trailer hookups at Oceano. This is the older campground, with planted trees now rising toward maturity; it is surrounded by dunes. The newer campground 2 miles north on a flat behind the dunes still has young vegetation. The park also has a sanitation station for camping vehicles. Visitor count is half a million annually, and space is hard to get in summer. Camping limits are 7 days in summer, 30 in winter.

A recent acquisition of 600 acres to the south expands the park to more than 1,500 acres. This new area, mainly high dunes behind the beach, will be open to dune buggies.

Near the old campground a dune-entrapped lagoon, now fresh water, has good fishing in spring for bluegill, crappie, and black bass. It is an interesting wildlife preserve as well, with muskrats and many waterfowl. The beach, more than 5 miles long, is also popular with fishermen—perch and sometimes steelhead are caught in season. Vehicles are allowed on one portion of the beach, but horses are not.

THE PISMO CLAM

Pismo clams are found on just about any beach from Half Moon Bay south to Baja California, but Pismo Beach is most famous for these succulent shellfish. On this section of coast the Pismo reproduces better than anywhere else.

Recommended style of digging is with a blunt-pointed fork, working along the edge of the water line. The clams lie with their hinges seaward, hence you are working across their broadest surface and have a better chance of finding them. You can also keep an eye out for incoming waves. Some people use a long-tined rake which is pulled along with a rope. This is legal but apt to be hard work. Skin-divers have become adept at spotting the shellfish with a face mask, then diving down to dig them out with a short tool.

A female clam spawns about 15 million eggs each year. Free-swimming embryos hatch and apparently drift with the tides and currents for months before they begin to metamorphize into clams. The newly hatched young are very sensitive to pollution and changes in salinity and temperature. Being almost microscopic, they are eaten in great numbers by all sorts of organisms. Sharks and other surf fish eat many before their shells are hardened, certain rays use their wings to suck them out of the sand, and even after shells have grown, moon snails bore in and work the meat out with their rasping tongues. Crabs can crack the shells of 1-inch clams. Gulls, if they catch a clam exposed on the beach, fly with it up to a height of 50 feet or so and drop it on the rocks to break the shell.

But the worst predator is man. Park rangers and Fish and Game biologists some years ago tried to work out a rotating system, in which some of the beaches would be kept closed a number of years to rebuild their Pismo populations. The program failed. On the day when one of these beaches was reopened to public clamming, people came in thousands. Today official policy is to allow clamming at all beaches, except a few breeder strips which can be watched.

The name Pismo comes from an Indian word meaning tar. Deposits of tar are present along this coast and were used by Indians for varied purposes. Pismo was adopted as a place name during the Mexican period in California, and "clams from Pismo" eventually became "Pismo clams."

For further information: Area Manager, c/o Morro Bay State Park, State Park Road, Morro Bay 93442.

Access: At the south end of the town of Pismo Beach, take the State 1 offramp from U.S. 101, and follow signs to the beach.

Supplies: Dunes Center concession near the main park entrance has food, fuel, clamming forks for rent, dune buggy supplies. Pismo Beach is a sizable resort city with all amenities.

Southern Coast Region

A great shallow embayment is created along California's southern coast where the shoreline curves eastward before resuming a north-south direction about at San Diego. At one time much of the water area offshore was land, and some of the old mountain ranges are still apparent as the Channel Islands: Santa Catalina Island, San Clemente, and other smaller islands. These configurations have far-reaching effects on the use of the shoreline for recreation. The cold currents from the north are to some extent shunted seaward, which means warmer water and less fog. The islands tend to act as breakwaters which, with the relatively shallow water, inhibit surf action except in heavy storms. The offshore kelp beds, rarely disturbed, are natural incubators for fish, and the warmer water breeds a greater variety of them.

Given such geographic advantages, it is easy to understand why most of the south coast parks are beach parks. With few variations, the visitor to the south coast parks will find broad, sandy beaches, usually below coastal bluffs; sunshine, warm water, and safe swimming. At more heavily used beaches, lifeguards may be expected during the summer and often on holiday weekends.

But the surf is not completely safe. Some beaches shelve quickly. Riptides—swirling local currents which may develop almost anywhere, but especially south of Point Fermin—are common.

In general, these south coast parks are well-maintained, with good facilities, but quality varies simply because not enough money has been appropriated to develop all of them. They are usually small. Heavy population took over much of the land before any serious thought was given to public use.

Few of the southern parks have camping, since day use of the small acreages serves more people; also, the state usually owns little land besides the beaches. In recent years the park administration has worked to expand camping facilities, despite these space problems. Considerable ingenuity has been employed, but unavoidably camping along the south coast will generally be in crowded and cramped campgrounds, with little privacy and no nature experience except that offered by the beach itself.

Rules must be strictly enforced to benefit all, and there may even be unexpected restrictions. Still, the sites get heavy use, and reservations must be made well in advance. With the great popularity of camping vehicles in recent years, such camping has become a substitute for the older practice of renting a cottage at the beach for a vacation.

Los Angeles County beaches are not included in this chapter but are listed in the section which begins on page 108.

Surfers *ride waves at Huntington State Beach (see page 101). This is at southern end of 2-mile beach.*

Beach *strollers, fishermen, surfers share San Onofre State Beach (see page 102), opposite photo.*

Patina of age *that enhances some of buildings at La Purisima Mission actually has been acquired since the 1930's, when restoration work began. In foreground are priests' quarters. La Purisima is one of state's finest historic parks.*

La Purisima Mission State Historic Park

La Purisima ranks with Columbia and San Juan Bautista as one of the state's most important historic parks. Each offers more than one or two historic buildings and, through restoration and preservation of a complex of buildings, gives a realistic impression of life in an earlier phase of California history. La Purisima is the best historic monument anywhere which explains the mission system.

California's missions continue to be a major tourist attraction, but in almost all other cases the only structure retained or restored has been the mission church. Obviously the church was important, since each mission resulted from the dedicated work of a few priests; but these men were also administrators, teachers, builders, and businessmen. Each mission had to be a self-sustaining unit, producing to meet virtually all needs.

Some needs, such as for iron tools, could not be satisfied by the mission's resources, and most missions had to produce some commodity which could be traded for necessities. Often, as at La Purisima, it was hides; but by virtue of acquiring a master weaver who trained Indian assistants, this mission also developed a brisk business in woven wool blankets.

Restoration of La Purisima began with a Civilian Conservation Corps project under federal guidance in the 1930's, and it has continued intermittently ever since. Not quite all of the buildings of the original establishment have been restored, but there are many more than will be found elsewhere to depict the various elements of mission life. With the attention to authentic detail which has been shown in the careful furnishing of the interiors, you literally do visit a mission of the early 1800's, lacking only its priests, its soldiers and majordomos, its Indian workers.

This effect is heightened by the fact that La Purisima is off the beaten track, and its surroundings have not been spoiled by commercial buildings shouldering close. The land around La Purisima is still open country devoted to agriculture and grazing as it was 150 years ago, so that the mission establishment can still be visualized as the center of a great rancho of thousands of acres. Luckily, the state owns 800 acres for the park, which insures that modern civilization cannot encroach too closely.

The visitor to La Purisima should plan on several hours to tour it. There is a great deal to see—the two chapels, the priests' and novitiates' quarters, the soldiers' barracks, and many other buildings besides just a church and bell tower. You will see authentic restorations of the shops, olive press, soap and tallow factory, water system, grain mill—even the bakery. Even the ruts of the old Camino Real are still discernible where it passed through the mission compound.

A sizable parking area is close by the park offices, and a small museum contains many artifacts and exhibits explaining mission life. This is a good place to start and to pick up the informative park folder for better understanding of the full-scale exhibits in the buildings. The park has a 17-unit picnic ground in a shaded grove near park headquarters.

The animals in the corral are breeds from the mission period—Mexican cattle and sheep which have descended from Spanish sheep left on Channel Islands by early explorers. Occasionally their wool is clipped, cleaned, carded, and woven into blankets on the mission looms by park employees.

Group guided tours may be arranged for, and school groups may tour the park without charge, as may any children under 18. A small fee is charged adults.

Access: Use State 246, which passes directly by the park. From U.S. 101 at Buellton, go about 12 miles northwest; or from State 1 at Lompoc, go about 4 miles southeast.

Gaviota State Park

Once a small beach park of eight acres, Gaviota now has additional uplands which expand it to 3,000 acres. The new area has not been developed as yet, but hikers use the fire trail.

Gaviota beach has long been popular and it gets heavy use year-round, particularly on weekends. The protected cove is almost always warm, and the surf is gentle.

Activities: Camping, picnicking, surf play and swimming, fishing, hiking, skin-diving. A total of 59 improved campsites are provided, 20 of them in a grove of trees for tent campers and 39 more set aside for vehicle camping, but with no hookups (showers). Camping limits are 7 days in summer, 30 in winter.

The sizable picnic area is located under a pergola just back from the beach with barbecue pits nearby.

You may fish from the long pier at the north end of the beach, or in the surf. The pier has an electric winch and crane for launching or lifting small boats. A 65-foot charter boat is available for trips to the Channel Islands or along the coast.

For further information: Area Manager, Gaviota Area State Parks, Route 1, Box 238, Goleta 93017.

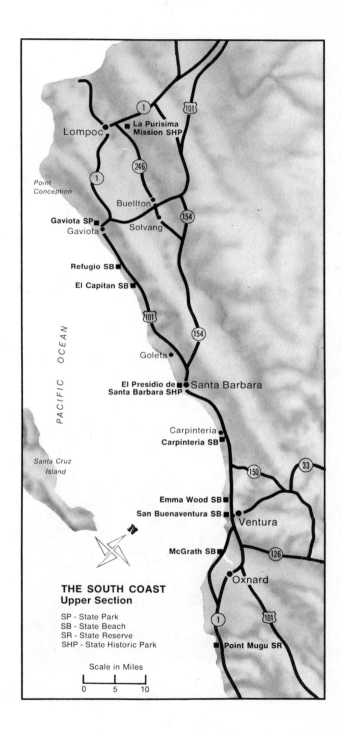

THE SOUTH COAST
Upper Section

SP - State Park
SB - State Beach
SR - State Reserve
SHP - State Historic Park

Scale in Miles
0   5   10

Access: The park is about 35 miles north of Santa Barbara on U.S. 101 where the highway breaks away from the coast northward.

Supplies: Goleta or Buellton. A concessionaire in the park has a snack bar and bait and tackle shop and rents small boats.

Refugio State Beach

A wide beach, a rocky point to protect it, and a few acres of lawn and wooded land behind it make up Refugio State Beach. Climate here is mild, and the 39-acre park is usable most days of the year.

Activities: Camping, picnicking, swimming and beach play, hiking, surf fishing. One campground has 60 improved campsites, another has 46 with trailer hookups (showers). Limit on camping is 7 days in summer, 30 days in winter. There is also a group camp which may be reserved.

Lifeguards on duty during summer months conduct aquatic safety programs for visitors. There is surf fishing from the beach.

For further information: Area Manager, Gaviota Area State Parks, Route 1, Box 238, Goleta 93017.

Supplies: From concessionaire in park, or Goleta.

Access: The beach is off U.S. 101 some 20 miles north of Santa Barbara.

El Capitan State Beach

The sycamore grove near the entrance of El Capitan State Beach is a landmark along this portion of coast. A beautifully developed small park of 133 acres, with excellent facilities, El Capitan has a beach below bluffs. Most facilities are on high ground.

Climate is moderate much of the year. Surf is gentle, and the water is warm.

Activities: Camping, picnicking, hiking, swimming, beachcombing, surf fishing, self-guided nature trail.

Two camping areas provide 85 improved campsites (showers). The old campground is in the sycamore grove, and a new one has been built higher up on the bluff. Some sites in the latter have ocean views. Camping limit is 7 days in summer. A picnic area has 35 sites near the beach.

For further information: Area Manager, Gaviota Area State Parks, Route 1, Box 238, Goleta 93017.

Access: Park entrance is on the ocean side of U.S. 101 between Refugio and Goleta beaches, 18 miles north of Santa Barbara.

Supplies: Snack concession in park; Goleta.

El Presidio de Santa Barbara State Historic Park

Although the Spanish mission system included four presidios—San Francisco, Santa Cruz, Santa Barbara,

---

SOLVANG—SCANDINAVIA TRANSPLANTED

At the foot of the Santa Ynez Valley some 35 miles north of Santa Barbara is the Danish town of Solvang. Although it is today a major tourist attraction, it was founded in 1910 by a group of midwestern educators of Danish descent who chose the spot as a place to retain their native culture.

They picked the quiet valley because its climate was mild, it was off the beaten track, and there was good soil for farming. When they built their houses, they followed old country style of architecture. They named their village Solvang—"sunny valley" in Danish.

Inevitably, touring Americans discovered the charm of this little island of foreign culture and came to buy the native handicrafts. Solvang's population is still under 2,500, but on a nice weekend this figure is magnified many times over by visitors.

Solvang is easily reached by State 154, the San Marcos Pass route, from Santa Barbara, or you can turn east from U.S. 101 at Buellton and drive about 4 miles to Solvang. On the outskirts of the town is the Santa Ines Mission, founded in 1804 as a link between Santa Barbara and La Purisima.

and San Diego—virtually nothing remains of them today. The state owns a small parking lot and museum in Santa Barbara which memorializes one of the sites which was an important part of the mission system.

The museum is in El Presidio Adobe at 122 East Canon Perdido in the downtown part of the city. The building is an original part of the married soldiers' quarters of the Presidio established in 1782.

Carpinteria State Beach

One of the safest beaches for children, Carpinteria has a reef about 2,000 feet out which eliminates the surf. This is an old, established park, well used for years, with a wide variety of attractions on its 50 acres. It started out as farm land and was once a bean field with a slough running through; then sand was hauled in, trees were planted, and the slough was converted into a lagoon.

The park has a wide stretch of sand backed by small dunes much loved by sunbathers. Lifeguards are on duty in summer and during other periods of heavy use. Climate is mild all year, and the water is warm.

Activities: Camping, picnicking, water play and swimming, surf fishing. The campground has 77 improved sites (showers) and an additional 48 sites with hookups for trailers. Camping limit is 7 days in summer, and you cannot make reservations. A large picnic area with more than 80 sites is separate from the campground. The park is closed for day use at 10 P.M.

For further information: Area Manager, Channel Coast State Parks, 901 South San Pedro Street, Ventura 93003.

Access: Turn west from U.S. 101 onto State 224 at the town of Carpinteria. Signs mark the way.

Supplies: Concessions in park have food and supplies during season, also bicycle, surfboard, chair, and umbrella rentals. Otherwise Carpinteria, just outside the park entrance, is a supply point.

Emma Wood State Beach

A long, narrow, little-developed camping strip and beach, Emma Wood State Beach gets considerable casual day use. The beach is somewhat rocky but has fine sandy stretches. The park is warm and sunny much of the time.

Activities: Camping, picnicking, swimming, surf fishing, some tide pool study. Camping area has 200 unimproved sites, portable toilets, and water from tanks. Camping limit is 15 days. Picnicking is permitted in unoccupied campsites.

Swimming is reasonably safe, with lifeguards provided at the southern end of the beach during the season. Surf fishing is popular where space permits.

For further information: Area Manager, Channel Coast State Parks, 901 South San Pedro Street, Ventura 93003.

Protected beaches *of Santa Barbara County, like Refugio, may be less crowded than many other south coast beaches.*

Access: The park is off U.S. 101 about 3 miles north of Ventura. A left turn into the entrance is not permitted, so northbound traffic must turn around at Solimar and come back about a mile.

Supplies: Camp store concession in park in the summer, otherwise Ventura.

San Buenaventura State Beach

A large beach park, San Buenaventura has been developed to handle a big day-use crowd of visitors. A new picnic area is well-designed and attractive. Beaches are small crescents separated by ridges.

Climate is mild, surf gentle, and water warm; lifeguards are on duty during summer.

Activities: Picnicking, swimming and surf play, fishing, beachcombing. Picnic areas are laid out in groups of four with redwood screens extending out for privacy and wind protection. Each unit has its own table and barbecue, and ground is turfed. Commodious parking aprons are on the perimeter.

The park has one of the longest fishing piers on the West Coast.

Access: The park is reached from U.S. 101 in Ventura city limits. Watch for signs.

McGrath State Beach

A 2-mile section of broad beach and coastal strip near the mouth of the Santa Clara River, McGrath is backed by low dunes. It has been developed primarily as a camping park.

Weather is usually mild, but it may be windy.

Activities: Camping, swimming, beach play, beachcombing, picnicking in off season. The campground is in the open behind the dunes, with new plantings; 174 improved sites (showers) are laid out with "cul-de-sacs" for each small group. There is a sanitation station for camping vehicles.

The long beach is good for surf fishing when not too crowded. Swimming is popular, with lifeguards in summer. Nature programs and walks are conducted in summer.

For further information: Area Manager, c/o San Buenaventura State Beach, 901 South San Pedro Street, Ventura 93003.

Access: Take the Channel Islands Boulevard turnoff from State 1 about 7 miles south of Oxnard.

Supplies: Oxnard.

Point Mugu State Recreation Area

With a dramatic coastline which includes 3 miles of ocean frontage, backed by the abruptly rising Santa Monica Mountains, the relatively new Point Mugu State Recreation Area is close to being an all-purpose park for recreation-hungry southern Californians. Its 6,500 acres are still rather undeveloped, with primitive facilities, but the park gets heavy use.

There may be fog in late spring and summer along the coast penetrating a mile or so into the coastal canyons. Inland temperatures may rise to 90° in summer but normally are in the low 80's, cooler on the coast. The higher elevations of the park may be chilly and windy in winter, but the park is usable all year.

Activities: Camping, picnicking, hiking, beachcombing and surf play, surfing, surf and rock fishing, swimming, and nature study.

With present development, the park divides into two sections—the Big Sycamore Canyon section at the south end and the beach area about a half mile to the north. Big Sycamore Canyon has 50 unimproved campsites and a 50-unit picnic ground, with trails leading into the mountains to peaks 1,500 feet and higher. To protect the delicate wildlife region, no dogs are allowed on interior trails. There is parking for 65 cars. Campfire programs are presented in summer. Camping limit is 7 days in summer, 30 in winter.

The shoreline section comprises about a mile and a half of usable beach and a rocky section about the same length. There are 50 primitive campsites on the beach in the open. The beach has no picnic facilities, and day use visitors must park on the highway shoulder. Lifeguards are on duty in summer.

Point Mugu *is really two parks. The beach section is crowded with camping vehicles and surfers, but just back from the coastal cliffs are thousands of acres of rolling, open country, with massive trees that invite climbing.*

For further information: Area Manager, Point Mugu State Parks, 35000 Pacific Coast Highway, Malibu 90265.

Access: The park is on both sides of State 1 in Ventura County, about 5 miles north of Los Angeles county line. A sign marks Big Sycamore Canyon entrance on the east side of the highway.

Supplies: Small store across the street from Big Sycamore Canyon.

Bolsa Chica State Beach

A 3-mile-long beach strip between the ocean and highway, Bolsa Chica is intensely used in summer and on warm weekends any time. Exclusively a day-use park, the beach is open from 8 A.M. until midnight but has a curfew at 10 P.M. for persons under 21 unaccompanied by adults.

Activities: Picnicking, beach activities, surfing, swimming. Surf fishermen catch corbina and barred perch. The park has 100 fire rings for beach fires, and there are portable toilets.

Access: In the town of Huntington Beach, turn off Pacific Coast Highway at Warner Avenue.

Supplies: Two snack bar concessions provide food and soft drinks, umbrella and surf mat rentals.

Huntington State Beach

A wide, spotlessly clean beach with 2 miles of ocean frontage, Huntington will be expanded when a new freeway is built and old highway right-of-way becomes available.

The park property abuts directly on the highway, with a high industrial fence between and turnstiles for visitors on foot. The park has a 1,500-car parking capacity, but as many as 2,000 extra can be accommodated by shoulder parking and turnstiles, with cooperation of the city beach to south. The park is full every day of the summer. Usable most days, it is open all year.

Activities: Picnicking, beachcombing and beach activities, swimming. Fire rings are provided for 550 fires. An annual entry ticket may be purchased for $10. Lifeguards are on duty in summer. There are food and soft drink concessions.

Access: The beach is just south of Bolsa Chica State Beach. A turnoff sign on Beach Boulevard is visible from State 1.

Corona del Mar State Beach

A wide, sandy beach with palm trees and sand dunes, Corona del Mar is operated by the city of Newport Beach just south of the breakwater. Total area of this day-use beach park is 26 acres.

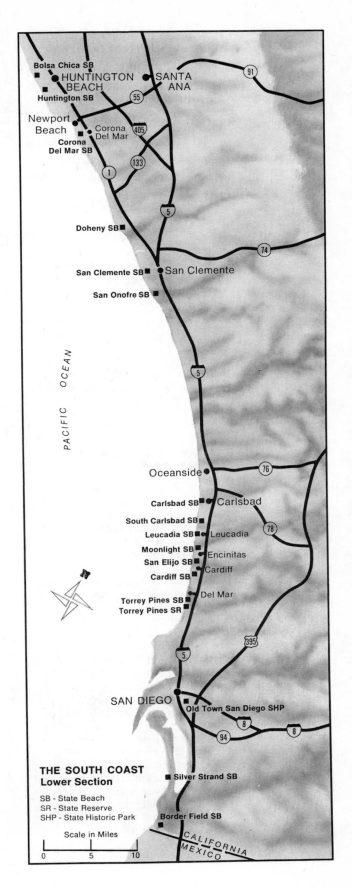

THE SOUTH COAST
Lower Section

SB - State Beach
SR - State Reserve
SHP - State Historic Park

Scale in Miles

0   5   10

Weather here is sub-tropical, with the park usable much of the year. It is very popular in summer.

Activities: Picnicking, swimming, beach activities, boating and water-skiing outside swimming areas. Several small boat harbors and launching facilities are situated nearby. Fee is $1.50 for parking on the large aprons. Hours are 8 A.M. to 10 P.M.

Two concessions offer food and rent beach equipment.

Access: Drive from Pacific Coast Highway to Marguerite Avenue in Corona del Mar, turn south to Ocean Boulevard, and go west to the park entrance.

Doheny State Beach

A popular and usually crowded 62 acres, Doheny is one of the few south coast parks that offers camping and also has a safe beach with good surfing. Another 1,500 feet of beach to the south is under consideration for addition to the park.

The lagoon at the north end of the park is a wild bird habitat. Just to the north is the Orange County small boat harbor at Dana Point.

Activities: Camping, picnicking, beach play, swimming, surfing. Surf fishing for corbina and perch has deterior-

COLLECTING COWHIDES AT DANA POINT

Just north of Doheny State Beach are the impressive headlands of Dana Point, from which the pleasant coastal town on State 1 takes its name. Richard Henry Dana was here on May 7, 1835, and he devotes several pages in his *Two Years Before the Mast* to a description of the point, the surrounding country, and the collection of hides.

San Juan, as the point was called in those days, was an exposed anchorage, very dangerous if a storm came up, and above the cliffs a great barren tableland extended inland. In Dana's words, "There was a grandeur in everything around . . . a silence and solitariness . . . not a human being but ourselves for miles." In the distance "the only habitation in sight was the small white mission of San Juan Capistrano with a few Indian huts around it." (The mission ruins are still there, and they are a popular visitor attraction.)

Trade in cowhides from huge ranchos was the major commerce on the coast at that time. Dana, up on the tableland to handle the hides because there was no road down the cliffs to the anchorage, speaks of working on the giddy heights from which "we pitched the hides, throwing them as far out into the air as we could; and as they were all large, stiff, and doubled, like the cover of a book, the wind took them and they swayed and eddied about, plunging and rising in the air, like a kite when it has broken its string."

ated in recent years with changes that have occurred in coastal configuration.

The park layout was revised recently, with the camps now east of San Juan Creek lagoon and the day-use area to the west. Campground facilities were brand new in 1971, with 115 improved sites (showers). Camping limit is 7 days in summer, 30 in winter. Rangers patrol the area at night, and there is a weekly campfire program in summer and sometimes on off-season holidays. A sanitation station for trailers and campers is provided.

The day-use area, also completely remodeled with new structures, has 189 picnic tables, 63 barbecue pits, and 80 fire rings on the beach. A parking apron has a 700-car capacity. Two group picnic areas are available for reservation (50 or more people).

Access: You reach the park near the junction of State 1 and Interstate 5 at Capistrano Beach or 1 mile south of Dana Point on State 1; signs mark both routes.

Supplies: Concessions in both camping and day-use area; snack bar; surfboard rentals.

San Clemente State Beach

Located close to the rapidly developing urban areas to the south of Los Angeles, San Clemente—although classified as a beach—is really a dual-purpose park. It has both camping and day-use facilities on the coastal ledge above the beach. Trees and shrubs were planted on the uplands some years ago, so that today there is plant cover to shade and separate the facilities.

The climate is sub-tropical, with summer fog which generally remains offshore; it may be windy in winter, sometimes stormy. The park is extremely popular, and campsites are extremely difficult to get in late spring, summer, early fall, and on long weekends through the year, so reservations are important.

Activities: Camping, picnicking, beachcombing, beach play, swimming, surfing, skin-diving, and surf fishing.

The park has two campgrounds, one with 85 sites for mixed vehicle/tent camping (showers), the other with 72 sites for trailers, including hookups. Camping limit is 7 days in summer, 30 days in winter. The day-use area has 26 picnic units in the groves. Two group camps are available by reservation. In summer there are nature talks.

The beach is below the cliffs, which are high and crumbly, so you should stay on the trails for safety's sake. The Santa Fe railroad runs below the cliffs, but the beach trail has a pedestrian underpass.

The park has excellent lifeguard services during periods of high use, but sometimes there are riptides—inexperienced swimmers should discuss them with the guards before venturing into deep water.

For further information: Area Manager, Orange Coast State Parks, 3030 Avenida del Presidente, San Clemente 92672.

Supplies: San Clemente.

Access: From Interstate 5 in San Clemente, you go about a half mile to the beach. There are signs.

San Onofre State Beach

A new park which until 1971 was part of the Marine Corps' huge Camp Pendleton base near Oceanside, San Onofre is an excellent surfing beach which was transferred to the state on a 25-year lease by presidential executive order.

The beach is narrow and is underwater at high tide. There is only mobile lifeguard service. Surfers will find good action for big boards, knee boards, and rubber surf-riders. Fishing is excellent for all coastal surf fish.

This section of coast has been little used for many years, and rattlesnakes may be encountered. The steep, high bluffs are very treacherous, and you must stick to the trails.

Climate is mild year-round except for occasional storms in winter.

Activities: Camping, surfing, surf fishing. Campsites are above the bluffs in an open area, unimproved but suitable for vehicle campers. Campers must bring their own water, and no open fires are allowed.

For further information: Area Manager, Orange Coast State Parks, 3030 Avenida del Presidente, San Clemente 92672.

Access: Take the Basilone offramp from Interstate 5 to old U.S. 101 on the west side of the freeway, and drive south about 2 miles to the park uplands area.

Supplies: San Clemente, 5 miles north; limited supplies at camp store.

San Diego State Beaches

Seven small parks known as San Diego State Beaches are scattered along 13 miles of coast southward from Oceanside. They are operated under a single management headquarters at Carlsbad. These parks are not in the city of San Diego but in the county. All are easily accessible from the Pacific Coast Highway, old U.S. 101 (now county route S-21). Signs giving directions are not consistent, so when in doubt ask directions locally.

This is a beautiful section of the California coast, particularly since Interstate 5 has taken away most of the through highway traffic and discouraged much of the commercialism which once marred the area. Most days have sun, and the sparkle of gentle surf in contrast to the deep blue of the ocean and the white beaches creates the sort of picture beloved by southern California chambers of commerce.

In general these beaches are much the same—fairly wide, sandy expanses below steep coastal bluffs. In most cases the bluffs are precipitous, up to 100 feet high, and composed of unstable, crumbly soil. Climbing on them

South Carlsbad *offers plenty of room for rough-and-tumble game of touch football, also has camping facilities.*

or negotiating them anywhere except on designated trails or stairways is dangerous.

Two of the parks, San Elijo and South Carlsbad, have camping areas with improved facilities—tightly planned layouts between the highway and the cliffs. Statewide park rules apply, but some special rules are necessary to keep the campgrounds usable by large numbers of people. Motorcycles may be used only for necessary travel to and from campsites; no motor vehicles may be driven on the beaches. When laundering clothes you must use the coin-operated dryers in the campground washroom. Drainwater must be caught in a container and dumped in the restroom toilets. Pets must at all times be on a 6-foot-maximum leash or in the camping shelter. Camping limit is 7 days in season. Both of the camping parks have sanitation stations for campers and trailers. A maximum of two vehicles and eight persons

San Elijo *is one of the most developed of the seven San Diego State Beaches, offering camping as well as day use. San Elijo and adjacent Cardiff State Beach together have about 2 miles of coast available for public use.*

may occupy a campsite. Reservations are necessary in season.

All the beaches have swimming, and surfing is popular. Leucadia and Cardiff have no lifeguards. Torrey Pines has mobile lifeguard service at the north end only. During the summer, special surfing areas are designated. Riptides are a danger, and those unfamiliar with them should talk to the rangers or lifeguards before going into deep water.

Surf fishing for perch, bass, corvina, and halibut is often rewarding, though sand sharks are a nuisance.

From north to south, the seven parks are as follows:

Carlsbad: Relatively undeveloped, this park does have drinking water, restrooms, fire rings, parking, and lifeguards in summer. Total area is 10 acres with 4,400 feet of beach. Northernmost of the seven units, it is accessible from Carlsbad overcrossing on S-21.

South Carlsbad: Known as La Costa State Beach before remodeling; character similar to San Elijo, with 226 improved campsites (showers) available for day use when not occupied. The park has a camp store concession. More than 12,000 feet of beautiful beach below bluffs are included in this park, located a few miles south of the city of Carlsbad.

Leucadia: Formerly known as Ponto State Beach; no facilities except parking and fire rings. The area is excellent for surfing, with a mile of beach. Total park area

is 11 acres. Turn west off the main highway in Leucadia onto Fulvia Avenue at the city roadside park.

Moonlight: Very attractive day–use development with permanent restrooms, dressing rooms, lifeguard towers, and picturesque landscaping on land near beach level on cove. Facilities include a children's play area, a snack bar, fire rings on the beach, and two parking aprons. There is good surfing. Total area is 13 acres, with a third of a mile of beach. The park is west of Encinitas on B Street.

San Elijo: Adjacent to Cardiff State Beach, with all facilities including a food concession. Total area is 39 acres, with a beautiful, open beach 9,000 feet long.

San Elijo was remodeled a few years ago to provide 171 improved campsites (showers). A day-use area is at the north end. Planning the campground created a problem with local residents who had homes on the slopes above ocean views. This was solved by lowering the level of the top of the bluffs about 4 feet and using the dirt removed to provide additional parking space for day-use activities at Torrey Pines. Planting in the campground now screens campers from view of residents.

The park is at Cardiff on the Coast Highway.

Cardiff: No facilities. Total area is 11 acres, with 3,800 feet of beach. The park is 1 mile south of the town of Cardiff.

Silhouetted *Torrey pine at state reserve is typical of twisted character of these trees. Trail drops down to beach.*

Torrey Pines: Kiosk at entrance also serves Torrey Pines Reserve (see following). The southern part of the 4½-mile-long sandy beach is beneath the cliffs of the reserve. There are no facilities except portable restrooms. Parking is available through the underpass on the east side of the highway. Access is from the foot of Torrey Pines Grade, directly off county route S-21.

Torrey Pines State Reserve

It is a mystery why the trees for which Torrey Pines State Reserve is named grow here and nowhere else on earth except on Santa Rosa Island 175 miles to the northwest. The pines are the main feature of the park, with their wind-distorted shapes scattered over the mesa above the ocean, silhouetted against the sky or the yellow, eroded cliffs.

Most dendrologists today agree that California's wealth of rare tree species results from changing weather conditions over eons of time which have gradually reduced the ecological zone in which they can survive. The Torrey is not closely related to any of the state's mountain pines but seems to be nearer to the Digger and Coulter pines of the foothills. Its present habitat was once a 6-mile strip, but many of the trees were cut for firewood before Ellen Scripps of San Diego purchased the original property which began the reserve. Additions

through the years have expanded the park to nearly 900 acres, with 3,000 trees, and negotiations are going forward for another 160 acres with 1,500 trees.

Wildflowers on the mesa are special, too. Among the scattered trees you will find spectacular stands of wild buckwheat, sea dahlia, and bush poppy. And aside from the pines, many rare plants not found elsewhere grow in the reserve. More than 200 species of birds also have been identified in the various parts of the park. The salt marsh east of the highway along the estuary is a waterfowl refuge.

Climate is sub-tropical, usually warm and sunny, but not excessively hot in summer.

Activities: Picnicking, hiking, and nature study. The reserve has a handsome new 48-unit picnic ground with ramadas near the museum. A paved road leads to nearby parking from the park entrance. A number of trails

---

THE DANCING GRUNION

On certain spring and summer nights you can see hundreds of silvery fish dancing on their tails at beaches on the south coast. These are the grunion, who come up on shore to deposit eggs in the damp sand. Their schedule is predictable, and on the nights they are to dance people arrive with burlap sacks to catch them before they can return to the ocean.

The schools are apt to come in great numbers, but individual fish stay on the beach only about a minute. Shouts from grunion-hunters herald each new batch of the little silvery fish, and there is much running back and forth with flashlights. Grunioners must have a fishing license and may use only their hands. The season is closed in April and May. There is no limit, but Fish and Game personnel request that you don't take any more than you can use.

The grunion eggs lie buried in the sand for about 10 days. New high tides come in and uncover the eggs, which hatch almost immediately, and the baby grunions ride the waves down into deeper water. They grow rapidly and in a year are ready to lay eggs themselves, to start the whole process over again.

Grunion are members of the silverside fish family. They are generally seen only in southern California below Point Conception and into Baja California, although a few appear as far north as Monterey Bay.

They are small fish, about 5 to 6 inches in length, and it is thought they stay close to shore during their 3 to 4 years of life. Since their reproduction is entirely dependent upon correct analysis of complicated tidal factors, marine biologists assume they have some mechanism which either detects tiny changes in water pressure resulting from tidal cycles or reacts to the magnetic attraction of the moon. Grunion runs can occur during the summer months during about a 10-day period following the maximum full moon and following a new moon.

thread through the groves and ravines, some down to the beach, others to viewpoints.

The Fat Man's Misery Trail of the Canyon of the Swifts is a novelty. Clearance between the rocks is only a foot in some places, so if you have too much girth you had better not try it. But even a fat man can make the easy climb up High Point Trail to the oldest known pines in the park—one estimated a seedling in 1585, the other in 1635. Here, too, you have a magnificent view up the coast framed by the twisted trunks.

The number of vehicles in the reserve is restricted to the capacity of the parking lot—133 cars maximum. Other parking is prohibited. To avoid being denied entrance, get to the reserve early during the vacation season or on holiday weekends.

Access: The reserve is just south of the city of Del Mar at the foot of Torrey Pines grade on S-21 (the Coast Highway). The park entrance is on the west side of the highway, from where you either proceed uphill to the reserve area or go through an underpass to the beach parking lot.

City museum *adjacent to site of 1769 presidio attracts visitors to Old Town San Diego State Historic Park.*

Old Town San Diego State Historic Park

In 1835, according to Richard Henry Dana, Old Town was a cluster of some "forty dark brown looking huts . . . and three or four larger ones, white-washed, which belonged to the gente de razón." By this time the Presidio which marked the first Spanish foothold in California was already in ruins, and the town had reverted to a slow, sleepy existence dependent on whalers and fur trappers from the back country. Now this area in San Diego is a state historic park.

The site of the Presidio is just above Old Town, in a city-owned park where there is a handsome, mission-style museum which many visitors mistake for the old mission. It is well worth a visit when you are in the vicinity. The presidio hill actually was the site of Father Serra's first mission in California—a rough, bushwood shelter erected in 1769 and later rebuilt up the river a few miles.

The state park comprises roughly a six-block area near the intersection of Interstate Highways 5 and 8 in the San Diego city limits. Funds for restoration have not been lavish, but the park administration is slowly re-creating the old area.

There is parking and a visitor's center, and several of the old adobes are now open to visitors. A number of shops are located here; the Bazaar del Mundo is a Spanish-style shopping arcade with something of the atmosphere of a Mexican marketplace.

Park headquarters is at 416 Wallace Street. Here you can get information and stop at the visitor's center before touring the park.

Silver Strand State Beach

At Silver Strand you can enjoy a beach that was fashionable in the Gay Nineties, when the more daring of the fashionably outfitted men promenading along the sand were photographed with derby, walrus mustache, and cigar. Silver Strand comes close to being the perfect beach park, and with the completion of the new San Diego-Coronado bridge it gets more use than ever. It is truly a strand, or perhaps more accurately a big sand bar, which gradually built up through many thousands of years to connect the mainland to Coronado.

The west side of the park is one long beach, taking its name from the glitter of millions of tiny seashells in the sand. On the other side are the quiet waters of San Diego Bay. The highway and a railway run through the middle, but three pedestrian underpasses connect the two parts. Weather is sub-tropical, with an occasional storm in winter across the open Pacific. The park averages only nine days a year without sunshine.

Activities: Picnicking, swimming, beach activities, water-skiing, boating, beachcombing, clamming, grunion scooping during runs, surf fishing.

The ocean beach area is 5 miles long, with a main

observation tower 40 feet high and several additional lifeguard towers. Swimming is permissible but should be attempted only by experienced swimmers—the beach shelves sharply, and this entire section of coast is subject to riptides and powerful currents. Some Pismo clams are taken, but competition is keen.

The beach has 230 fire rings and another 130 family picnic units, some under ramadas, on both sides of the highway. A huge parking apron accommodates 1,800 cars. All facilities are modern and generous, with a number of restrooms, concession buildings on both the ocean and bay, and two first aid stations.

The bay side has shallow and quiet water, best for children, and north of the park the city offers boat launching for water-skiing on the bay.

Surf fishermen work along the entire strand for croaker, sea bass, perch, corbina, and halibut.

Access: From San Diego, drive across the San Diego-Coronado (toll) bridge, which is also State 75. Follow the highway directly to the park.

Border Field State Beach

At the southwest corner of the United States, abutting the international border and in sight of the Tijuana bull ring in Mexico, is Border Field State Beach. Its 372 acres include 6,000 feet of beach.

The state acquired this beach by transfer from the federal government; the land previously was Navy property used as an emergency landing field.

The warm climate makes the park usable year-round except during winter storms.

Activities: Sunbathing, basket picnicking, beach and surf play, surf fishing. Until funds are available for development, facilities are limited to portable toilets and litter cans. Rangers patrol the area, but currently, due to lack of facilities, no use fee is charged.

Access: From the city of Imperial Beach, take Interstate 5 to Palm Avenue, drive west on Palm to 19th Street, turn south onto Monument Road and continue to the park entrance on the west.

OCEAN FISHING IN CALIFORNIA

California offers four kinds of salt-water fishing—surf, rock, pier, and party-boat. Some party boat fishing out of the southern seaports yields big game fish such as marlin and swordfish. Northern fishing is to a great extent concentrated on anadromous fish such as salmon, steelhead, and striped bass.

The state licenses about a million anglers each year, and competition can be keen, particularly for salmon. At popular spots such as Smith River near Crescent City, during heavy salmon runs skiffs may be anchored gunwale to gunwale all the way across the river mouth, with fishermen lining the bank elbow to elbow. Nevertheless, some 50 and 60-pound salmon are taken.

About a quarter million surf fishermen work the beaches, mostly in southern California, where the coast is better suited for the sport and the variety of fish is greater. At these southern beaches surfperch, corbina, spotfin, and yellow croakers are most common, although a few other species are also caught. Best season is April to October. On the northern beaches surfperch is predominant, but in good spring striped bass runs these fish may sometimes be taken from the shore of San Francisco Bay with lures and bait. A specialized kind of northern fishing is netting surf smelt.

Although there is some rock and breakwater fishing on the southern coast, this sport is more commonly practiced on the central and northern coasts. This is simply because there are more rocky sections and fewer beaches suitable for surf fishing, except in places such as Monterey and Morro bays. Catches include rockfish, cabezon, greenling, sea trout, and sometimes halibut. There is no particular season.

Many rock fishermen use the simplest of tackle—just some long poles with short lines to lower into the holes. Fairly strong tackle is a must to clear snags, and many experienced rock fishermen use small bags of sand for sinkers because they mean little loss if snagged.

A few northern coastal cities have piers for fishing, but most piers for this kind of sport are on the central and southern coast, with the majority of them south of Point Conception. Where these piers are open to the public, no license is required, but a California fishing license is required for all other kinds of fishing, including party boat fishing.

About 500 licensed party boats operate from California coastal towns—generally at any small harbor where commercial boats also base. Rates vary, but the charge is around $12 per day and up, depending on the size of the boat, provision of tackle, location, and other factors. Despite the expense, this kind of fishing is popular because it is apt to be most productive.

Party boat fishing is usually in pursuit of schools. In the north these are predominantly striped bass and salmon, and hence are dependent on runs. Lingcod, halibut, and other species may sometimes be caught in this kind of fishing. In southern waters seasons vary but are generally best from mid-spring through mid-fall. The range of fish is wide—from marlin and swordfish to tuna, yellowtail, albacore, bass, bonito, barracuda, and some of the species caught in northern waters, such as rockcod and lingcod. A large percentage of the party boat catches all along the coast comes from the less glamorous species such as cod, bass, and various deep-water rockfish which, though relatively small, are excellent eating.

Los Angeles County

Los Angeles County has few state parks—partially because the flat lowland, so suitable for development, grew so rapidly that no one realized the necessity of setting aside land. Nor is the terrain particularly suited to park development—there are few naturally wooded areas except in the higher mountains to the north and east. But the area does have excellent beaches, great sections of which have been reserved and developed for public use. They are heavily used for swimming, sunbathing, and other beach activities including surfing, diving, and fishing.

Six historic parks in the area give insight to all periods of California history, beginning with the founding of the Pueblo in 1781. El Pueblo de los Angeles State Historic Park, now surrounded by downtown Los Angeles, is where the city began.

Angelenos give heavy use to the mountain parks in the back country outside the county borders (see page 117) and also the many national forest facilities in these mountains. Finding a place to camp close to home on a weekend or holiday is difficult, and there has been much interest in establishing a camping park in the Santa Monica Mountains.

Placerita Canyon State Park

Famed desperado Tiburcio Vasquez often used Placerita Canyon for his forays and horse-stealing operations in the 1860's and 1870's. Many of his exploits were later attributed to Joaquin Murieta, whose legend was created by a California newspaperman from the records of several desperados.

With state and county cooperation, the park has been expanded to about 350 acres and is now operated as a regional park under the jurisdiction of the Los Angeles Department of Parks and Recreation. It is heavily wooded with oaks, sycamores, and cottonwoods; the upper portion, undeveloped, is a game refuge and bird sanctuary.

The park has picnic facilities and some historical exhibits harking back to the early gold mining and oil prospecting days. The handsome new Nature Center has outstanding ecology exhibits, with tours and lectures conducted by the staff.

Access: The park is in the southwest San Gabriel Mountains, 6 miles east of Newhall. From Golden State Freeway (Interstate 5), take State 14 about 7 miles to Placerita Canyon Road.

Los Encinos State Historic Park

Slightly off the beaten track, a short distance from the busy Ventura Freeway, is a quiet and lovely 5-acre park which has many claims to historic importance. Los

Rocky *promontory at Leo Carrillo State Beach (see page 112) makes launch platform for sand jumping.*

Fine *beaches of Los Angeles County offer good swimming, surfing, other beach activities. Redondo Beach (see page 115) in opposite photo is typical.*

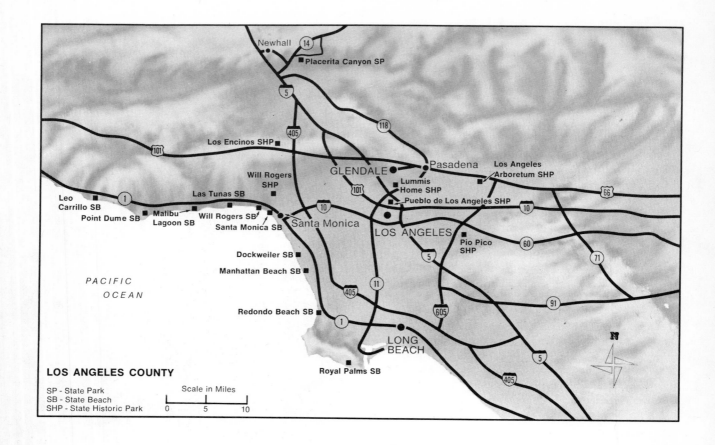

LOS ANGELES COUNTY

SP - State Park
SB - State Beach
SHP - State Historic Park

Scale in Miles

0   5   10

Encinos was first visited, recorded, and named by Governor Gaspar de Portola and Father Juan Crespi in 1769. Portola named the valley "Santa Catalina de Bononia de los Encinos" (*los encinos* means "live oaks"), and Father Crespi's diary specifically mentions the springs and pool which made the site highly attractive. In fact, a large Gabrieleno Indian village was here when Portola and Crespi passed through.

In 1845 Governor Pio Pico gave 4,460 acres of the surrounding land to Vicente de la Osa, and the nine-room adobe ranch house he built in 1849 in the center of his domain still stands. Today it is a museum furnished to show the succession of ownerships.

Two Basque brothers—Philippe and Eugene Garnier —came into possession of the de la Osa rancho in 1872, and they built the two-story French provincial house of native limestone. Now it is being restored to house another museum.

About 1878 the Garniers had some business reverses when there was a bad drought, and eventually the rancho came into the ownership of the Amstoy family, who subdivided the rancho into building lots in 1945. In 1949 the state bought the five-acre heart of the rancho for its historic significance.

A rather crude stone hut in the park is believed to have been built in 1788 by the mayor of Los Angeles

as a shelter for his cattlemen. Later it was used as a stagecoach stop by the Butterfield Stages, then as a sheepherders' shelter, and finally as a blacksmith shop. It is now restored as the latter.

There are limited picnic facilities at the park, and tours are conducted every half hour in the afternoons (except Monday and Tuesday) from 1 to 4 P.M., Sundays from 1 to 5 P.M.

Access: Take Balboa offramp south from Ventura Freeway to Ventura Boulevard. The park entrance is near the intersection of Ventura and Balboa at 16756 Moorpark Street.

Will Rogers State Historic Park

The ranch house in which the famous comedian-philosopher Will Rogers lived for seven years before his untimely death was deeded to the state in 1944, with 187 acres of hills and thick eucalyptus forest. The rambling, rustic home is preserved as a museum of Rogers' life, and there are guided tours every half hour.

The estate includes the polo grounds and stables, which are still used, and riding trails laid out by Rogers. Horses may be rented in the vicinity.

Fee for tours is 25 cents, with no charge for those under 18. The park is open from 9 A.M. to 5 P.M.

Access: A one-way entrance road leaves Sunset Boulevard about 4 miles from U.S. 101, some 15 miles from Los Angeles Civic Center.

Los Angeles State and County Arboreta (Scientific Reserve)

Much of the Los Angeles State and County Arboreta consists of branches at Descanso Gardens in La Canada and South Coast Botanic Garden on the Palos Verdes peninsula. These excellent botanical gardens are wholly owned and operated by the county; gardeners and botanical students who wish more information can contact the main office in Arcadia. The part of this park owned by the state but operated by the county is at Arcadia, where three historic buildings are open to the public—the Hugo Reid Adobe and the "Lucky" Baldwin Queen Anne Cottage and Coachhouse.

Hugo Reid was a Scotsman who came to California in the 1820's and married into one of the great landholding families, eventually obtaining a large land grant himself. He built the adobe in 1839, and through the years it had a number of changes which made restoration particularly difficult. The finished work, however, is superb, and the old house carefully reflects the period in which it was built, complete with enclosed garden and even wikiups for the Indian servants who once lived there.

"Lucky" Baldwin traveled to Nevada from Indiana to strike it rich in the Virginia City silver mines. He built a great fortune and was active in San Francisco and Tahoe as well as in southern California. He operated Rancho Santa Anita as a true ranch and objected vigorously to being called "Lucky," claiming his success came from hard work and good judgment. When the Bank of California failed through its manipulation of Virginia City mining stock, Baldwin was wiped out except for his Arcadia property, to which he retired. The opulent and attractive Victorian architecture of the cottage and coachhouse delight visitors.

Access: From San Bernardino Freeway, drive north on Baldwin Avenue. The address is 301 North Baldwin Avenue, Arcadia 91006.

Lummis Home State Historic Park

His love for the Southwest and his lifetime of work as an editor, author, poet, historian, and librarian made Charles Fletcher Lummis beloved of Californians and westerners. The Lummis Home (El Alisal) on its 3 acres of land near the Pasadena Freeway is the work of his own hands, with help from his sons and an Indian boy or two when he had funds to pay for assistance. Its rocks were hand-hauled from the Arroyo Seco river bed.

Lummis (1859-1928) was a native of Massachusetts. Beset by illness in New Mexico when he was 29, he followed the motto, "I am bigger than anything that can happen to me," and lived for another 40 productive years.

The park is operated by the City of Los Angeles, and it is also the headquarters of the Los Angeles branch of the California Historical Society. It is open to the public and contains a collection of Mayan and North American Indian artifacts and early California furnishings.

Access: The park is at 200 East Avenue in Los Angeles, close to the Pasadena Freeway.

Lummis Home *in Los Angeles, now an historic park, was built by a California writer and historian.*

Pio Pico State Historic Park

The home of the last Mexican governor of California has been preserved and restored to its original grace as the center of Pico's 9,000-acre Rancho Jamul. Pio Pico State Historic Park is open to the public without charge from 10 A.M to 5 P.M. daily except on major holidays.

Pico was a native, the son of an army sergeant, born at Mission San Gabriel in 1801. He was instrumental in the Mexican rebellion of 1831 and was governor at the time of the U.S. invasion, but rather than oppose superior force, he retired to his home in Los Angeles. He adapted fairly well to the Yankee system and was in business locally for many years, but his open-handedness and faith in unworthy acquaintances reduced him to a pauper by 1880. He lived with relatives and friends until his death in 1894; he is buried at La Puente.

The adobe home was the property of the city of Whittier for many years and attempts were made to restore it, but funds were inadequate. State restoration specialists have done an excellent job in recreating the period interiors and exteriors.

Access: Turn west off San Gabriel Freeway (Interstate 605) at Whittier Boulevard; the adobe is about a quarter mile further on the left.

RESTORING HISTORIC BUILDINGS

When you visit one of the state's historic parks and see a building which is accurate for its period, you are seeing the results of a meticulous process of reconstruction. Specialists in the State Office of Architecture and Construction search through old books, drawings, and photographs; study old records and diaries; sift dirt in courtyards; and carefully uncover old foundations. Park historians often help in this process, as do outside agencies such as historical societies, archeologists from colleges and universities, and, in the case of mission property, the Catholic church.

If only a single hinge or door lock remains of a building, it is used as a pattern, and state prison shops which specialize in this kind of work make exact replicas. When adobe walls must be rebuilt, new bricks are made from the crumbled material around the old walls. If this supply is insufficient, the pit from which the original clay was taken is sought out, so that any new materials match perfectly.

The Reid Adobe in the Los Angeles Arboretum (see page 111) is an example of the care given in the restoration of the state's historic buildings. The site was studied and excavated for months before any construction was started. A whole series of changes made through the years since the 1830's had to be cleared away before the outlines of Reid's original rancho home were clearly defined. Some of these changes were revealed by the discovery that the walls contained adobe from three different sources. When reconstruction was started, adobe bricks were sun dried just as they were during the original construction. Local oak was hand hewn for thresholds, jambs, door and window lintels. From the Angeles National Forest came alder poles for the roof, and native tules were laid across them. Fresh cowhide strips were cut to make the bindings for the roof. Finally, asphalt from the tar pits was poured over the framework to make it waterproof, just as Reid's men had done to the original structure.

The only variations from original construction methods are those which cannot be seen but which will make the building last longer. A modern binder is used in adobe brick—it does not change the appearance but makes the brick resistant to crumbling.

El Pueblo de Los Angeles State Historic Park

Comprising more than 40 valuable acres in downtown Los Angeles where the heart of the city once lay, the Pueblo is considerably more than an historic park. Olvera Street, which retains the authenticity of the Mexican Quarter, is a colorful center for Mexican works of art and souvenirs. Band concerts are given from 2 to 4 P.M. every Sunday during summer from the old bandstand in the square.

A number of buildings have been restored and are open to the public, including the firehouse with its horse-drawn equipment. Work is going forward on others as funds are available, and the life of the city will be represented from its founding in 1781, with a population of 44 people, up to the present day.

Access: Bounded by Spring, Macy, Alameda and Arcadia Streets, the Pueblo is just north of the Santa Ana Freeway, a few blocks from the four-level interchange. Parking is a problem.

Leo Carrillo State Beach

Although designated a state beach, Leo Carrillo is an all-round park and the only state park in Los Angeles County offering camping except Joshua Trees east of Lancaster (see page 118). Originally the only developed parts of the park were the beaches and small scenic headlands on the seaward side of the highway, but in 1963 campgrounds in the Sequit Arroyo flat across the highway were added. (Carrillo was once known as Sequit Beach.) The arroyo has sizable stands of sycamore, live oak, and sumac—a few trails give access to the remainder of the 1,200-acre park's chaparral-covered foothills.

The climate is sub-tropical; except during winter storms, the park is usable all year. In winter there are many vacant campsites, which must be reserved in vacation season and often on holiday weekends as well.

Wrought iron *craftsman works at trade on Olvera Street in Pueblo de Los Angeles, where the city began.*

Point *and small cove beach at Leo Carrillo State Beach has been used many times as motion picture setting.*

Activities: Camping, picnicking, hiking, beachcombing and beach activities, swimming, scuba and skin-diving, surfing, and both surf and rock fishing. The arroyo campground has 140 improved campsites on the arroyo flat and side slopes, most with shade and semi-privacy. The camping limit is 30 days in winter, 7 in summer. No picnic facilities are provided, but there is a concession at the beach; picnickers may use campsites when un-occupied, or the beach, where fires are not permitted.

Sequit Creek has water in it about a mile upstream, and a trail leading to it. In summer there are weekly campfire programs and nature walks and talks. A sanitation station is available for camping vehicles. Access from the campground to the beach is through a highway underpass.

Leo Carrillo has long been a popular ocean-sport park, and Los Angeles County provides lifeguards all year. Submerged rocks and riptides make some swimming areas unsafe, so swimmers should check with lifeguards

before entering the water. New park buildings and a big parking area have recently been added at the west end of the beach.

For further information: Area Manager, Point Mugu Area State Parks, 35000 Pacific Coast Highway, Malibu 90265.

Access: Entrances are on both sides of State 1 about 15 miles north of Malibu and a mile south of the Ventura County line.

Supplies: Concessionaire has limited stock; Malibu Beach and Oxnard have supplies.

Los Angeles Beaches

Along the great crescent of Santa Monica Bay almost all of the coast is sandy, with broad, gleaming beaches. About half of this stretch has been set aside for public use—some of it is state land, some local, some held in combination. Altogether these beaches, including those just south of the mouth of the San Gabriel River, have an annual visitor count of about 50 million—southlanders visit their beaches many times a year.

The state owns 10 beaches here, and over the years it has turned them over to local administrations for more efficient operation. Most of these beaches are operated by Los Angeles County, although the city of Los Angeles has a few, and one or two are controlled by other municipalities. These are day-use parks, in most cases offering excellent swimming, often good surfing, and broad expanses for sunbathing and beach play. Skindivers like some of them, and there may be surf fishing when the visitor attendance is not too high.

In general the beaches are much alike—usually wide, sandy strips below coastal bluffs—but facilities vary. Some charge a fee, others do not, usually depending upon what facilities are provided. Almost all have lifeguards on duty during the season of peak use. Several have fishing piers. Volleyball posts are almost standard equipment, but there may be little else except the lifeguard towers. Some have picnic areas and parking aprons.

With such heavy use, administration is somewhat strict. No fires are permitted unless fire rings are furnished. No alcoholic beverages are allowed on the beach, not even beer. Picnickers are responsible for their own litter.

Going from north to south, these are the state beaches in Los Angeles County:

Point Dume: More than a mile of beach excellent for swimming, skin-diving, and fishing; operated by the county. Surfing is poor because of the location on a curve of a point. This area was once known as Westward Beach. The park is 34 acres.

Recent improvements provide an access road, large parking apron, permanent restrooms, and lifeguard towers. The beach is on the seaward side of State 1 about 18 miles west of Santa Monica.

Corral (also known as Solstice): Not state park land but owned by the Division of Highways; operated by the county. Facilities are primitive. The beach is on State 1 some 4 miles west of Malibu.

Malibu Lagoon: About 35 acres of sand and two-thirds of a mile of ocean frontage which incorporates the old Surfrider Beach, world renowned among surfers; operated by the county, Malibu Lagoon is located on the

Beneath cliffs *at northern end of the city of Santa Monica is Will Rogers State Beach. The city of Los Angeles operates this day-use beach. Point Dume juts out toward the ocean in the distance.*

south side of State 1 at Malibu, 11 miles west of Santa Monica.

The Surfrider area is reserved for surfing, but the remaining beach offers excellent swimming. There are restrooms, concessions, and parking along the highway.

The place-name Malibu is said to be derived from Chumash Indian "Maliwu," which was the name of one of their villages here. Spanish coastal explorer Juan Rodriguez landed at Malibu Lagoon in 1542 to fill his water casks.

Las Tunas: Very small, only .3 mile of beach and two acres total area. Relatively undeveloped, the beach has parking along the roadside and offers swimming in open areas, plus skin-diving and spear fishing. The beach is on State 1 about 6 miles west of Santa Monica.

Will Rogers: Almost contiguous with Santa Monica, about a half mile west, between the ocean and the palisades; operated by the city of Los Angeles. Busy State 1 occupies the inward side of the beach, but a broad band of sand is left free, with parking, lifeguard towers, and restrooms. There are many snack shops, beach equipment rental establishments, and restaurants along the highway.

Santa Monica: Encompasses virtually all the ocean front at Santa Monica, and since the 1860's has been one of the most popular beaches in the Los Angeles area; operated by the city.

Santa Monica has some picnic and barbecue facilities, plus play equipment and many concessions, restaurants, and amusement facilities nearby. It is adjacent to Ocean Avenue.

Dockweiler: Named after a chairman of the State Park Commission in the 1930's; operated by the city of Los Angeles.

A long, broad stretch of sand beneath coastal bluffs, with parking above and stairways leading to the beach. There are lifeguard towers and volleyball standards. This beach usually is not too heavily used, perhaps because it is directly under the flight path of Los Angeles Airport. It is on the west side of Vista del Mar Boulevard in Playa del Rey.

Manhattan: Includes entire beach at city and adjacent El Porto vicinity, comprising 44 acres of sandy beach slightly more than 2 miles in length; county operated. There are restrooms, playgrounds, and volleyball facilities.

The beach offers excellent swimming and normally fine surfing at several points. A long fishing pier is at the foot of Manhattan Beach Boulevard, and there are three parking aprons. Take the Rosecrans Avenue offramp west off San Diego Freeway.

Redondo Beach: Mostly owned by the state, but supplemented by small parcels owned by city and county to a total of 85 acres and almost 2 miles of beach; county operated. There is good swimming and sometimes fine surfing. Facilities include restrooms and play areas plus

---

OLD PICO #4

California's first commercial oil fields were located north of Los Angeles at Newhall. Just south of town near the old U.S. Highway 99 in Pico Canyon is the parent commercial well from which it all started—Pico #4.

Pico was spudded in by Demetrious G. Scofield, who later became first president of Standard Oil of California. On September 26, 1876, at a depth of 300 feet the well began producing 30 barrels a day. It was deepened to 600 feet with the first steam drilling rig in the state, and its flow increased to 150 barrels. The state's first refinery was constructed nearby.

In 1967 Old Pico #4 was designated a National Historic Landmark by the U.S. Park Service. But it hasn't retired completely—it still produces a barrel of oil a day.

---

two city-owned piers, of which Monstad is flood-lighted for night fishing. An extensive parking apron is operated by the city, and there are many concessions. Located at the city's westerly boundary, the beach is reached by Torrance Boulevard and Pacific Coast Highway.

Royal Palms: A small beach close to San Pedro, with limited facilities; operated by the city of Los Angeles. Royal Palms is at the foot of Western Avenue where it joins Paseo del Mar 2 miles northeast of Point Fermin.

Non-state beaches: Other coastal parks operated by Los Angeles County are the *Point Vicente Fishing Access* for surf and rock fishing, also used for scuba and skin-diving; *Torrance Beach* near the Palos Verdes cliffs; *Hermosa Beach* with excellent surf, good swimming, and wide sand; and *Marina del Rey* swimming area in the harbor, in conjunction with the marina. This park has public showers and picnic-barbecue facilities, with a large parking area.

Zuma Beach is the largest county-owned beach, just north of Point Dume off State 1. It has parking for about 2,000 cars (50 cents) and modern facilities. Zuma is an excellent swimming beach, but occasionally in summer it has riptides. Fishing and skin-diving are good, but surfing is only fair.

The county also operates the beach at *Avalon* on Santa Catalina Island, with lifeguards on duty all year. Other facilities have been turned over to concessionaires.

In addition to the state beaches under control of the city of Los Angeles, the city also operates *Cabrillo Beach* in San Pedro, which has picnic areas, fire pits, and a section for surfing; and *Venice Beach*, a small developed park with picnic areas, shuffleboard courts, and the Venice Beach Pavilion. Here, too, are the huge Venice Fishing Pier and an area set aside for surfing.

Southern Desert
& Mountains

The "backyard" parks of California's southland include two quite different kinds of areas—mountain parks which get their maximum use during regular vacation seasons and desert parks which are too hot for most people in summer but attract many winter visitors. Both get their greatest use from the heavily populated urban areas in the Los Angeles-San Diego strip.

With the exception of Elsinore, an artificial lake that is strongly watersport-oriented, the parks closest to the urban centers are all in the back-country mountains at elevations of 5,000 feet and higher. They get much heavier rainfall than the lower elevations nearer the coast, so they are heavily wooded—in fact, they compare in character with many of the Sierra parks farther north. In San Diego County, for instance, annual rainfall is only 10 to 13 inches along the coast, but it often reaches 45 inches in the higher mountains. In some of the parks a high proportion of this precipitation falls as snow, but all get snow periodically, so skiing, tobogganning, snow-hiking, or at least "snow bunny" fun is usually available in winter. In late spring and summer these same parks will have pleasant days, pure air, and chilly nights as a rule.

The desert parks are far flung. Mitchell and Picacho are close to Arizona. Anza-Borrego, with a half million acres, is larger than the rest of the state park system combined. For good reason it is divided into six patrol areas which rangers cover in four-wheel-drive vehicles. Among the desert parks, Salton Sea is a special case, with heavy use even during summer heat.

The desert parks are not dangerous if, as at any time when you are in an unfamiliar environment, you use common sense. Desert varmints will rarely be encountered in the vicinity of people, but if you are exploring normally unfrequented country, you might come across a sidewinder. Flash floods can result from thunderstorms —usually they occur in summer, but nonetheless it is foolish to camp in the bottom of a wash at any time.

An adequate supply of water and a reserve supply of fuel are essential. Experts exploring desert wild areas usually travel with at least two vehicles which keep together. Thousands of people do explore the wilder desert areas each year and enjoy a unique experience. You can, too—but learn a little about what to expect from someone who knows before you start out. Make sure a ranger or other dependable person knows where you are going and when you expect to return.

Red Rock Canyon State Park

Fascinating high desert country which has been the scene for a number of western movies is now a state park.

Hikers *can have high-mountain backpacking experience at Mt. San Jacinto Wilderness State Park (see page 120) and adjacent national forest land.*

Huge *Anza-Borrego park, opposite photo, preserves wide range of desert plants (see page 123).*

The area is near the Garlock Fault, the largest cross-state fault in California, and in a region of many secondary faults. Old lake beds containing chemical deposits have been broken and upthrust in some places, then wind-eroded, to form the beautiful layered sculpturing.

High desert climate prevails, and the canyon is in an air movement channel. Weather is usually sunny, hot in summer; it may be windy any time and can be quite cold in winter if arctic air is moving southward down the valleys east of the Sierra.

Currently the park includes almost 2,000 acres, but more land is being acquired. Accessibility is facilitated by the old U.S. Highway 6, which ran through the canyon before it was realigned and renumbered. It generally followed the stage route from Los Angeles to the old mining towns on the east side of the Sierra in the 1860's and 1870's.

Activities: Camping soon (possibly 1972-73), picnicking, hiking, rockhounding in surrounding areas, and nature study of desert life and wildflowers. Previously unregulated use of "off-the-road" vehicles is being curtailed.

Fifty unimproved campsites will be provided west of the old townsite of Ricardo, off the old highway, but facilities will be primitive. Picnicking in designated areas is basket picnicking for the time being, and you must bring your own water.

Many rockhounds comb this whole section of desert, although rock-hunting is not permitted within the park.

For further information: Area Manager, High Desert State Parks, 17102 Avenue J East, Lancaster 93534.

Access: Turn west off State 14 onto the old highway, 23 miles north of Mojave, or 16 miles south from Freeman Junction where State 178 joins State 14.

Supplies: Mojave or California City.

Joshua Trees State Park

A desert recreation area that also functions as a reserve for the protection of a Joshua tree forest, Joshua Trees State Park encompasses nearly 3,000 acres in eastern Los Angeles County. The park lies on the western side of a small ridge at about 2,700 feet altitude, and it is gently sloping, open, and sandy, with little vegetation except mesquite and Joshua trees. There is a striking view of Mt. San Antonio and the San Gabriel range to the south.

Joshua trees are rapidly disappearing in the whole vicinity as real estate development increases. The trees, *Yucca brevifolia*, are long lived but slow growing and are found only in arid regions of four western states. They were a source of food for desert Indian tribes who ate the flower buds roasted and also the fruit. A truly gigantic Joshua tree would be 50 feet high, but most mature specimens are only 20 to 25 feet.

Aside from the desert camping experience, with its clear air and quiet, this park should also be considered for day use for picnicking in spring. In good years, wildflower displays are outstanding in early spring.

This is the rim of the high desert, so it can be very cold in winter and quite hot in summer. It may be windy. Spring and fall are the best seasons.

Activities: Camping, hiking, picnicking, kite-flying. A 25-unit picnic area is located near the park entrance, with a 50-unit unimproved campground beyond. Camping limit is 30 days. The park is closed in summer. Roads through the park are easily passable but unpaved. Water for cooking and drinking is available from tanks.

For further information: Area Manager, c/o Joshua Trees State Park, 17102 Avenue J East, Lancaster 93534.

Access: From State 18 in Lancaster, turn east on Avenue J and drive 18 miles. Signs direct you to the park.

Supplies: Lancaster.

Joshua tree, *backdrop of San Gabriel Range make striking setting for camping at Joshua Trees State Park.*

Ranger discusses high desert plant life on tour near Mitchell Caverns.

Mitchell Caverns State Reserve

Caverns located in the Mojave Desert not far from the Arizona state line may have been used by Indians as a cool hideout for thousands of years. Now you can see Mitchell Caverns on tours conducted by rangers at this state reserve.

The park is 270 miles northeast of Los Angeles by road. High (4,300 feet) and rocky, it includes more than 5,000 acres, mostly on the steep eastern slopes of the Providence Mountains. Although limited camping facilities are available, this is primarily a day-use park.

Tours of the limestone caverns are conducted daily at 1:30 P.M., with three tours a day on weekends; they last one and a half hours. The tour takes you first through El Pakiva cavern, then through a tunnel to Tecopa cavern. Inside the caverns, the temperature remains at 65 degrees. The easily negotiated interior trail winds for 700 feet through a continuous display of magnificent formations enhanced by an excellent lighting system. Enroute the geologic story is told by the guide. You may take photographs on the tour. Tour fee is 50 cents for those 18 years and older, 25 cents for those under 18.

In addition to the caverns, the recreation area offers high desert flora extending over two life zones. Sunsets and sunrises across the desert from vantage points near park headquarters often are spectacular. A 1½-mile nature trail loops past the entrance to caverns.

Climate can be bitter here in the winter, so the best seasons are spring and fall; but due to the altitude, even summer temperatures rarely exceed 100 degrees.

Activities: Hiking, high-desert nature study, geology study, and picnicking. A six-unit unimproved campground is located on the bluffs close to the main parking apron, and there are additional sites for overflow vehicle camping. There are also four picnic sites. Water supply is limited, so campers should bring as much as they can carry.

When no camping space is available, the ranger can direct you to one of two Bureau of Land Management campgrounds within 20 miles.

For further information: Area Manager, Mitchell Caverns State Reserve, P.O. Box 1, Essex 92332.

Access: The park is about 23 miles in from Essex on U.S. 66 (now being converted to freeway as Interstate 40, which will pass about 6 miles closer to the park). The road is mostly paved, with easy passage over desert flats; it is dusty in places.

Supplies: There are a few desert hamlets along the way to the park, but Needles to the east and Barstow on the west are the only sizable towns along the highway. Barstow is 130 miles away, and Needles is 70 miles.

Heart Bar State Park

High mountain ridges, wooded flats, and open meadows make up Heart Bar State Park. Located in a mountain valley, headquarters are at an elevation of 6,700 feet; surrounding ridges are more than 8,000 feet high.

The park includes more than 4,000 acres acquired with funds from a 1964 bond issue, but it has been little developed. The name "Heart Bar" derives from the ranch which the state purchased for the park. Climate here is warm in summer, with cool nights; often there is heavy snow in winter.

Activities: Camping, picnicking, riding, hiking. A main campground of 100 unimproved sites is about a mile in from the highway, surrounded by parklike stands of large pines, with unpaved roads. A picnic area is located near the park entrance. There is a group campground for horsemen and another for youths.

Camping limit is 15 days in summer, 30 in winter. Some use is developing in winter for the growing sport of snow-hiking, but the road is not plowed, and the park is not accessible if snow gets too deep.

Both the west branch of the Santa Ana River and Fish Creek provide trout fishing in season.

For further information: Area Manager, Heart Bar State Park, Star Route, Angelus Oaks 92305.

Access: Leave Interstate 10 at Redlands and take State 38 about 35 miles; 14 miles beyond Camp Angelus you reach the park. The only sign is at the park entrance. The last 20 miles of road are steep and curving, but the surface is good.

Supplies: Piped water in park. There are no nearby sources of supplies except an occasional roadside store.

Mt. San Jacinto Wilderness State Park

A high-altitude, wilderness park of more than 13,500 acres, Mt. San Jacinto ranges in altitude from 5,500 feet at the park headquarters at Idyllwild to 10,830 feet at the summit of San Jacinto Peak. The terrain is rugged, and much of it is heavily forested by large pines at higher altitudes. A trail climbs up three peaks higher than 10,000 feet—views are superb on clear days, though smog often obscures the landscape.

Big yellow pines *and high mountain atmosphere are among attractions of Heart Bar State Park, 6,700 feet high.*

Tramway *up Mt. San Jacinto lets you climb the peak the easy way. You rise a mile in horizontal distance of 2 miles.*

Only two campgrounds are accessible by automobile—Idyllwild and Stone Creek—but there are many primitive camping areas along the riding and hiking trails. The character of the park is like that of a national forest primitive area, which it once was. It is, in fact, surrounded by other national forest land, and on the west it borders San Bernardino National Forest Wild Area.

A tramway climbs the steep eastern scarp of the mountain. It operates seven days a week except in August, when it is closed for overhaul.

Once there was a great amount of Indian activity around the peaks, with many trails. Some pictographs and other symbols have been found.

The park has typical high mountain climate, with warm days and cool nights in summer. In winter severe storms and snowfall may be experienced.

Activities: Hiking and backpacking, horseback and animal packing, camping, mountain climbing, rock climbing in Forest Wild Area. There is a small picnic area near headquarters at Idyllwild.

The 33-unit campground above headquarters is improved with full facilities (showers) and even remains open in winter (with primitive facilities), getting some weekend use. Summer limit is 15 days. Stone Creek campground a few miles to the west, off Highway 74, has 50 unimproved sites. There are also many forest service campgrounds in the vicinity, both for auto and hike-in camping.

Horses are available for rental nearby, but before entering the wilderness area either on horseback or on foot you will need a permit. Apply in person or write the park headquarters at Idyllwild or the Long Valley Ranger Station in Palm Springs.

Many inveterate fishermen work the streams in the park, but this is frustrating, even with planted trout, because of competition. Snow sports are popular in winter.

For further information: Area Manager, Mt. San Jacinto Wilderness State Park, P.O. Box 308, Idyllwild 92349.

Access: You can reach park headquarters at Idyllwild either by State 74 from Hemet, turning onto a good forest service road at Mountain Center, or by a steep climb from Banning.

Supplies: Idyllwild.

Lake Elsinore State Recreation Area

A lake which had disappeared by evaporation and seepage through fissures was refilled in 1964 with state funds, and now Lake Elsinore State Recreation Area offers a variety of water activities. Much of the lake shore is now heavily commercialized with motels, resorts, and private camping facilities.

The emphasis is on boating at Elsinore, rather than on a nature experience. Facilities are operated by a concessionaire.

RECREATION IN THE WILDERNESS

California has 21 designated primitive and wilderness areas in its national forests. No roads or vehicles are allowed in these areas, and no timber cutting is permitted. Horses and pack animals may be taken in under strict regulations, but much of the use of these vast, wild territories is by backpackers.

Several of California's state parks are adjacent to primitive and wilderness areas, and when you are visiting a park you may want to make a trip into one of them with the park as a base. You will need a visitor's permit. Overuse of some of the areas and violations of regulations have necessitated stricter control of use. You are required to state which wilderness you plan to visit, where you will enter and when, how long you will stay, how many will be in your party, and whether travel will be on foot, on foot with pack animals, or on horseback.

Permits are obtained from the national forest headquarters for the area you plan to visit. You need a permit for each visit, but there is no charge. If overcrowding is a problem, you may be refused a permit and advised of areas which are not overloaded.

Mount San Jacinto Wilderness State Park is the only wilderness within the California state park system. In line with new forest service controls, the state is imposing the same controls at San Jacinto.

Located in a pocket valley between coast range ridges, the park has 3,000 acres and is at an altitude of 1,200 feet. Climate is usually equable, but it may be hot in summer.

Activities: Camping and picnicking, with 56 sites in a combination campground (standard $3 fee for camping, $1 for picnicking).

The park offers the usual water sports related to boating—fishing, power boats, water-skiing—and bicycling. There is a large boat ramp, with a launching fee of $3.

Access: The park is at the north end of the lake; east-west State 74 passes by the entrance. The park also is accessible by north-south State 71.

Supplies: Many local sources. Concessionaire rents a wide range of water-sport items and also bicycles.

Palomar Mountain State Park

The beautiful, densely wooded park on top of Palomar Mountain is somewhat like Cuyamaca (page 125)—but its annual rainfall of up to 40 inches makes the vegetation more lush. Palomar's trees are outstanding, with excellent specimens of big cone pine and spruce, firs, cedars, and oaks. The park includes slightly less than 2,000 acres, and it is adjacent to portions of Cleveland National Forest.

Highest point in the park is Boucher Hill, at 5,438 feet, and the remainder of the park is not much lower. From Boucher Lookout, you can look across the intervening ridges to the Pacific Ocean.

Nearby Palomar Observatory has a museum and photo gallery open daily to visitors from 8 A.M. to 5 P.M. The road to the observatory is marked.

Cold and snowy in winter, the park gets its major use from May to November, but some hardy souls come early in the season for fishing in the small lake and nearby streams.

Activities: Camping, picnicking, hiking, fishing from late winter to early summer, some "snow bunny" activity in winter.

There are two campgrounds—Cedar Grove, which is heavily wooded with considerable privacy at the sites, and Doane Valley, where sites are on the edge of a meadow above Doane Pond. The campgrounds have a total of 51 improved sites (showers) between them, and there is a sizable picnic area at Silver Crest near the park entrance, with a superb view across the surrounding mountain ranges. There are also a few picnic sites at the pond.

A 25-DAY CROSS-COUNTRY RUN

California had many stage lines before the coming of the railroads, and even for many decades afterward the old Concords still rolled through the more isolated back-country towns and up the steep mountain grades. The Butterfield Stages of the Overland Mail Company, with their 3,000-mile dash across a great segment of the continent, were the most famous of all the lines—even though their service only lasted from 1858 until interrupted by the Civil War in 1861.

The route was a great southern loop, from the farthest west railhead at that time, Tipton, Missouri, through Arkansas, Texas, Arizona, and Mexico, then north into California through the Borrego Desert to Vallecito. The station at Vallecito is now restored and open to visitors in the San Diego County Park. The stages continued through Box Canyon, Warner Springs, Elsinore, swung west through Los Angeles, and headed north to San Francisco over a route which roughly parallels U.S. 99.

The emphasis was on mail delivery, and passengers had a rough time of it. The entire trip was scheduled to take 25 days, and average speed was five miles an hour. Continuous runs of 48 hours were not unusual, and stops were only long enough to change teams. John Butterfield, company president, admonished his drivers: "Remember, boys, nothing on God's earth must stop the United States Mail."

Passage cost each traveler in the neighborhood of $200, and only 40 pounds of baggage was allowed a passenger.

A self-guided 1-mile nature trail follows the creek into lower Doane Valley. During summer and on spring and fall weekends, the rangers program nature walks, interpretive talks, and campfire sessions. The park has 14 miles of trails, and horseback riding is permitted on the trail from lower Doane Valley to the lookout station.

Doane Pond is stocked with trout in the spring and channel catfish in summer. The pond is small, but it draws a good crowd when the fish are biting. Swimming is not permitted.

For further information: Area Manager, Cuyamaca Rancho State Park, Cuyamaca Star Route, Julian 92036.

Access: Near Lake Henshaw, take County Route S-7, a long, winding climb. The Rincon Springs road is shorter, but it is steeper and difficult for heavy camping vehicles.

Supplies: At Lake Henshaw, a recreation center.

Salton Sea State Recreation Area

More than 16,000 shoreline acres around the northern edge of Salton Sea comprise the state's most popular boating park. Salton Sea State Recreation Area gets year-round use—though temperatures of more than 100 degrees are not uncommon here in summer, this is the best fishing season. The surface of the sea is 234 feet below sea level—only 46 feet higher than the lowest point in Death Valley.

In past geologic ages, a prehistoric sea filled the entire valley and was hundreds of feet deep. In 1905 an irrigation canal from the Colorado River flowed into the depression. The present level of Salton Sea seems to have about stabilized with replenishment of irrigation water from adjacent agriculture, but the water also leaches minerals from land, making the sea gradually more salty.

Steep temperature gradients often occur between the Imperial Valley and areas to the west, creating strong winds. Salton Sea is shallow, and waves up to 10 feet in height are experienced at times. A storm-alert system is in effect at the park.

Activities: Camping, picnicking, swimming, sunbathing, fishing from boats, and water-skiing. Two campgrounds at Mecca Beach near park headquarters have 50 improved camping sites (showers), mostly in shade. Here there is also a sizable picnic area with ramadas. A sanitation station is available for campers and trailers.

At Mecca Beach there is a launching ramp in protected Varner Harbor, and there is a big parking apron. A concessionaire offers rentals, food and supplies, a snack bar, and ice and fish-storing facilities.

South of headquarters there are another 164 unimproved campsites scattered along the shore at Corvina, Salt Creek, and Bombay beaches, with additional primitive camps at these beaches and elsewhere suitable only

At Salton Sea *the emphasis is on motorboating for water-skiing and fishing—but some prefer a quieter approach. This is the state's most popular boating park, and it gets year-round use despite hot summer temperatures.*

for camping vehicles. The park, with these primitive sites, can accommodate more than 2,000 family groups.

In the 1950's the Department of Fish and Game planted corvina, sargo, and gulf croaker in the sea, where they have thrived, but fishing is declining because of leaching.

For further information: Area Manager, Salton Sea State Recreation Area, General Delivery, North Shore 92254.

Access: Park headquarters is about 12 miles south of Mecca on State 111, which parallels the park for several miles farther south, with access to other beaches.

Supplies: Available at many nearby communities.

San Pasqual Battlefield State Historic Park

The site of the only real pitched battle between two nations on California soil is San Pasqual Battlefield. Historical exhibits commemorate the event at the site.

In 1846 a small invading army of dragoons and a few marines under General S. W. Kearney, worn and starving after an almost continuous march from Fort Leavenworth, were met here in the rain by a smaller group of Mexican cavalry. Heavy casualties were inflicted on both sides, with Kearney's losses almost a third of his force. The Mexicans, however, did not follow up the attack,

and Kearney managed to continue on until reinforcements from San Diego reached him.

Access: The park is in a small valley about 7 miles east of Escondido on State 78.

Anza-Borrego Desert State Park

An outstanding reserve for hundreds of species of rare desert trees, plants, and animals, Anza-Borrego Desert State Park comprises nearly half a million acres in the western part of the Colorado desert. Situated about 60 airline miles northeast of San Diego, the park is rugged and colorful, with many fascinating canyons and washes to explore and some mountains rising to more than 8,000 feet in height.

There are few paved roads, although the park is crossed by several public highways. Within the park boundaries it is permissible to drive on 600 miles of unimproved roads through canyons and washes, some of them passable only with dune buggies and four-wheel-drive vehicles but many negotiable with conventional passenger cars. There are many additional miles of hiking and riding trails.

Travelers have crossed through the Borrego Springs area for nearly 200 years, beginning with the Spanish leader Anza, who made several trips with parties across the Colorado Desert between 1774 and 1776. (The park name commemorates Anza and also the bighorn sheep which once frequented the springs vicinity—*Borrego*

Sandstone canyon *in Anza-Borrego is one of many intriguing byways for exploring in this huge expanse of desert.*

it is not easily apparent, the park teems with desert wildlife. A few bighorn sheep still roam the higher ridges, and the lucky visitor may sight one. There are also antelope, cougar, even a few deer, and a wide range of smaller animals.

Desert ecology is frail, so visitors must use care to preserve it. Always dispose of litter and garbage in trash receptacles; if none is nearby, carry litter and garbage out of the area to a container. It is against park rules to bury litter and garbage, as animals dig it up later and scatter it.

Geologically and scenically, the Split Mountain-Fish Creek Canyon area is one of the more interesting in the park. It is easily accessible from Ocotillo Wells on State 78. On the road to the canyon there is a turnoff over a very rough road which leads to a foot trail by which the famed Elephant Trees can be reached—a hike of about a mile. There is a sizable grove of these oddities—perhaps the best anywhere.

At sensible speeds the wash up Fish Creek Canyon can be negotiated easily by passenger car. Traversing the narrow canyon, with its vertical and even overhanging walls rising 600 feet, is a memorable experience. Farther upstream is the narrower and even more dramatic Sandstone Canyon, which only small four-wheel-drive vehicles can ascend.

Palm Canyon, with its little oasis of native palms between dry canyon walls, is probably the most popular spot for casual visitors to the park. A good foot trail leads from the main campground up the canyon, and a self-guided nature trail leaflet is available at the trailhead.

Anza-Borrego is open all year, but in summer it is often very hot, and it may be cold in winter. It gets heavy use in spring and fall, with an annual total of about 500,000 visitors. In these seasons daytime temperatures range from about 60 to 80 degrees but fall sharply at night 20 degrees or more. Occasional sandstorms may be expected, and on rare occasions there may be a desert cloudburst. Average annual rainfall is five inches at Borrego Springs, but it varies greatly with elevation.

Because the park is so large and is still true desert, even though it is developed to some extent, visitors may occasionally have problems. You should notify someone, preferably a ranger, if you are going off the beaten tracks and when you expect to return. If you do have trouble, stay where you are. Rangers are patrolling constantly in four-wheel-drive vehicles.

Activities: Camping, picnicking, hiking, horseback riding and trail packing, nature study, exploring with vehicles. (Riding and pack animals are permitted in the park but not in Palm Canyon or established campgrounds.)

The main campground is at the mouth of Borrego-Palm Canyon, not far from park headquarters, in a protected area with 117 improved campsites (showers) —there are ramadas but few trees. Surrounding ridges

comes from the Spanish word for these sheep.) Kit Carson and the Mormon Battalion in the Mexican War crossed the park area. The Butterfield Stages, as well as cattle drovers, stopped here for many years. San Diego County has reconstructed the old Butterfield Stage stop at Vallecitos and maintains a small park there on the western edge of the state land.

Vegetation is sparse and typically desert. In good years, wildflower displays—particularly ocotillo—may be spectacular in late winter and early spring. Although

shade campsites in late afternoon. The park has 52 trailer hook-up units, but there is no trailer sanitation station.

There are 25 improved campsites at Tamarisk Grove, Box Willow has 10 unimproved sites with tap water available, and Sheep Canyon has three sites but no water. All of these campgrounds have ramadas. Sheep Canyon is not accessible by conventional vehicle. Seven other primitive campgrounds, with portable toilets but no water, are accessible to family cars. You must camp in designated areas to protect the ecology.

The park folder contains an excellent map of the various trails, roads, camp areas, and special features of the desert.

For further information: Area Manager, Anza-Borrego State Park, Borrego Springs 92004.

Access: Several good state and county highways cross the park. Headquarters is west of the town of Borrego Springs up Palm Canyon Drive. Other highways give access to many interesting points; for specific instructions, visitors should get a detailed map of this part of southern California or write for the park folder.

Supplies: The town of Borrego Springs in the center of the park is a sizable winter resort area with several good restaurants, motels, a golf course, a small airport, markets, and other amenities. There is a small commercial center at Ocotillo Wells (access to Fish Creek Canyon), and several other small settlements are scattered around the park perimeter. Four-wheel-drive vehicles, dune buggies, and trail bikes can be rented at several points.

Cuyamaca Rancho State Park

From the top of Mt. Cuyamaca in Cuyamaca Rancho State Park, you can see—on a clear day—from the Pacific Ocean to the Salton Sea. The trail up Mt. Cuyamaca is one of a network of 75 miles of trails which make this mountain park popular with hikers.

Located about 40 miles east of San Diego on the western slopes of the Laguna Range, Cuyamaca Rancho stretches over some 20,000 acres. Altitude is from about 3,500 feet to the top of 6,515-foot Cuyamaca Peak. The western sides of the ridges often are rocky and chaparral covered, but canyons in the park are heavily forested with oaks, sycamores, and various conifers. There are many open meadows. Cuyamaca Rancho shares its border with Anza-Borrego State Park at one point, and it also has a small section of shoreline on Cuyamaca Lake. Cleveland National Forest surrounds the park.

COLOR IN THE DESERT

The rich colors and delicacy of wildflower blooms in what seems the inhospitable environment of the desert have a special appeal. The trick is to know when to go and where to look to see them. In areas which have only a few inches of rainfall annually—and in some years practically none—wildflowers bloom only in conjunction with rainfall at the right time.

Rain in the desert is most likely from mid-December through January, sometimes in February or March. Hence you can normally expect desert wildflower displays in March, plus or minus a few weeks. There will be variations because of altitude—high altitude means later bloom—and also a few weeks' variation, all other things being equal, between the southern Colorado Desert and the northern Mojave Desert.

Perennial trees and shrubs are more consistent, not being dependent upon rain for germination of seeds. You can be fairly sure you will see excellent displays of scarlet ocotillo in the Anza-Borrego area, creamy Joshua tree flowers in Joshua Tree National Monument and Joshua Trees State Park, and brilliant yellow blooms on the palos verdes through much of the Colorado Desert—all in April. If you go into the high Mojave Desert in May, park your car and explore some of the ridges. You will find all sorts of delightful little rock gardens in the pockets.

Best poppy displays are usually in April in the fields and foothills west of Lancaster and Palmdale. But these are subject to rain patterns, too.

Several travel services (such as automobile clubs) provide information on where wildflowers are in bloom, and newspapers often report this information.

Fragile *dune primrose illustrates charm of delicate blooms in the harsh environment of the desert.*

THE DESERT BIGHORNS

The desert bighorn sheep is fascinating for his ability to survive in an inhospitable environment. The careful and persistent amateur naturalist may sight these animals at Picacho State Recreation Area and at Anza-Borrego State Park.

Naturalists believe bighorn sheep evolved in Mongolia, crossed the frozen Bering Sea during past ice ages, and eventually spread out through North America as the ice receded. Before the coming of Europeans, there were millions of bighorns existing on the fringes of forage areas inhabited by more massive herds of antelope, elk, and buffalo.

Several sub-species evolved in the various sections of the continent, and a few sizable groups still exist in Canada and in wild portions of western mountain ranges. There may even be one or two small groups still living in the higher Sierra Nevada.

They are timid animals. The great curving horns of the males are poor defensive weapons, primarily being used against each other in struggles for domination. Agility is their best defense, for they can climb cliff faces on the most meager ledges. They also have developed extremely keen eyesight.

With the coming of western civilization, the bighorn's defenses were almost useless. Man's domestic animals, particularly his sheep, crowded them out of their natural feeding places and passed on to them diseases against which they had no resistance. Entire herds of the wild sheep were wiped out. Hunters sought the sheep as meat and as trophies. Today probably no more than 5,000 are left in North America.

In recent years the bighorn has had lots of attention from naturalists, and intensive efforts are being made to save him. Waterholes are being provided, and studies are being made by biologists from the State Department of Fish and Game, the U.S. Park Service, and the Bureau of Land Management. Surprisingly enough, it appears that these bighorns in the dry, barren mountains of the Southwest deserts may prove to be the largest group left on the continent.

Several small, intermittent streams (depending upon rainfall) run through the park, and there are a number of springs.

Essentially a hiking and camping park, Cuyamaca Rancho receives a great deal of day use, and group camping is popular. Besides the trail up Mt. Cuyamaca, there is an easier hike to the top of Stonewall Peak and a pleasant trail to Green Valley Falls.

Wildlife in the park includes deer, an occasional cougar, and many smaller animals native to intermediate mountain altitudes. Golden beaver introduced in 1947 are flourishing.

An all-year park, Cuyamaca Rancho is warm and sometimes hot in summer, but it can be cold and often has snow in winter. (When there is snow, the park has an influx of snow-lovers.) Used heavily by San Diegans and other southern Californians, the park has an annual visitor total of more than half a million. It gets particularly heavy use on weekends.

Originally this region was inhabited by Diegueno Indians, whose culture is portrayed in an Indian museum here. The northern end of the park was mined during the Julian gold rush in the 1870's.

Activities: Camping, hiking, horseback riding, picnicking, nature study, campfire programs, fishing in the Green Valley Falls area in late winter and early spring and in Cuyamaca Lake, where rental boats are available. The California Riding and Hiking Trail passes through the park.

In addition to nature interpretation programs, the park offers an exhibit of natural science displays at the Nature Den, an excellent Indian museum, and a tour of the old Stonewall Mine.

There are two campgrounds, one at Green Valley near the southern edge of the park and another at Paso Picacho, higher up. The campgrounds have a combined total of 179 improved sites (showers). There are sizable picnic areas at both places. The campsites are mostly shaded.

Several group campgrounds are used by Boy Scouts, Girl Scouts, horsemen's associations, and others. Los Caballos Campground beneath Stonewall Peak has 16 specialized campsites for horsemen.

For further information: Area Manager, c/o Cuyamaca Rancho State Park, Cuyamaca Star Route, Julian 92036.

Access: You approach the park on State 79 either from Julian to the north or Descanso on Interstate 8 to the south. Nine miles of Route 79 passes through the park.

Supplies: Descanso or Julian.

Picacho State Recreation Area

A picturesque and rugged desert area with several miles of frontage on the Colorado River, Picacho State Recreation Area is located near the southeastern corner of the state. Volcanic activity plus aridity have created a wild and almost barren landscape here, but there is a wealth of wildlife and growth in the washes. Accessibility to the park is somewhat difficult.

The park takes in more than 5,000 acres of land, including outstanding desert scenery with views of the multicolored Chocolate Mountains.

Imperial Dam downstream has slowed the Colorado River so that it has silted up about 12 feet, resulting in overflow lakes and marshes in many places along the shores. Two of these lakes are within park boundaries, several more close by on the Arizona side. The park lies within the Imperial National Wildlife Refuge, and all the kinds of wildlife found at Anza-Borrego are found at Picacho, plus wild burros. You can see displays of wildflowers in late winter and spring.

This area was visited as early as 1540 by exploring parties under Coronado. It was an Indian habitat for many centuries. The old town of Picacho was a gold-mining center in the 1880's, but most of the townsite is now covered by water from the elevated Colorado.

Picacho is open all year, but it may get as hot as 120 degrees in summer, when there are also occasional thunderstorms creating flash floods. During other months, its climate is usually dry and warm, making this an excellent off-season park. Mosquitoes are a problem from April to October.

Activities: Fishing and boating are the most popular pastimes, but many visitors like the warmth and isolation of the area and use the park for camping and exploring. A small marina with launching ramp and rental boats is located near park headquarters. Boat fishermen catch black bass, channel catfish, crappie, and bluegill. Waterfowl hunting is allowed in season.

Despite the dams, the river is deep and swift, Only strong swimmers should attempt it. Rafting from Blythe to Imperial Dam is a popular sport, and some parties use Picacho as a stopover.

One road traverses the park. It is rough and unpaved but passable in passenger cars. Travel is slow, so one-day visitors should start early. A number of hiking trails lead to points of interest.

The headquarters campground has 50 improved sites, with water, shaded by tamarisk groves. There are two group camps, which must be reserved, and several other informal camping areas for overflow visitors. A picnic area near the river has tables, fire rings, and water.

For further information: Area Manager, c/o Picacho State Recreation Area, P.O. Box 1207, Winterhaven 92283.

Access: About half a mile from the Colorado River on the California side, turn north off Interstate 80 at the Imperial Dam sign; follow the signs to Picacho. The road is paved about 6 miles, then becomes rough, sandy, and dusty, with many curves and dips, for 18 miles. The road from Ogilby via Gavilan Wash to 4-S Ranch is not recommended except for four-wheel-drive vehicles.

Supplies: A snack bar and limited grocery store are located at the marina. Fuel and supplies are available at Yuma or Winterhaven. There is some rental equipment for fishing at the marina concession. Water is piped to several points in the park.

Rafting *from Blythe to Imperial Dam is a popular Colorado River sport. Rafts usually are made from oil drums upstream and dismantled at end. View here is from Picacho State Recreation Area looking across to Arizona shore.*

Index

Admiral William H. Standley State Reserve, 21-22
Alameda Memorial State Beach, 52
Andrew Molera State Park, 87
Angel Island State Park, 40, 49-50
Ano Nuevo State Beach, 55
Anza-Borrego Desert State Park, 116, 117, 123-125
Armstrong Redwood State Reserve, 24
Arroyo de los Frijoles State Beach, 54, 55
Asilomar State Beach, 84
Atascadero State Beach, 90-91
Austin Creek State Recreation Area, 24-25
Avalon Beach, 115
Avila State Beach, 92-93
Azalea State Reserve, 15

Baker State Beach, 48
Bean Hollow State Beach, 54, 55
Benbow Lake State Recreation Area, 17
Benicia Capitol State Historic Park, 51
Benicia State Recreation Area, 50
Bethany Reservoir, 7
Bidwell Mansion State Historic Park, 60, 61
Big Basin Redwoods State Park, 56
Bliss State Park, 27, 35-36
Bodie State Historic Park, 38
Bolsa Chica State Beach, 101
Border Field State Beach, 107
Bothe-Napa Valley State Park, 63
Brannan Island State Recreation Area, 68
Butano State Park, 41, 56

Cabrillo State Beach, 115
Calaveras Big Trees State Park, 36-38
Cardiff State Beach, 104
Carlsbad State Beach, 104
Carmel River State Beach, 85
Carpinteria State Beach, 99
Carrillo State Beach, 109, 112-113
Castaic Lake, 7
Castle Crags State Park, 27-28
Castle Rock State Park, 55
Caswell Memorial State Park, 70
Cayucos State Beach, 90
Clear Lake State Park, 58, 62
Coe State Park, 80-81
Columbia State Historic Park, 68-69
Colusa-Sacramento River State Recreation Area, 62
Corona del Mar State Beach, 101-102
Cowell Redwoods State Park, 57
Cuyamaca Rancho State Park, 125-126

D. L. Bliss State Park, 27, 35-36
Del Norte Coast Redwoods State Park, 11-12
Delta region, 59, 65, 68
Dockweiler State Beach, 115
Doheny State Beach, 102
Donner Memorial State Park, 32-33
Dry Lagoon State Park, 13

El Capitan State Beach, 98
El Presidio de Santa Barbara, 98-99
El Pueblo de Los Angeles, 112, 113
Elsinore State Recreation Area, 121
Emma Wood State Beach, 99

Fees, 6
Fishing
  Abalone, 83
  Grunion, 105
  Ocean, 107
  Trout, 39
Folsom Lake State Recreation Area, 63-64
Forest of Nisene Marks State Park, 80
Fort Humboldt State Historic Park, 14, 15
Fort Point, 50
Fort Ross State Historic Park, 24
Fort Tejon State Historic Park, 75
Frank's Tract State Recreation Area, 68
Fremont Ford State Recreation Area, 72
Fremont Peak State Park, 83

Gaviota State Park, 97-98
George J. Hatfield State Recreation Area, 72
Governor's Mansion, 66, 67
Gray Whale Cove State Beach, 53
Grizzly Creek Redwoods State Park, 15, 16
Grover Hot Springs State Park, 36

Half Moon Bay State Beaches, 54
Hatfield State Recreation Area, 72
Hearst San Simeon State Historic Park, 88-89
Hearst State Beach, 89-90
Heart Bar State Park, 119-120
Hendy Woods State Park, 22
Henry Cowell Redwoods State Park, 57
Henry W. Coe State Park, 80-81
Hermosa Beach, 115
Hugo Reid Adobe, 111
Humboldt Redwoods State Park, 16-17
Huntington State Beach, 95, 101

Ide Adobe, 59-60
Indian Creek State Reserve, 22, 23
Indian Grinding Rock State Historic Park, 67, 68
Indian Museum, 66-67
Ingram Creek Aquatic Area, 7

Jack London State Historic Park, 42-43
James Phelan State Beach, 48-49
Jedediah Smith Redwoods State Park, 5, 10-11
Jetty State Beach, 82
Joshua Trees State Park, 118
Julia Pfeiffer Burns State Park, 87-88

Kern River State Recreation Area, 74
Kettleman City Aquatic Area, 7
Knowland State Arboretum and Park, 52
Kruse Rhododendron State Reserve, 23

La Purisima Mission State Historic Park, 96-97
Lake Del Valle, 7
Lake Elsinore State Recreation Area, 121
Lake Oroville State Recreation Area, 7, 61-62
Lake Perris, 7
Lake Tahoe, 27, 33-36
Las Tunas State Beach, 115
Leo Carrillo State Beach, 109, 112-113
Leucadia State Beach, 104
Little River State Beach, 15
London State Historic Park, 42-43
Los Angeles Arboreta, 111
Los Angeles Pueblo, 112, 113
Los Coches Rancho Wayside Camp, 86-87
Los Encinos State Historic Park, 109-110
Lummis Home State Historic Park, 111

MacKerricher State Park, 19-20
Mailliard State Reserve, 21-22
Malakoff Diggins State Historic Park, 26, 31-32
Malibu Lagoon State Beach, 114-115
Manchester State Beach, 22-23
Manhattan State Beach, 115
Manresa State Beach, 81
Marin Headlands State Park, 47
Marina del Rey, 115
Marshall Gold Discovery State Historic Park, 64-65
McArthur-Burney Falls Memorial State Park, 28-29
McConnell State Recreation Area, 71-72
McGrath State Beach, 100
Millerton Lake State Recreation Area, 73-74
Mitchell Caverns State Reserve, 119
Molera State Park, 87
Montana de Oro State Park, 92
Montara State Beach, 54
Monterey State Beach, 84
Monterey State Historic Park, 77, 83-84
Montgomery Woods State Reserve, 21-22
Moonlight State Beach, 104
Morro Bay State Park, 91
Morro Strand State Beach, 90
Mount Diablo State Park, 51-52
Mount Tamalpais State Park, 46-47
Mt. San Jacinto Wilderness State Park, 117, 120-121

Natural Bridges State Beach, 78-79
New Brighton State Beach, 79

Oakland Zoo, 52, 53
Old Sacramento State Historic Park, 67
Old Town San Diego State Historic Park, 106
Oro Grande Aquatic Area, 7
Oroville State Recreation Area, 7, 61-62

Palomar Mountain State Park, 121-122
Patrick's Point State Park, 13-14
Paul M. Dimmick Wayside Camp, 22
Peace Valley Aquatic Area, 7
Pelican State Beach, 10
Pescadero State Beach, 54, 55
Petaluma Adobe State Historic Park, 44
Pets, regulations, 6
Pfeiffer-Big Sur State Park, 87
Phelan State Beach, 48-49
Picacho State Recreation Area, 126-127
Pio Pico State Historic Park, 112
Pismo State Beach, 92, 93
Placerita Canyon State Park, 109
Plumas-Eureka State Park, 30-31
Point Dume State Beach, 114
Point Lobos State Reserve, 4, 76, 85-86
Point Mugu State Recreation Area, 100-101
Point Vicente Fishing Access, 115
Pomponio State Beach, 55
Portola State Park, 55
Prairie Creek Redwoods State Park, 8, 12-13
Pyramid Lake, 7

Red Rock Canyon State Park, 117-118
Redondo State Beach, 108, 115
Redwood National Park, 9
Redwoods, 17
Refugio State Beach, 98, 99
Reid Adobe, 111
Reservations, 6
Reynolds Wayside Camp, 18
Richardson Grove State Park, 17-18
Ritter Canyon Aquatic Area, 7
Robert Louis Stevenson State Park, 62-63
Royal Palms State Beach, 115
Russian Gulch State Park, 20-21

Sacramento parks, 65-66
Sacramento River, 59, 65
Salt Point State Park, 23-24
Salton Sea State Recreation Area, 122-123
Samuel Taylor State Park, 44-45
San Antonio Mission, 89
San Buenaventura State Beach, 99
San Clemente State Beach, 102
San Diego Old Town, 106
San Diego State Beaches, 103-105
San Elijo State Beach, 104
San Francisco parks, 47-49
San Gregorio State Beach, 54
San Joaquin River, 59, 65
San Juan Bautista State Historic Park, 82-83
San Luis Obispo, 89
San Luis Reservoir State Recreation Area, 7, 72-73
San Mateo State Beaches, 53-55
San Miguel Mission, 89
San Onofre State Beach, 94, 102-103
San Pasqual Battlefield State Historic Park, 123
San Simeon State Beach, 90
Santa Barbara Presidio, 98-99
Santa Cruz Mission State Historic Park, 77-78
Santa Monica State Beach, 115
Seacliff State Beach, 79-80
Seal Rocks State Beach, 49
Sequoias, 17
Sharp Park State Beach, 53
Shasta State Historic Park, 30
Silver Strand State Beach, 106-107
Silverwood Lake, 7
Smith Redwoods State Park, 10-11
Smithe Redwoods State Reserve, 18
Soledad Mission, 89
Solvang, 98
Sonoma Coast State Beach, 9, 25
Sonoma Mission, 43
Sonoma State Historic Park, 43-44
South Carlsbad State Beach, 103, 104
Squaw Valley State Recreation Area, 33
Standish-Hickey State Recreation Area, 18-19
Standley State Reserve, 21-22
Stevenson State Park, 62-63
Stinson State Beach, 45-46
Sugar Pine Point State Park, 34-35
Sugarloaf Ridge State Park, 41-42
Sunset State Beach, 81
Sutter's Fort State Historic Park, 66

Tahoe State Recreation Area, 33-34
Taylor State Park, 44-45
Thornton State Beach, 53
Tomales Bay State Park, 44, 45
Torrance Beach, 115
Torrey Pines State Beach, 105
Torrey Pines State Reserve, 105-106
Trinidad State Beach, 14-15
Tule Elk State Reserve, 74, 75
Turlock Lake State Recreation Area, 70-71
Twin Lakes State Beach, 79

Upper Feather River Basin, 7

Van Damme State Park, 21
Venice Beach, 115

Weaverville Joss House State Historic Park, 29-30
Westport-Union Landing State Beach, 19
Will Rogers State Beach, 114, 115
Will Rogers State Historic Park, 110-111
William B. Ide Adobe State Historic Park, 59-60
Wm. R. Hearst State Beach, 89-90
Wood State Beach, 99
Woodson Bridge State Recreation Area, 60

Zmudowski State Beach, 81-82
Zuma Beach, 115

PHOTOGRAPHERS